D1432796

ENGLAND

UNDER

PROTECTOR SOMERSET

ENGLAND

UNDER

PROTECTOR SOMERSET

AN ESSAY

BY

A. F. POLLARD

NEW YORK / RUSSELL & RUSSELL

1966

FIRST PUBLISHED IN 1900
REISSUED, 1966, BY RUSSELL & RUSSELL
A DIVISION OF ATHENEUM HOUSE, INC.
L.C. CATALOG CARD NO: 66—15433

Reprinted from a copy in the collections of
The New York Public Library

PRINTED IN THE UNITED STATES OF AMERICA

942.053
P771

CONTENTS

CHAPTER I

THE COUP D'ÉTAT

CHAPTER II

THE PROTECTOR'S TASK

v

CHAPTER III

PRINCIPLES AND METHODS OF GOVERNMENT

CHAPTER IV

SOMERSET AND THE RELIGIOUS REVOLUTION

CHAPTER V

FOREIGN RELATIONS

CHAPTER VI

THE ATTEMPTED UNION WITH SCOTLAND

CHAPTER VII

THE PROTECTOR AND THE LORD HIGH ADMIRAL

CHAPTER VIII

THE PROTECTOR AND THE SOCIAL DISCONTENT

CHAPTER IX

THE PROTECTOR'S FALL

CHAPTER X

REACTION

CHAPTER XI

TRIAL AND EXECUTION OF THE PROTECTOR

CHAPTER XII

THE PROTECTOR'S WORK AND CHARACTER

APPENDIX

ENGLAND

UNDER PROTECTOR SOMERSET

CHAPTER I

THE COUP D'ÉTAT

THROUGHOUT Thursday, the 27th of January 1546–7, in the thirty-eighth year of his reign and the fifty-sixth of his age, Henry VIII. lay on his death-bed in the royal palace at West-minster. Parliament was in session, and three days before had attainted of treason the most experienced of his advisers.[1] Of the Privy Council, besides the Duke of Norfolk, three members only were absent. Bishop Thirlby of Westminster was resident as ambassador at the court of Charles V.; Dr. Nicholas Wotton, Dean of Canterbury, had been sent on the conclusion of peace in the pre-vious year to renew diplomatic relations with France; and his brother, Sir Edward Wotton, was Treasurer at Calais.[2] Within the palace the Earl of Hertford, Sir William Paget, and Sir Anthony

---

[1] *Lords' Journals*, i. 287–289.
[2] *Acts of the Privy Council*, ed. Dasent, vol. i. *ad fin.*

Denny nervously watched and waited for their master's dying breath. The first, Lord Great Chamberlain of England and uncle to the heir-apparent, had in his keeping Henry's will; the second, principal secretary to the king, was also his most trusted confidant and the recipient of his last real or fabricated wishes; and the third, chief gentleman of the chamber, was one of the commissioners who, five months before, had been empowered to affix to public documents a stamp in lieu of the royal signature. Towards evening Denny ventured to remind Henry of his approaching end and persuaded him to send for Cranmer. Henry was speechless when the archbishop arrived from Croydon,[1] and while Cranmer was administering to the dying monarch the last consolations of religion, outside in the gallery Hertford and Paget[2] were scheming to override the provisions of his will and grasp the sceptre slipping from his hands.

His will.   The heir to the throne was a child of nine, and for nine years more, by royal usage and by Henry's will, that minority was destined to endure. Until then, Henry fondly hoped that his will would still be law and his dead hand control the government. Taking full advantage of the statutes which, passed in the twenty-eighth and thirty-fifth years of his reign, empowered him to entail his kingdom like a fee, Henry had placed second and third in succession to the crown two daughters, from whom

[1] Strype's *Cranmer*, ed. 1820, i. 179.
[2] Paget to Somerset, 7th July 1549, printed from *Cotton MS.*, Titus F. iii., in Strype's *Eccles. Mem.*, II. ii. 430.

the stigma of illegitimacy cast by Acts of Parliament had never been removed; had limited the right of both by conditions, neglect of which destroyed their claim; and had trampled on hereditary right by postponing, if not excluding, the title of the descendants in the Scottish line. By a still more extraordinary use of the powers lavished on him, he had nominated a body of sixteen [1] who were to govern during Edward's minority, not by their constitutional right as Privy Councillors, but in virtue of their appointment as executors to Henry's will. Pronounced a forgery in the interests of the Stuart claim, the instrument in which these singular provisions were embodied has since been considered suspicious in origin and doubtful in validity.[2]

Its genesis is not, indeed, beyond reproach. On 31st August 1546, in order to relieve Henry of the labour of signing State papers, Sir Anthony Denny, Sir John Gates, and William Clerc had been commissioned to sign such documents with a dry stamp and fill in the signature thus made with ink.[3] Last but one in an extant list [4] of " such billos, warrauntes, letters, and other writings, to the number of four score and six, which the kinge's

Was it genuine? Arguments against its authenticity.

---

[1] It is curious that sixteen was also the number of the councillors appointed on 9th Sept. 1543, to "direct and order" the Governor (Arran) and the Queen-dowager of Scotland during the minority of Mary Stuart.

[2] See Brit. Mus. *Harleian MS.* cf. *Addit. MS.* 4712, No. 29, 849, " A Brief Tractate of the Invalidity of Henry VIII.'s Will."

[3] Rymer's *Fœdera*, original ed.

[4] *State Papers, Henry VIII.*, 1830, i. 892–898.

Majestie caused me, William Clerc, to stamp with his Hieghnes' secrete Stampp, at dyverse tymes and places in this moneth of Januarie, anno 38vo Regni dicti Regis nostri, Henrici Octavi, etc.," occurs "your majestie's last will and testament, bearing date at Westminster, the thirtie daie of December last past, written in a booke of paper, signed above in the beginning and beneath in the end, and sealed with the signet in the presence of th' Erle of Hertford, Mr. Secretarie Pagett, Mr. Denny, and Mr. Harbert, and also in the presence of certain other persons whose names are subscribed with their own 'hand, as witnesses to the same, whiche testament your majestie delyvered then, in our sightes with your own hande, to the said Erle of Hertford, as your own dede, last will, and testament, revoking and adnulling all other your Hieghnes' former willes and testaments." But the statutes [1] in virtue of which Henry VIII. drew up the terms of his will, required that such a will should be signed with his Majesty's own hand, and on the ground that the will was stamped and not signed, Maitland of Lethington, writing to Cecil on 4th January 1566–7 a letter [2] which was the first enunciation of the Stuart claim, declared that the will was manifestly invalid. Moreover, the commission giving Henry's assent to the Act of Attainder against Norfolk, which occurs last in Clerc's list, and was further declared by Paget to have been signed with the stamp, was on that

---

[1] 28 Hen. VIII. c. 7, and 35 Hen. VIII. c. 1.
[2] Printed in Burnet's *Hist. Reformation*, ed. Pocock, iv. 533–6.

ground treated in 1553 as null and void, and the duke resumed his seat in the House of Lords, and was succeeded in his titles and dignities by his grandson without that Act of Attainder ever having been reversed.

These objections would be fatal to the validity of Henry's will, were it not for the fact that the only document now extant purporting to be his will, and certainly that on which his executors acted, is not signed with a stamp, but is signed in writing.[1] It is now in the Record Office,[2] and a careful examination by experts has resulted in the conclusions that there is no trace of the indenture of a stamp, that the two signatures at the beginning and end of the will are not sufficiently uniform to have been made with a stamp, and that both differ materially from signatures known to have been so made. It does not, however, necessarily follow that the signature is Henry's, and the evidence of haste afforded by the

---

[1] In the text of the will it is said to be "signed with our own hand."

[2] The will was ordered to be enrolled on Wednesday, 2nd February 1546-7, and each of the executors was "to have exemplification under the Greate Seale of the same, for the doing whereof the saide wille was presently delivered by them unto the saide Lord Chancellour" (*Acts of the Privy Council*, ed. Dasent, ii. 11). Besides the original, there is in the Record Office (Augmentation Books, 469) a copy which also gives the signatures, but only in the hand of the copyist. There is also a copy of the "exemplification," originally belonging to Lord Cobham. Another contemporary copy of the will is in the British Museum, *Stow MS.*, 576, fol. 11 *et seqq.* The will is printed by Fuller, *Church Hist.*, ed. Brewer, 214-229, in Hilkiah Bedford's *Hereditary Right*, 1713, in Bayly's *Life and Death of John Fisher*, 1655, in Rymer's *Fœdera*, ed. 1713, xv. 110 *sqq.*, and also separately and anonymously in 1713.

writing, the absence of Gardiner's name from the list of executors, the production of the will from Hertford's custody, and the suppression of some of its clauses, have been urged as conclusive proofs that Hertford, probably with Paget's connivance, not merely forged the signature, but dictated the terms, of the will.

These arguments inconclusive. This theory is altogether untenable. Apart from the infamy of such a proceeding, of which nothing in Hertford's career suggests that he was capable, the objections to it are insuperable. For the provisions of the will opposed a serious obstacle to his ambition; it named him fifth in order of precedence, the position he was entitled to as Lord Great Chamberlain; placed him on an equality of power with the other executors; and recognised no claim arising from his kinship to the young prince. His first task was to remove a barrier which would not have existed had there been no will at all, or had the will been manifestly invalid; and in setting the will aside no doubt of its validity was suggested, though such a doubt would have materially smoothed Hertford's path. Moreover, when at the time of his fall every conceivable charge was raked up against him, not only was this forgery not mentioned, but his enemies took their stand upon the terms of the will and accused Hertford of violating its provisions.[1]   Nor was this omission due to igno-

---

[1] See *Troubles Connected with the Prayer-Book of 1549*, Camden Soc., pp. 113–118.   The will was read to the Council on several occasions, and was then transferred to Wriothesley's keeping : on his fall it was sent to the Treasury (*Acts of the Privy Council*, ii. 59,

rance on their part, for several of them were present when Henry handed the will to Hertford; and if Hertford forged the will he must also have forged the signatures of the ten witnesses. The will could only be produced from his custody because it was to him that Henry had entrusted it; the clauses suppressed were those providing for perpetual masses for the benefit of Henry's soul, not those relating to Hertford's position; and if Hertford had dictated the terms of the will, he would not have inserted such as needed suppression in his own interests.

There remain two hypotheses to account for the Other sug-
gestions. discrepancy between Clerc's implied statement that the will was stamped and the fact that the only will extant is signed in writing. Either the illegality of a stamped will was suggested some time shortly before Henry's death, and another was hastily drawn up and signed in writing by the king, in which case all trace of, and all reference to, two wills has disappeared; or Clerc made a mistake in including in his schedule of stamped documents one which, though drawn up possibly at the same time as the others, was signed in writing and not like the others with a stamp.[1]

60). That the will now extant is that on which the executors acted is proved by a comparison of it with the long extract entered in the *Acts of the Privy Council*, ii. 39–41.

[1] Alfred Bailey's *Succession to the Crown*, 1879. This view is strengthened by the fact that while in Clerc's list Henry's will is categorically stated to have been signed at the beginning and at the end, as it is in the Record Office document, no such assertion is made with regard to the remaining eighty-five documents.

Hertford's previous career.

Whichever be the true account of the origin of the will, its contents afforded Hertford little ground for satisfaction.   His long and faithful services, his relationship to Edward, the success which had attended his military enterprises, and his popularity with the masses, constituted in his own eyes an indefeasible claim to a position at least equal to that enjoyed by John, Duke of Bedford, or Richard, Duke of Gloucester, during the minorities of Henry VI. and Edward V.   The height to which he had already climbed suggested to him, and placed within his reach, the attainment of a position of still greater eminence.   Born about 1505, he was the eldest surviving son of Sir John Seymour of Wolf Hall, Wiltshire, who claimed a shadowy descent from a hypothetical Norman invader, but served in Henry VII. and Henry VIII.'s wars in the comparatively humble capacity of a knight.   His mother, a daughter of Sir Henry Wentworth of Nettlested, boasted among her ancestors the Clares and the Cliffords, Hotspur and Edward III.   Both Oxford and Cambridge[1] have claimed the Protector among their *alumni*, but the first authentic mention of him is as *enfant d'honneur* to Mary Tudor on her marriage to Louis XII. of France in 1514.   Chapuys afterwards referred to Hertford having been in Charles V.'s service,[2] which perhaps means nothing more than that he was with his father in attendance

---

[1] Wood's *Athenæ Oxon.*, ed. Bliss, i. 210; Cooper's *Athenæ Cantab.*, i. 107.

[2] *Letters and Papers of Henry VIII.*, ed. Brewer and Gairdner, x. 1069.

upon that monarch during his visit to England in 1522. In the following year he first saw active service in the French war; he was present throughout Suffolk's campaign, assisted in the capture of Bray, Roye, and Montdidier, and was knighted at Roye on 1st November. Two years later he became Master of the Horse to Henry's natural son, the Duke of Richmond, and in July 1527 he went in the retinue of Cardinal Wolsey on his embassy to France.[1] Parsimony was not among Henry's faults, and Seymour's services were lavishly rewarded by the grant of many a manor in Wiltshire, Somersetshire, and Yorkshire. Nor was it less a mark of royal favour when the king borrowed of him large sums of money which he did not repay,[2] and his advance in Henry's graces is marked by his successive appointments as esquire of the royal household, esquire of the body, and gentleman of the privy chamber. Still more important for his advancement was the selection of his sister Jane to be lady-in-waiting to Catherine of Aragon, and to her successor, Anne Boleyn. On 10th September 1535, Henry honoured the Seymours by a visit to their paternal home at Wolf Hall,[3] and on 30th May 1536, after refusing a less honourable connection, Jane became Henry's third wife, Cranmer issuing a dispensation to remove the dis-

The marriage of his sister to Henry VIII.

---

[1] *Chronicle of Calais*, Camden Soc., p. 37.

[2] See *Letters and Papers of Henry VIII.*, vols. iv. v. and vi. *passim*. Most of the facts in Hertford's career down to 1540 have been gleaned from this source.

[3] See for Henry's various visits to Wolf Hall some excellent papers by the late Canon Jackson in *Wiltshire Archæol. Mag.*, vol. xv.

ability involved in the somewhat remote affinity of the two parties. A week later Sir Edward Seymour was created Viscount Beauchamp of Hache, and to support this dignity was granted several manors in Wiltshire, including the Duke of Somerset's present seat of Maiden Bradley. In July he became Governor and Captain of Jersey, and in August Chancellor of North Wales. At the end of the year he succeeded to his father's estates, in the following May he was sworn of the Privy Council, and six days after the birth of the future Edward VI. he was created Earl of Hertford.

The death of Queen Jane was naturally a blow to her brother's influence, but it did not affect his position as uncle to the king's only son, and though the imperial ambassador described him as "young and wise" but "of small power," his rise continued without interruption. After taking part in the trial of the Poles, he was in March 1539 sent to secure the defences of Calais and Guisnes, and in December to escort to London Henry's fourth wife, Anne of Cleves. No authority attaches to the assertion of the Spanish chronicler [1] that Hertford instigated the fall of Cromwell which followed Henry's disgust with his German bride. Cromwell was father of his sister's husband,[2] and that Hertford, who shared Cromwell's religious views, not

[1] *Spanish Chronicle of Henry VIII.*, ed. Martin A. S. Hume, 1888. The author was a Spanish merchant, Antonio de Guaras (Hume's *Year after the Armada, and other Essays*, 1896, p. 77), but the *Chronicle* is a ridiculous farrago of impossible stories.

[2] Hertford's sister Elizabeth married, as her second husband, Cromwell's son Gregory.

only passed unscathed through the ensuing period
of reaction but continued to grow in power, speaks
volumes for the circumspection with which he
walked and the personal popularity he enjoyed
among his colleagues. Throughout 1540 he took
an active part in the business of the Privy Council
and on 9th January 1540–1 was elected a Knight
of the Garter. Another fruitless mission to determine the boundaries of the English Pale in France
followed, and during Henry's absence in the north,
from July to November, Hertford was associated
with Cranmer and Lord Chancellor Audley in the
management of affairs. In November he and the
archbishop were the recipients of the charges against
Catherine Howard which ultimately brought her to
the block and impaired the influence of her relative,
the Duke of Norfolk. In September 1542, Hertford
was made Warden of the Scottish Marches, a sphere
of activity destined to become very familiar to him;
but for the present "the country knew not him, nor
he them," and in December he asked to be relieved
of his charge. On his return he was appointed
Lord High Admiral, but almost immediately he relinquished the post to his future rival, John Dudley,
Viscount Lisle, receiving instead the more dignified
office of Lord Great Chamberlain of England.

Before the end of the year (1543), however, the His services
Scots entered into a fresh alliance with France, and in the
French and
in March 1543–4 Hertford was entrusted with the Scottish
command against them. He was directed to throw wars.
the blame of the war upon Cardinal Beaton, and to
proclaim Henry guardian of the infant queen and

protector of the Scottish realm. At the end of
April his army embarked at Berwick, and on 3rd May
the fleet entered the Firth of Forth. Next day ten
thousand men landed at Leith, and on the 5th
Lord Evers arrived with four thousand horse, who
had marched overland from Berwick. The Provost
of Edinburgh offered Hertford the keys of the city
on condition that all who wished might depart with
their effects; but Hertford demanded unconditional
surrender, declaring that he had come "to punish
the Scots for their detestable falsehood," and to
"show the force of his highness' sword to all such as
would resist him." The Scots replied with defiance,
and on the following day Canongate was blown in.
The castle held out, but the city was pillaged without resistance for two days, and then the English,
lading the ships at Leith with their spoil, sailed for
Berwick, which they reached on the 18th.[1]

In the following July Hertford received a signal
mark of confidence by being appointed lieutenant of
the realm under the new queen, Catherine Parr, who
was regent during Henry's absence in France. In
August he joined the king before Boulogne, and is
said to have materially contributed to the capture
of that town by bribing the French commander,
De Vervins.[2] In October and November he and
Gardiner made futile endeavours to keep Charles V.

[1] Full details of this expedition have been accessible by the
recent acquisition by the British Museum of the official correspondence relating to it (see Appendix). An account was published in the
same year as *The Late Expedition into Scotland*, London, 1544, 8vo.

[2] *Mémoires de Vieilleville*, ed. 1822, and the Preface to Nott's
Works of Surrey, 1815–16, 2 vols. 4to.

to his engagements with England; and when these
proved unavailing, Hertford was sent to Guisnes to
provide for its defence in the war which England
had now to wage single-handed with France. In
January 1544–5 he took command at Boulogne,
and on 6th February performed a brilliant achievement by surprising and routing a French force
double his own numbers which had been sent
against the town.[1] Having thus rendered Boulogne
safe for the time, he was in the spring sent to the
Scottish border[2] to restore the confidence that had
been shaken by the rout at Ancrum Moor, and to
revenge on the Scots their victory. Lack of munitions and men postponed the projected invasion,
and through the summer Hertford remained on the
borders guarding against the risk of a French or
Scots invasion. At length, on 6th September, he
crossed the border, and a list of monasteries and
castles burnt marked his course and shocked even
Englishmen accustomed to the horrors of border
warfare.[3] It was an act of revenge with no ulterior
object, and by the 27th of the month Hertford was
back at Newcastle. On the 10th October he was
summoned to Parliament, and after four months'
close attendance at the Privy Council he was once
more sent to Boulogne to retrieve the blunders of
his rival Surrey. Three months later he concluded

[1] Herbert's *Life and Reign of Henry VIII.*, ed. 1719, p. 250; see
also various letters from Hertford in *Harleian MS.* 284.

[2] Rymer, xv. 72.

[3] *State Papers,* v. 448–452; compare Hooper to Bullinger in
Original Letters (Parker Society), vol. i. p. 37, under wrong date,
January 1545–6, which should be January 1544–5.

peace with the French commissioners, and in July he was once more in London. A mission in September and October to carry out the stipulated destruction of fortifications at Boulogne [1] closed his active service under Henry VIII., and from the date of his return in the latter month until Henry's death [2] he was absorbed in that unrecorded struggle for predominance in the councils of his successor that raged beneath the peaceful surface of affairs.

The fall of the Howards. One after another, by death and by attainder, his rivals had been swept from Hertford's path, and his influence, backed up by that of Catherine Parr, began, not without peril to themselves, to mitigate the severity of the reaction which had set in on Cromwell's fall. But the Howards still survived, a bar alike to religious change and to Hertford's ambition. He and Norfolk stood face to face, the representatives of rival claims and opposing forms of religion. In case of a minority, who should be Protector but his father, Surrey is reported to have asked; and the clash of such pretensions might well have precipitated a civil war. Suddenly, on the 10th of November, the French ambassador informed his Government that violent dissensions had broken out among the English magnates, and that the justices of the peace had been ordered to inquire into treasonable practices that were suspected.[3] On 2nd December Surrey was summoned to meet

[1] *Correspondance Politique de Odet de Selve, 1546–1549*, ed. 1888, pp. 31, 34; *State Papers*, Henry VIII., i. 877, 879.
[2] *Acts of the Privy Council*, ed. Dasent, vol. i. 535 *ad fin.*
[3] *Odet de Selve*, p. 55.

his accusers before the Privy Council, and on the 12th he and his father were committed to the Tower. On the 31st a commission was issued for taking the indictments, and on 13th January 1546–7 Surrey was condemned for treason. He was executed on the 19th.[1] On the 18th a Bill of Attainder against Surrey and his father had been introduced into the House of Lords. It passed its second and third readings on the 19th and 20th, and on the 24th was returned from the Lower House. On Thursday the 27th, in virtue of a stamped commission, it received the royal assent.[2]

Hertford's last serious rivals were thus removed, and the manifest advantage he derived from their fall has naturally involved him in the suspicion of having procured it. Nevertheless, there can be little doubt that it was due to Surrey's folly rather than to Hertford's intrigues. For in spite of personal rivalry and religious differences the relations between Hertford and Norfolk were of a friendly

Hertford's alleged complicity.

---

[1] *Wriothesley's Chronicle*, Camden Soc., i. 177. Other authorities give the 21st as the date. For his trial see *Stowe MS.* 396.

[2] *Lords' Journals.* The entry gives a most suspicious reason for the royal assent being given to the Act, viz., in order that Norfolk's offices might be conferred on, and exercised by others "in sacratissimam solemnitatem coronationis principis Edwardi que jam instat" (i. 289). Such a reference could not have been made unless Henry's ministers had been sure of his speedy death, and were already using his authority. The chief of Norfolk's offices, those of Lord Treasurer and Earl Marshal, were granted to Hertford on 10th February. The informality of this assent (see pp. 4–5) has been suggested as a reason why Norfolk was not executed. But probably it was thought that Norfolk would soon die without the executioner's intervention. He was then seventy-three years old.

character, and when the latter proposed a series of matrimonial alliances between the two families Hertford offered no objection, and he was not among the enemies at whom the duke hinted in his letter to Henry from the Tower. Between Surrey and Hertford, indeed, there was no love lost. Hertford had taken part in the condemnation of Surrey three years before for his midnight frolic in the city,[1] but it was Surrey who, detesting Hertford as an upstart, had scorned the proposed marriages between his and Hertford's children. He had dedicated poems and made other advances to Hertford's wife, which she had haughtily declined, and he had been enraged beyond bounds by his recall from the French command in Hertford's favour. But his fall was due to other causes. By quartering with his own the royal arms,[2] by claiming the protectorate for his father, he had roused Henry's jealous fear for his son's secure succession, and it was Henry himself who drew up the charges against him. In this task he was aided by Lord Chancellor Wriothesley; but both Wriothesley and Sir Richard Southwell—Surrey's original accuser—were staunch adherents of Surrey's own religion, and bitter enemies of Hertford.

[1] On 1st April 1543 Surrey was charged before the Privy Council with breaking windows in the city and shooting stones at peaceable citizens, and was sent to the Fleet. His companion in this prank was Sir William Pickering, afterwards ambassador to France and a suitor for Elizabeth's hand (*Acts of the Privy Council*, i. 104 ; Bapst, *Deux Gentilshommes Poètes à la cour d'Henri VIII.*, p. 269).

[2] There was also the hideous charge that Surrey had urged his sister, the Duchess of Richmond, to assume the same relation to Henry VIII. as Madame D'Etampes held to Francis I.

Hertford was now beyond question the most His position at Henry's death. powerful of Henry's councillors, and to strengthen his position still further he formed an alliance with the king's principal secretary. Sir William Paget, a man after Henry's own heart, was an admirable type of those Tudor officials who " sprung rather from the willow than the oak," [1] served with equal fidelity Henry VIII., Edward VI., Mary, and Elizabeth. Of great ability and untiring industry, he had few scruples, and no determinate religious opinions. But he knew the inner workings of the king's mind as no other man knew them, and was master of all the secrets of the court. His relation with Hertford was one of mutual interest, and together they were supreme in Henry's council. When the French ambassador was unable to see the king, it was with Hertford and Paget that he negotiated, and a few months later Paget told the same diplomatist that " neither Wolsey nor Cromwell had such freedom of speech with the king as he had at the time of his death." [2] So great, indeed, was Paget's prestige that the distribution of dignities in the new reign was determined solely by what he declared had been Henry's intentions.[3]

Henry died about two o'clock on the morning of The accession of Edward VI. Friday, the 28th of January, and scarcely was the

---

[1] When William Paulet (1485?–1572), who became successively Baron St. John, Earl of Wiltshire, and Marquis of Winchester, was asked in old age how he had survived so many storms and changes, he replied, " Ortus sum e salice, non ex quercu" (Naunton's *Fragmenta Regalia*, p. 95).

[2] *Corr. Pol. de Odet de Selve*, p. 195.

[3] *Acts of the Privy Council*, ii. 12–22.

breath out of his body when Hertford and Paget, in a hasty consultation in the gallery, concerted the final arrangements for securing a monopoly of the new king's authority.   They decided to keep secret for the present the news of Henry's death, and to suppress a portion of his will, and Hertford purchased Paget's help in seizing the Protectorate by a promise to be guided by his advice in preference to any other.   Then, handing over to Paget Henry's will, the earl set out to secure the person of Edward VI., who was at Hertford.   On the way back at Enfield, on Sunday the 30th, Hertford received an important accession of strength in the person of Sir Anthony Browne, who " gave his franke consent, after communication in discourse of the state, that his grace should be protector, thinking it . . . both the surest kynde of governement and most fyt for this commonwelth." [1]   Browne's adhesion was significant, not merely because, as Master of the Horse, he was a man of some power, and stood eighth of the executors in order of precedence, but because, as a staunch Catholic, he was one of those on whom Henry VIII. is said to have relied to check the progressive tendencies of Hertford and the reformers. About eleven o'clock the next morning the royal party resumed its journey towards London.

There meanwhile the secret of Henry's death had been well kept.   Parliament had, according to its usual custom, adjourned over Friday, but on Saturday it had met and transacted business, quite unconscious that its power had been annulled and its

[1] Tytler, i. 169.

existence legally ended by Henry's death. It met again on Monday, at eight o'clock, and then Lord Chancellor Wriothesley announced, with tears in his eyes, the king's decease. When he had ended, Paget, who as Secretary of State had a seat on the Woolsack in the House of Lords, read aloud the greater part of Henry's will, including the order for the succession, the names of the executors, and the directions for the payment of the royal debts. Then the Lords of the Privy Council and others "came out of the Parliament Chambre into the Palace of Westminster Hall,"[1] where the Garter King of Heralds proclaimed the new king, Edward VI. At ten o'clock the Lord Mayor and Aldermen assembled in their scarlet gowns in the Guildhall; thence they rode to St. Magnus Church Corner where a like proclamation was made by Clarence herald, and again at the conduit in Fleet Street. At three o'clock "the kinges majestie . . . rode in at Algate, and so along the wall by the Crossed Friars to the Towre Hill, and entred at the Redd Bulwarke, where Sir John Gage, Constable of the Towre, and the Lieutenant, receaved his Majestie on horsebacke, the Erle of Hertford ryding before the king and Sir Anthonie Brown riding after the kinge; and on the bridge next the Wardgate my Lord of Canterburie, my Lord Chauncelor, with other great Lordes of the Counsell, receaved his Majestie, and so brought him to his Chambre of Presence, where they were sworne to his Majestie."[2] An hour or so later Henry's executors met to choose a master.

[1] *Wriothesley's Chronicle*, Camden Soc., vol. i. p. 178.　　[2] Ibid.

Henry's
arrange-
ments for
the govern-
ment during
his son's
minority. The death of Henry VIII., besides voiding all commissions and dissolving Parliament, had also terminated the existence of his Privy Council, and the body which now met in the Tower would in ordinary circumstances have been nominated by the new king, and have held office in virtue of his summons. But Edward VI. was a minor, and his council was not a body selected by him, but a number of executors acting in virtue of their appointment by the late king's will. In default of a ruling sovereign his place was taken, so to speak, by Henry's will, which, like a written, rigid constitution, limited the powers and controlled the action of the executors. Between the lines of his will has been read Henry's determination to maintain the compromise in Church and State which he had established.[1] With natural pride he regarded this settlement as the best possible for his throne and his people, and with Tudor arrogance he disliked the idea of mere subjects interfering with his handiwork. To place this scheme on a surer basis than The executors to his
will. the doubtful fidelity of his executors to their instructions, he sought, we are told, to create a governing body in which two opposing tendencies acting with equal force should neutralise each other and produce a stable equilibrium. The Catholics would restrain the zeal of the Reformers, and the Reformers would check the reactionary desires of the Catholics, and the result would be that Henry's work would remain intact. With this end in view, the executors were selected from both parties. The Reformers

[1] Froude.

were represented by Cranmer, Hertford, Russell, Lisle, Denny, and Herbert; the Catholics by Wriothesley, Tunstall, Browne, and possibly the two Wottons; a third party, consisting of St. John, Paget, and North, possessed no pronounced views, and might be trusted to turn the balance between the other two. The remaining two executors, Montagu, Chief Justice of the Common Pleas, and Bromley, Chief Justice of the King's Bench, were expected as judges to take little part in party conflicts, and as a matter of fact rarely attended the council.

If such was Henry's design, his plan was singularly faulty. The equilibrium he sought to establish proved to be of that unstable character in which the least disturbance destroys the balance, and overturns the whole construction. The balance had, indeed, been destroyed when Surrey was sent to the block and Norfolk to the Tower. "Nor is any one wanting," wrote Burcher to Bullinger, "but Winchester alone, and unless he be caught the evangelical gospel cannot be restored."[1] Gardiner's head remained upon his shoulders, but his exclusion from the list of executors was quite as effective in shattering the power of the Catholic party, and has been plausibly represented as due to the machinations of the Reformers. Foxe's story, based partly upon Paget's statements during the subsequent proceedings for Gardiner's deprivation, that Henry VIII. had conceived a hatred for the bishop owing to his

Gardiner's exclusion from the number.

---

[1] *Original Letters*, Parker Soc., ii. 639.

alleged plot against Catherine Parr,[1] and had remarked, when his attention was called to the omission of Gardiner's name, that he could rule him but
no one else could, has been carefully examined and
pronounced a fabrication.[2]   But Gardiner had more
than once been under Henry's displeasure; he had
certainly been implicated in the well-known "plot
of the prebendaries" against Cranmer; he had been
excluded from the commission appointed to draw up
the "Institution of a Christian man"; on one occasion he had been supplanted by Bonner in an important diplomatic mission; and a few months before
Henry's death the French ambassador records a
violent quarrel in the council between the bishop
and Viscount Lisle, which caused the former to
absent himself from that body.   Nor can there be
any reasonable doubt that Henry was in full possession of his faculties when he omitted Gardiner's
name from the list of his executors.[3]   The issue
has, moreover, been obscured by the tacit assumption that Henry's executors included all the members
of his Privy Council, and that Gardiner alone by a
special dispensation was excluded.   Such was not
by any means the case.   Of Henry's Privy Council
no less than ten besides Norfolk and Gardiner do
not appear among the list of executors.   William
Parr, Earl of Essex, and brother to the queen, as
pronounced a Reformer as Gardiner was a Catholic,

---

[1] See Mr. J. Gairdner in the *Dictionary of National Biography*,
s.v. Catherine.

[2] S. R. Maitland, *Essays on the Reformation*, ed. A. W. Hutton, 1898.

[3] Gardiner himself stated that at this time "he had no access to
the king" (*State Papers, Henry VIII.*, i. 884).

was not among the number; Henry Fitzalan, Earl
of Arundel, the king's Lord Chamberlain; Bishop
Thirlby of Westminster; Sir William Petre, his
second secretary; Sir Richard Rich, formerly Solicitor-
General and Chancellor of the Court of Augmentations; Sir Thomas Cheyney, Sir John Gage, Sir
John Baker, Sir Ralph Sadler, and Sir Anthony
Wingfield, were all members of Henry's council,
who were not appointed executors. Most of them,
it is true, were made assistant-executors, but as the
latter were only to be called in when the others
thought fit, their position was not one of any importance. Two others, Bonner, who had been almost
as prominent as Gardiner himself, and Dorset, who
had married Henry's niece, were excluded both
from Henry's council and the list of his executors.

But the fall of the Howards and the exclusion The election
of Gardiner were not the only circumstances which of a Protector.
rendered the balance of parties in the council an
illusion. For of the conservative party two, Sir
Edward and Dr. Nicholas Wotton, were absent, Sir
Anthony Browne had already given in his adhesion
to Hertford, and Tunstall was a personal friend who
had long been associated with the earl in the
government of the Scottish borders, and subsequently nearly lost his life as he did his bishopric
for his fidelity to the fallen Protector. Accordingly, when the executors met in the Tower on
the afternoon of the 31st of January, they met only
to register a foregone conclusion. They had already
tacitly admitted Hertford's claim to superiority
when on the previous Saturday they had written

to ask his opinion about proclaiming a general pardon, and had deferred to his advice.[1]   Wriothesley alone is said to have offered a strenuous opposition to Paget's proposal that Hertford should be made Protector;[2] and even he acquiesced in the wish of the majority, signed the minute of the council nominating the Protector, and himself announced that step to the king, the assistant-executors, and to the peers in Edward's presence.

The executors evinced a becoming sense of the gravity of the occasion; the minute of the proceedings of their first consultation is headed " In the name of God: Amen," and before transacting any business they determined that one and all, considering " reverently and diligently the greate charge committed unto us, and calling to Almightye God, the only gevir of all grace, for his aide and assistence in all our proceedinges" should " take a corporal othe apon a boke" that they would " stand to and mayntaine the saide laste wille and testament of our said Maister and every parte and article of the same to the uttremoste of our powres, wittes, and connynges." " And to thintent we might the more assuredly answer and satisfie the charge

---

[1] Tytler, i. 17.

[2] There is no authority for the words Mr. Froude puts into Wriothesley's mouth on this occasion; but it is likely enough that some such thoughts were present to the minds of more than one of the executors.   The last Protector had been Richard, Duke of Gloucester, likewise uncle to a King Edward, and his shadow fell darkly across Somerset's career.   A considerable portion of the following passage has been transcribed by Mr. Froude altering and omitting *more suo* many sentences, without giving any indication of such changes.

committed unto us, it was ordered also this daye
that we shuld forbeare the taking of our othes to
the perfourmance of the wille tille the next morowe,
and then apon an other deliberate reading of it to
procede first to the geving of our othes to the
Kinges Majestie, and then to swere to thobserva-
cion of the wille as is affore saide." Then in the
interval between this solemn engagement to swear
to maintain every part and article of the will and
the actual taking of the oath, the executors, it
is said, proceeded to violate in an all-important
particular the spirit if not the letter of the will.
" And forasmuche as in the consideracion and de-
bating of the several poynctes of the charge of the
saide wille committed unto us, and of the grete
accompte which we have to rendre to God, to our
Souveraigne Lorde that now is, and to the hole
worlde for the same, it appeared unto us aswell
uppon thoccasion of the depeache of sundry letters
which were thought mete to be sent to themperour,
the French Kyng, the Regent of Flaundres and
others for the declaracion of the decease of our
said late Master, with request for the conservacion
of their amities, as appon sundry other greate and
urgent thinges to be presently depeached within
the realme and other the Kynges Majestes realmes
and domynions, that being a greate nombre ap-
poyncted to be executours with like and equal
charge, it shuld be more than necessarie aswel for
thonour, surety, and gouvernement of the moste
royal persone of the King our Souveraigne Lorde
that nowe is, as for the more certaine and assured

order and direction of his affayres, that somme
special man of the nombre and company aforesaide
shuld be preferred in name and place before others,
to whome as to the state and hedde of the reste
all strangers and others might have accesse, and
who for his vertue, wisedome, experience in things
were mete and hable to be a special Remembrancer
and to kepe a most certaine accompte of all our
proceedinges, which otherwise could not chose
within shorte tyme but growe into much disorder
and confusion : We, therefore, the Archebusshope
and others whose names be hereunto subscribed,
by oone hole assent, concorde, and agrement, uppon
mature consideracion of the tendrenes and proxi-
mitie of bludde between our Souveraigne Lorde
that now is and the saide Erle of Hertforde, being
his uncle, and of the grete experience which he
hathe in all affayres of this realme and all other
the Kinges Majestes realms, dominions, and cuntreys,
have by vertue of thauthorite gevin unto us by
the saide wille and testament of our saide late
Soveraigne Lorde and Master for the doing of any
Acte or Actes that may tende to thonnour and
suretie of our Souveraigne Lorde that nowe is, or
for thadvancement of his affayres, gevin unto him
the furste and chief place amonges us, and also
the name and the title of the Protectour of all the
realmes and dominions of the Kinges Majestie that
nowe is, and of the Governour of his most royal
persone ; with this special and expresse condicion,
that he shall nat do any Acte but with thadvise
and consent of the reste of the coexecutours in such

maner, ordre, and fourme as in the saide wille of our saide late Souveraigne Lorde and moste gracious Maister is apoynted and prescribed; which the saide Erle hath promised to perfourme accordingly." [1]

This declaration and appointment was subscribed by the thirteen executors who were present, including Wriothesley; there were three unimportant absentees, Bromley and the two Wottons. More than one were men of character, and it is not credible that they would have sanctioned Hertford's elevation, had they regarded it as an infraction of that will which they had just undertaken to maintain in every part and article. That it was contrary to Henry's intention has been inferred from the assumption that had Henry designed a Protectorate he would have himself appointed a Protector by his will. But the statute empowering Henry to devise his crown, enacted only that in case of a minority the young king should be under the guardianship of a council " of such your counsellours and Nobles of your Realme as your Majestie shall name and appoynte by your laste wille made in wrytyng . . ." [2] It gave Henry no express authority to nominate a Protector, and without that express authority overriding the ordinary law, by which all commissions issued by a king terminated with his death, it is not clear that Henry's nomination of a Protector would have been valid.[3] The will, moreover, contained no prohibition

Was it a violation of Henry's will?

---

[1] *Acts of the Privy Council*, ed. Dasent, ii. 4–6.
[2] *Statutes of the Realm*, Record edition, iii. 655–662.
[3] Thus Wriothesley as Chancellor " for avoiding of all questions

of the appointment of a Protector, and the executors could plead some of its phrases as an authorisation for their action. " We will," said Henry, " that our saide executors, or the most part of them, may lawfullie doe what theie shall think convenyent for the execution of this our will, without being troubled by our said sonne, or any other, for the same." " They shall," he proceeded, " and may make, devise, and ordaine, what things soever theie, or the most part of them, as aforesaid, shall, during the minorytie of our said sonne, thinke mete, necessarie or convenyent for the benefit, honour, and suretie, or the weale, profit, and comodite of our said sonne, his realmes, domynions, or subjects . . ." Finally, even if it be granted that Henry had forbidden a Protectorate, the council in setting aside his wishes did but follow the precedent set in 1422 when Parliament, ignoring the directions of Henry V., granted the Protectorate to John, Duke of Bedford, and during his absence in France, to Humphrey, Duke of Gloucester.[1]

The distribution of honours.

On the following day, Tuesday, 1st February, the executors met and took their solemn oath to observe the will. Then they proceeded to the royal chamber and announced their action to Edward, who gave his assent to Hertford's appointment as Protector " of his realmes and domynions and Governor of

and doubts" gave up the great seal to Edward VI. and received it back from his hands (*Acts of the Privy Council*, ii. 6) ; and Hertford insisted on the foreign ambassadors obtaining fresh credentials to Edward VI. So the spiritual jurisdiction of the bishops was renewed (*ib.*, p. 13), and similar commissions (*ib.*, p. 27).

[1] *Rotuli Parliamentorum*, iv. 174.

his persone."[1]   Next, Wriothesley declared it to
the peers, "who with oone voyce gave their consentes
to the same"; and thus the formalities necessary
for Hertford's recognition as Protector were completed.   For the next few days he and the council
were occupied in making arrangements for the
funeral of Henry VIII., and the coronation of his
successor.   On Sunday the 6th of February, Paget
made a detailed deposition before the council of
the honours Henry VIII. had intended to confer
on his executors and other courtiers, and on the
strength of this testimony Wriothesley was made
Earl of Southampton; Lisle, Earl of Warwick and
Lord Great Chamberlain in succession to Hertford,
his post as Lord High Admiral being taken by Sir
Thomas Seymour, who also became Baron Seymour
of Sudeley; Essex was created Marquis of Northampton; Sir Richard Rich became Baron Rich of
Leeze (Leighs); and Sir Edmund Sheffield, for
whose elevation it is difficult to account, was created
Baron Sheffield.   Hertford himself was made Duke
of Somerset, and was also given the barony of
Seymour of Hache and Norfolk's offices of Lord
High Treasurer and Earl Marshal.   Other dignities
which Henry had proposed to confer were not then
awarded; Russell had to wait for his promised
earldom, as had William Paulet, Baron St. John,
while Sir Thomas Cheyney, Sir Thomas Arundell,
and Sir John St. Leger were among the seven who
did not receive the baronies designed for them.
With some show of magnanimity they all refused,

---

[1] *Acts of the Privy Council*, ii. 8.

in consideration of the king's necessities, the revenues with which Henry was said to have intended to enrich them. Paget, perhaps to inspire belief in his deposition, claimed no title for himself.[1] He got it later, a reward for treachery.

Edward's coronation.

On Sunday, the 20th of February, Edward VI. was crowned. In consideration for his frail health and tender years some details of the elaborate ceremony were dispensed with; and among other changes the king's presentation to the people was placed before the administration to him of the oath. This innovation has been adduced to prove the absolutist tendencies of the Tudors and their advisers, and a desire on their part to obliterate what remained even of the form of popular election.[2] But popular assent to Edward's succession to the throne had already been given through the medium of Parliament. Edward VI. succeeded not merely by hereditary right but also by virtue of an Act of Parliament[3]—an Act passed not after his accession to legalise the fact, but before his predecessor's death, settling on him the succession to the crown. Edward VI.'s succession by virtue of a Parliamentary title was a fitting prelude to the movement towards constitutional liberty that was destined to mark the first three years of his reign.

[1] *Acts of the Privy Council*, ii. 13–22.

[2] Dr. Lingard and Canon Dixon, *Hist. Church of England*, ii. 413. "Hitherto the oath had been exacted before the consent of the people was demanded, to keep it in memory that the English monarchy was elective." Hallam also lends the weight of his authority to this view.

35 Henry VIII. c. i.

Somerset had barely seized the object of his ambition when, a fortnight after the coronation, the only statesman who had opposed his elevation himself forfeited his power and position. A convinced Catholic [1] of large ambitions and considerable abilities, Wriothesley inspired in his contemporaries a nervous dread of his designs. "I was afraid," wrote Sir Richard Morison, more than a year after Wriothesley's death, "I was afraid of a tempest all the while that Wriothesley was able to raise any. I knew he was an earnest follower of whatsoever he took in hand, and did very seldom miss where either wit or travail were able to bring his purposes to pass. Most true it is, I never was able to persuade myself that Wriotheseley could be great, but the King's Majesty must be in greatest danger." [2] His position as Lord Chancellor would have rendered him a serious obstacle to the religious and other changes that Somerset was contemplating, for he had been peculiarly identified with the reactionary policy of Henry's later years; but his ambition to take a constant and active part in the proceedings of the council caused him to overreach himself and brought about his fall. In order to relieve himself of part of his arduous legal duties, Wriothesley issued on 18th February a commission empowering Sir Robert Southwell, John Tregonwell, John Oliver, and Anthony Bellasis—all eminent civilians—to hear cases in Chancery during

[1] He with Rich had been unpleasantly prominent in the persecution of Anne Askew.

[2] *State Papers, Foreign Ser.*, Edw. VI., No. 491.

his absence. Actuated by the perennial jealousy between Chancery and common lawyers and by dread of the perpetual encroachments on the common law of injunctions, writs *subpœna* and case-made law, "divers studentes of the Commen Lawes" at once complained to the council, accusing Wriothesley of seeking to enlarge the jurisdiction of his court, and of thereby drawing business away from common lawyers.[1] The commission was only a repetition of one the Lord Chancellor had taken out three years before, but on this occasion he had issued his commission under the great seal without obtaining a warrant, which was both illegal and a direct violation of Henry's will. The question was referred to the judges, and they unanimously declared that Wriothesley had forfeited, "by the Commen Lawe," his office of Chancellor and incurred such penalty and fine as the king should please to inflict on him, "with also emprysonment of his bodye at the kinges will."[2] He aggravated his offence in that he "nat only menassed divers of the said lerned men and others for their service to the Kinges Majestie in this behalfe, but also used unfitting wourdes to me, the saide Protectour." Nor could he offer any other excuse than that he meant no evil in issuing the commission. Somerset, however, showed no disposition to deal hardly with his opponent. "Your Grace," wrote Gardiner, a sym-

---

[1] *Acts of the Privy Council*, ii. 48–58.

[2] The chief of the lawyers asked for their opinion was Sir Richard Rich, who became Lord Chancellor seven months later. See *Harleian MS.* 284, art. 7.

pathiser with Wriothesley, "showed so much favour to him that all the world commended your gentlenes,"[1] and a few weeks later the French ambassador observed Somerset and Wriothesley in friendly and confidential conversation.[2] He was deprived of the Lord Chancellorship, ordered to confine himself to his house, and compelled to enter into recognisances for four thousand pounds. But the fine does not seem to have been exacted, Wriothesley was paid the legacy left him by Henry VIII., and he was before long admitted a member of Edward's new Council.[3]

Wriothesley's fall was followed by the final step in Somerset's advance to power, and by an all-important revolution in the position of his colleagues. It has been already pointed out that the status of the governing body depended not upon a regular commission from the reigning sovereign, but upon the anomalous authority of a dead king. No one had questioned the necessity of granting new commissions to such officials as were not appointed by Henry's will, and even that authority had not been considered sufficient for the exercise of his office by the Lord Chancellor, who, " for avoiding of all questions and doubtes," had received again the great seal from the hands of Edward VI. But if the death of Henry VIII. caused questions and doubts to arise as to the validity of Wriothes-

Revolution in the position of the Protector and the executors.

---

[1] Gardiner to Somerset, in Foxe, vol. vi.

[2] *Corr. Polit. de Odet de Selve*, p. 147.

[3] Probably before the end of the year : the *Acts of the Council* does not give the exact date.

ley's appointment, it affected in like manner the
position of his colleagues.   The point may have
arisen during the discussion of the Lord Chancellor's misdemeanour, and it convinced the executors
that with their present status a commission issued
by them was not of sufficient authority to place
beyond cavil the legality of the use of the Great
Seal by Lord St. John, to whose custody it was now
entrusted.   A similar doubt occurred to the French
king; a defensive alliance between the two realms
was about to be concluded, when Francis I. raised
the question whether Edward VI., when he came of
age, might not repudiate the treaty on the ground
that the authority of the Protector and his colleagues was not sufficient to bind the king.

To satisfy these scruples the executors "made
humble petition to his Highnes that it would
please the same to graunte unto them his royall
assent for their establishment and confirmacion in
the romes of his Highnes Counseillours, and that
it wold likewise please his Highnes to graunte
unto them by a Commission to be signed with his
Graces owne hande suche powre and autorite as to
their saide romes for his Majesties honor and
suretye aperteigned; to thintent the same being
subscribed with their handes might be sufficient
warraunt to the Lord St. John, Lorde Greate
Master of his Highnes Household, and for the
while Lord Keaper of the Greate Seale of Englande,
to procede immediately to the ensealing and passing
under the saide Seale of the saide Commission, by
vertue whereof the Lorde Protectour and Counsail

afforesaide might have suche charge and powre to them committed by his Majeste as in the tenour of the same is at length expressed. Unto the which their peticion his Majeste did moste graciously condescend and graunte, and thereapon signed the afforesaide commission, which being by them subscribed was deliverde to the Lord St. John to be passed in due fourme under the Greate Seale. After thensealing whereof they did furder ordeigne that the saide Lorde St. John should cause a duplicate or exemplificacion thereof to be made furthe in like sorte under the saide Seale, which by thandes of Thomas Chaloner, one of the Clerkes of the Counseill, shuld thereapon the next day be deliverde to the Baron de la Garde repayreng to his master, the French king, for a testimonie of thundoubted powre and sufficiencie of the saide Lorde Protectour and Counsail to treate and conclude apon any matter wherein they shuld have to do on his Highnes behaulf." [1]

The commission alluded to was granted on 13th March, and eight days later it was entered in the Council-book. After confirming everything that had been done since the king's accession, it proceeded: "We for a full and perfect declar- cion of the auctorite to our saide uncle geven and appoincted as is afforesaide, do nominate, appoincte and ordeigne our saide uncle Governour of our saide persone and Protectour of our saide realmes and dominions and of the subjects of the same, untyl suche tyme as we shall have by the suffer-

The Protector's commission and powers.

---

[1] *Acts of the Privy Council*, ii. 64.

ance of God accomplished the age of eighteen yeares.
And We do also graunte to our saide uncle by theis
presentes full powre and autorite from tyme to
tyme, untill suche tyme as we shall have accomplished the saide age of xviii yeares, to do, procure
and execute, and cause to be doone, procured and
executed, all and every suche thing and thinges, acte
and actes, which a Governour of the kinges persone
of this realme during his minorite and a Protectour
of his realmes, dominions and subjects ought to do,
procure and execute, or cause to be done, procured
and executed; and also all and every other thing
and thinges which to thoffice of a Governour of a
king of this realme during his minoritie and of a
Protectour of his realmes, dominions and subjectes,
in anywise apperteigneth or belongeth; willing,
auctorising and commanding our saide uncle by
theis presentes to take apon him the name, title
and auctorite of Governour of our persone and
Protectour of our realmes, dominions and subjectes,
and to do, procure and execute, and cause to be
doone, procured and executed, from tyme to tyme,
untill we shall have accomplished the saide age of
xviii yeares, all and every thing and thinges, acte and
actes of what nature, qualite or effecte soever they be
or shalbe concerning our affayres, doinges, and procedinges, both private and publike, aswel in owte-
warde and foraine causes and matters, as also
concerning our affayres, doinges and procedinges
within our saide realmes and dominions, or in any
of them, or concerning any maner, causes or matters
of any our subjectes of the same, in suche like

maner and fourme as shalbe thought by his wisedome and discrecion to be for the honour, suretie,
prosperitie, good order, wealth or comodite of us, or
of any of our saide realmes and dominions, or of the
subjectes of any of the same." The king went on ^{The new}
to nominate twenty-six councillors,[1] but of these ^{Privy} ^{Council.}
councillors the Protector was given full power to
summon "suche and so many as he from tyme to
tyme shall thyncke convenient," and he could also
add new members at will.

The executors had regularised their position;
a living dog is better than a dead lion, and they
preferred to derive their authority from Edward VI.
rather than from Henry VIII., to be the Privy
Councillors of the one rather than the executors of
the other. But in so doing they gave themselves
a master. Instead of executors whose advice the
Protector was bound by the terms of his office to
follow, they sank into mere advisers who had no
veto on his proceedings, and with whose very
presence he could at pleasure dispense. No
longer *primus inter pares*, the Protector had attained
to an authority that was royal in everything except
name and prestige. So far as it affected the
government during the young king's minority,
Henry's will was torn in fragments and scattered
to the winds. The trammels that hampered
Edward's prerogative were removed, and his

---

[1] The Privy Council thus nominated was almost identical with
Henry VIII.'s Privy Council. Gardiner, Thirlby, and Wriothesley
were excluded, and the Protector no longer ranked as a councillor ;
but all the assistant executors were added, two only of whom,

uncle seized unfettered the royal power of the Tudors.

Sir Richard Southwell and Sir Edmund Peckham, had not been of Henry's Council.   Their names were :—

Thomas Cranmer, Archbishop of Canterbury (1489–1556).

William Paulet, Baron St. John (afterwards Earl of Wiltshire and first Marquis of Winchester), Lord Great Master of the Household (1485 ?–1572).

John Russell, Baron Russell and afterwards first Earl of Bedford, Lord Privy Seal (1486 ?–1555).

(a) William Parr, first Marquis of Northampton (1513–1571).

John Dudley, Viscount Lisle, Earl of Warwick and afterwards Duke of Northumberland (1502 ?–1553).

(a) Henry Fitzalan, Earl of Arundel (1511 ?–1581).

(a) Thomas, Lord Seymour of Sudeley, Lord High Admiral (1508 ?–1549).

Cuthbert Tunstall, Bishop of Durham (1474 ?–1559).

(a) Richard, first Baron Rich, afterwards Lord Chancellor (1496 ?–1567).

(a) Sir T. Cheyney (d. 1558).

(a) Sir John Gage (1479–1556).

Sir Anthony Browne (d. 1548).

(a) Sir Anthony Wingfield (d. 1552).

Sir William Paget, afterwards first Baron Paget (1505–1536), Chief Secretary and Comptroller.

(a) Sir William Petre (1505 ?–1572), Secretary.

(a) Sir Ralph Sadler (1507–1587).

(a) Sir John Baker (d. 1558).

Dr. Nicholas Wotton (1497 ?–1567).

Sir Anthony Denny (1501–1549).

Sir William Herbert, afterwards Earl of Pembroke (1501 ?–1570).

Sir Edward North, afterwards first Baron North (1496 ?–1564).

Sir Edward Montagu (d. 1557).

Sir Edward Wotton (1485–1550).

(a) Sir Edmund Peckham (1495 ?–1564).

Sir Thomas Bromley (d. 1555).

(a) Sir Richard Southwell (d. 1564).

(a) Denotes assistant executor.

CHAPTER II

THE PROTECTOR'S TASK

NEVER, perhaps, in the history of England save at The position of affairs at Henry's death. the accession of Queen Elizabeth has a statesman been confronted with a task so difficult as that which Somerset's ambition had impelled him to undertake. Seldom have England's foreign relations been so beset with dangers, or her internal condition been so pregnant with the elements of disintegration and disorder. The panegyrists of the "majestic lord who broke the bonds of Rome" have painted in glowing colours the glories of his reign, and have heightened the contrast by deepening the shadows that fell across the career of his successors. They have portrayed Henry as the deliverer of the Church from a bondage to the Bishop of Rome which she had long and impatiently borne, as the victor over his country's enemies, the even-handed dispenser of justice, the father of his people, who restored to England a proud position in the councils of Europe, and placed her internal affairs on a sure and lasting foundation. But the suppression of evidence required to produce this effect is not less colossal than that which has been employed to prove Henry VIII. a devotee to

domestic virtue and an unfortunate victim of the
female race; and a brief review of this neglected
evidence is an indispensable preliminary to an
attempt to remove the *suggestio falsi* which otherwise
vitiates any estimate of the statesmanship of the
Protector and the circumstances with which he had
to deal.

Foreign relations. Henry VIII. inherited a stable throne, an over-
flowing treasury, and the affections of a united
people.   He undermined the first, he emptied the
second, and alienated the third.   He mounted the
throne in close alliance with the most powerful
monarchy in Europe, and threatened by the hostility
of none; he left it without a sincere friend, and
with many a secret enemy.   The horizon was
clouded at every point.   Henry had failed to secure
The Empire and the Papacy. the support of the German Protestants, while he
had incurred the bitter hostility of the Emperor.
Charles V. was nominally at peace with England,
but he was only waiting for a suitable pretext and
a favourable turn in his own affairs to avenge the
insults Henry had heaped upon his aunt and cousin,
and Paget declared that in spite of appearances the
Emperor would help the Pope as soon as he could
to recover the spiritual allegiance of the schismatic
realm.   The Papal court was as hostile as ever;
Cardinal Pole was urging his restoration by force
of arms to the land of his birth, and Henry was
no sooner dead than Paul wrote to Charles V. in
an endeavour to persuade him to vindicate the
claim of Mary to the English crown, to which
Edward, being born in schism, could have no

legitimate title. The Emperor deliberated on this threatening scheme, and had his own position been less embarrassed, would doubtless have adopted it.

With France England's relations were even more France. strained. A war had just been concluded by a peace which settled nothing, and teemed with the germs of every sort of quarrel.[1] The limits of the English Pale in France had been defined with a looseness that gave rise to immediate and never-ending bickerings, and the fortifications of Boulogne were an equally prolific source of trouble.[2] But above all there was nothing to prevent the French abetting the Scots in their resistance to the invasion for which Henry was preparing at his death.[3] The acquisition of Boulogne—the one conquest of Henry's lavish wars—was a senseless, a costly, and a futile gain; futile because it was to be surrendered in eight years' time for a payment in money, costly because the expense of maintaining it during that period bade fair to exceed the sum for which it was to be restored,[4] and senseless because it rankled in the Frenchman's breast and made him eager to side with England's enemies whenever opportunity should offer.

[1] See the text in Dumont, *Corps Universel Diplomatique*, 1726, iv. 305–308, and in Rymer, *Fœdera*, orig. ed. xv. 93–98.

[2] The correspondence of the French ambassador, Odet de Selve, is almost exclusively occupied with these disputes.

[3] Odet de Selve, pp. 38, 50–51, 57, 58, 61, 64, 78, 80; *cf.* Brit. Mus. *Addit. MS.* 28595 *f.* 276 *b.*

[4] See a "Declaration of the Naval and Military expenses from September 1542 to September 1552," in *State Papers, Domestic*, vol. xx. No. 11.

With Scotland there was open war, and the result of bloodshed lasting almost throughout his reign was that Henry was no nearer the attainment of his objects than he was when it began. No effort had been made to relieve the murderers of Beaton, who were holding St. Andrews in the English interest, and within a few weeks of the commencement of the new reign the French were secretly sending aid to their ancient allies.[1] Peace or no peace with England, they had resolved to stand by the Scots in maintaining their independence, and with the accession of a new French king, Henry II., in March the defence of the Scots became the basis for schemes of a far-reaching character, which involved perils of the utmost gravity to England.

State of the defences.

While yet dauphin, Henry II. had declared that when he came to the throne he would offer ready money for the immediate restitution of Boulogne, and if the English refused he would make war and capture it within six weeks. The state of defence in which Henry VIII. had left the English Pale in France rendered it probable that his boast would prove no idle one; but fortunately for its power of resistance the Pale received prompt attention from the Protector. The commanders of the various forts in English hands reported on February 4th that their defences were all in a wretched condition;[2] nothing had been done to strengthen Blackness since the previous summer;[3] at Ambleteuse

---

[1] *State Papers, Foreign Ser.*, vol. i. No. 25 ; *Calais Papers*, Nos. 6–7, i.
[2] *Calais Papers*, Nos. 6–7.   [3] *Ibid.*, No. 39.

or Newhaven, Boulogneberg, and the forts called the Old Man and Young Man, things were just as bad, and even at Portsmouth Captain Edward Vaughan reported that extensive fortifications were necessary to render it at all secure against French attack.[1] At Calais the crews and artisans had received no pay since Michaelmas, and the amount owing was £2760, or at least £35,000 of our money.[2] Provisions, and especially corn, were scarce throughout the Pale, and its inhabitants were in a state of destitution.[3] Vigorous steps were taken to effect some amendment. Two commissioners, Sir Hugh Paulet and Sir John Harrington, were despatched to make a comprehensive survey of the whole Pale;[4] monthly musters were ordered to be held; £2500 were transmitted to Calais to relieve its immediate necessities; license was granted for the free exportation of corn from England, where it was eighteen shillings a quarter, to Calais, Newhaven, or Boulogne, where it was thirty,[5] and fortifications were rapidly begun wherever they were most needed.[6]

But if Henry VIII. had left his successor scanty means of defence against an attack which he had almost invited from the Emperor, the Pope, and the

(margin note) Henry's religious changes and oppressive government.

---

[1] *State Papers, Domestic Ser.*, vol. i. No. 19, dated 16th February. See *ib.*, No. 21, for "A Memorial of Necessary Defences." This Newhaven must of course be distinguished from the English port. Its French name appears to have been Ambleteuse; see p. 135, *note*.

[2] *Calais Papers*, No. 50.   [3] *Ibid.*, Nos. 10, 29.

[4] *Ibid.*, No. 50.   [5] *Ibid.*, No. 9.

[6] *Ibid.*, Nos. 39, 40, 41, 47.

King of France, the internal condition of England presented problems still more perplexing. The religious revolution, which originated in Henry's desire to put away an unattractive wife, had alienated at least a third of his subjects without conciliating the smaller proportion of doctrinal reformers. "Our king," wrote Hooper to Bullinger on 27th January 1545–6, "has destroyed the Pope, but not popery." [1] Priests still exacted the "ordinarie shott" before they would administer the sacrament,[2] and poor people were forced to beg before they could receive religious consolations or bury their dead.[3] Verily they exclaimed, "Simony hath lost his name," [4] and "No penny, no paternoster" became a proverb in the mouth of the poor. Never had the fires at Smithfield been more active than during the last years of Henry VIII., and in June 1546 his Lord Chancellor and former Solicitor-General racked with their own hands the schismatic Anne Askew.[5] At the same time the judicial murder of Fisher and More, and the spoliation of the monasteries, had rendered Henry anathema to every sincere Roman Catholic, and the two-faced tyranny of his later years was hideously exemplified on 30th July 1540, when six victims were dragged two and two on hurdles to execution through the streets of London; three were Roman Catholic priests to be hanged for

---

[1] *Original Letters* (Parker Society), i. 36.
[2] Crowley's *Works* (Early English Text Society), p. 155.
[3] *Four Supplications* (Early English Text Society), p. 86.
[4] *Ibid.*, p. 82.
[5] Anne's narrative in Foxe's *Acts and Monuments*.

treason, three were reformers to be burned for heresy.[1] The governing classes alone, the new nobility raised on the ruins and debauched by the spoils of the monasteries, had cause for satisfaction, and their support was compelled by a perfect fear which cast out love. Illegal fines and arbitrary imprisonment attended those who made show of resistance, if they were fortunate; if not, the scaffold or the block. Statute after statute swelled the long list of treasons; they were invoked against man and woman alike and became a fitting monument to the monarch who is said to have boasted that he never spared a man in his anger or a woman in his lust.

If this had been all the evil Henry did, the task of his successor had been comparatively easy. Judicial murders and the burning and torture of heretics could be summarily stopped Treason laws could be swept from the statute-book, and in any case they affected but a few. Other results, however, of Henry's rule were not so easily removed. To the social dislocation caused by the dissolution of the monasteries and the agricultural revolution Henry added the evils of a mountain of debt, a crippled revenue, and a debased coinage. According to Bacon's calculation, Henry VII. left in his treasury £1,800,000, or about £30,000,000 of our money; his successor bequeathed to Edward VI., instead of a surplus, a debt of some hundred thousand pounds. Forced loans and benevolences had proved unavailing to level up the ordinary revenue

Condition of the revenue.

---

[1] *Wriothesley's Chronicle* (Camden Soc.), i. 120, 121.

to Henry's requirements; the enormous wealth of
the monasteries disappeared in the abyss, and twice
had Parliament relieved him from his debts.   The
climax of financial infamy was reached when the
currency, which had remained intact throughout the
humiliations of the kingdom under John and the
confusion of the Wars of the Roses, was tampered with,
and the gold and silver coins of the realm debased.

Debasement of the coinage.   The debasement of the coinage is a matter of
such vital importance to the true understanding of
Tudor history as to necessitate a somewhat fuller
explanation.   From 1344 to 1816 England possessed the advantage or disadvantage of a bimetallic
system of currency.   From various causes the only
serious fluctuation in the value of gold and silver
during the fifteenth and early part of the sixteenth
century consisted in the gradual appreciation of
silver, and this the Government met by occasionally
reducing the weight of silver coins.   No attempt,
however, was made to tamper with the purity of the
coinage until 1543, when the alloy in gold coins
was increased by 2 dwt. in the pound.   The alteration in the silver coins was more serious, and the
alloy was raised from 1 in 13 to 1 in 5.   At the
same time the weight of both kinds of coin was
reduced; a pound weight of gold was coined into
twenty-eight instead of twenty sovereigns, and a
pound of silver was coined into forty-eight instead
of forty-five shillings.   Thus gold was reduced to
only ten times the value of silver; but in France it
was then worth 11·82 times the value of silver, in
Flanders 10·62 times, and in Germany 11·38, so

that while in England an ounce of gold would purchase only ten ounces of silver, in France it would purchase 11·82 ounces, in Flanders 10·62, and in Germany 11·38. The result was that gold began to be exported in large quantities over the sea.[1] The process of debasement once begun, the descent became easy and rapid. In 1545 the first French invasion since the time of Henry IV. illustrated the results of Henry VIII.'s foreign policy, and under pressure of this danger silver coins were issued, half of which consisted of alloy, and the weight of gold coins was further reduced by coining a pound weight of gold into 30 instead of 28 sovereigns. Again in 1546 both gold and silver coins were further debased; the former were issued with one-sixth alloy and the latter with two-thirds alloy.[2] Gold was thus reduced to only five times the value of silver, its exportation was immensely accelerated, and gold coins almost disappeared from England. The folly of this artificial appreciation of silver was accentuated by the fact that the large quantities of silver beginning to be imported from Mexico and Peru were producing an inevitable depreciation in its natural value. At Henry's death the coinage of England was more debased than it has been at any other

[1] This process was not novel, as Mr. Oman (*Trans. Royal Hist. Soc.*, New Series, vol. ix.) seems to think. Bishop William Smith, the founder of Brasenose, was about 1507 condemned to pay a fine of £1800 for having paid English gold to a foreigner, and the exportation of gold had been forbidden by statute 4 Henry VII., c. 23.

[2] See the accounts of Sir William Sharington, master of the mint at Bristol, in *State Papers, Edward VI., Domestic*, vol. ii. arts. 10–12,

time save for a few months during Northumberland's administration. The result was a rapid rise of prices, and the dislocation of commercial relations; but the evil fell most severely on the labouring classes, because, owing to the scarcity of employment caused by the substitution of sheep-farming for tillage, wages did not rise with prices.

The conventional explanation of this practical bankruptcy attributes it to the personal extravagance of Henry and the costliness of his foreign wars. It is pointed out that the household expenses, which had been £14,000 a year at his accession, rose to £56,000 before he died. These circumstances no doubt contributed to the result, but the true cause lay far deeper. It lasted throughout the Tudor period, was the hardest problem with which Elizabeth had to deal, and was at the root of the difficulties she bequeathed to the Stuarts. It impelled James I. and Charles I. to impose arbitrary taxes, and at the same time furnished Parliament with the means of resistance. Without it the constitutional struggle of the seventeenth century would have been of a totally different character, and without it the success of Parliament would have been highly problematical. This cause was the progressive decline in the revenues of the Crown. The ordinary royal income was still derived from the ancient taxes, tenths, fifteenths, and subsidies. There was also the right of purveyance, but owing to enclosures and the consequent decay of homesteads, and to the scarcity of meat and other provisions resulting from the conversion of arable land and

land employed in grazing oxen to sheep-farming,
the value of this right had been greatly reduced.
A similar fate had overtaken the tenths, fifteenths,
and subsidies. Originally the tenth levied on cities,
towns, and the royal domain, and the fifteenth
levied on rural districts outside the domain, had
been, as their name implied, direct variable taxes.
But through the English hatred of a direct variable
tax, these imposts were converted in the fourteenth
century into a fixed sum. In 1334 the commissioners arranged a composition with the counties
for the payment of the fifteenth and with the
cities and towns for the payment of the tenth,
and they agreed to pay a fixed sum which no
doubt at that time was equivalent to what would
have been paid had each taxpayer been separately
assessed by the commissioners. Henceforth it became the custom to grant tenths and fifteenths
with the stipulation that they were to be levied
according to the "ancient" manner, that is, the
method employed in 1334. The sum thus raised Methods of
was between £38,000 and £39,000, and from that taxation.
date a tenth and fifteenth meant that amount.
Various attempts were made at different times, but
in vain, to revive the practice of direct assessment.
During the fifteenth century a remission of £6000
was made for decayed towns, so that under the
Tudors a tenth and fifteenth meant about £32,000.
A process somewhat different in method, but similar
in result, had affected the subsidy. This tax consisted of two parts—a tax of four shillings in the
pound on revenue derived from land, and two

shillings and eightpence in the pound on the value of goods. No one was expected to pay both; the minimum income from land that was taxed was £20 a year. All others were taxed *in bonis*, which included crops from land as well as merchandise and other movables, and the minimum income taxed from these sources was £3 a year. The assessment was entrusted to commissioners appointed by officers of state, and these commissioners were usually justices of the peace and other local gentry. They were as a rule very lenient in their assessment; the subsidy became in practice a fixed sum equal to the last one granted, and the commissioners, while granting a rebate to those whose incomes had fallen, in all probability rarely demanded an increased payment from those whose worldly goods had multiplied. The result was that the subsidy, which was originally worth £120,000, had by Elizabeth's time sunk to £70,000, and in the seventeenth century it was little more than £50,000. The effect of the importation of precious metals from America, of the general rise in prices, on the royal revenue thus becomes obvious. Nominally it might remain the same, but really and relatively to the general wealth of the nation it continuously and rapidly decreased.[1]

Somerset's measures. These facts must be remembered in extenuation both of Henry's debasement of the coinage and Elizabeth's parsimony. They also explain the feeble-

[1] See this subject treated at greater length in Dowell's *History of Taxation*, 4 vols., 2nd ed., 1888, cap. iii. 70, 71, and compare the Account of the Revenue among the manuscripts of the Society of Antiquaries, No. 209.

ness of the efforts which Somerset made to remedy
that debasement, and excuse to a large extent his
comparative failure in other departments of government. To do anything at all, in face of the appalling difficulties Henry had bequeathed him, was no
small achievement. But to restore the coinage to
its original purity—a duty the partial fulfilment
of which cost Elizabeth five years' revenue—was an
absolute impossibility with an empty exchequer,
with the pressure of debts, the repayment of which
Henry had solemnly adjured his executors to make
their first care, with wages in arrear, with the defences in need of immediate attention, and with a
revenue which Henry had permanently crippled by
alienating a considerable portion of the royal domain.
Nevertheless Somerset effected a slight improvement; he reduced the household expenses during
the first six months of Edward's reign to £21,000,
as compared with the £28,000 to which they
amounted during the last six months of Henry's
reign,[1] though he had to reckon with the excep-
tional charges of the coronation. This economy
was maintained so long as Somerset ruled.[2] He
then turned his attention to the coinage; he was
unwilling that the young king's image should be
dishonoured by appearing on debased coinage that
occasioned sarcastic comment in popular ballads,[3]
and accordingly the coins which he was obliged to

[1] Strype's *Ecclesiastical Memorials*, II. ii. 156.

[2] When Warwick became supreme, the expenses rose from
£46,000 a year to over £100,000.

[3] See Oman, *The Tudors and the Currency*, in *Transactions of the
Royal Historical Society* New Series, vol. ix.

issue at once were cast in Henry VIII.'s dies.   In 1549, however, the alloy in silver coins was reduced from two-thirds to a half, and gold coins were raised from $\frac{20}{24}$ carats fine to $\frac{22}{24}$ carats.   But the treasury was unable to support even this reformation, and at the same time that the coins were purified their weight was reduced; the new sovereign weighed only 170 grains as against 192 grains, and the "testoon" or shilling was reduced to two-thirds its former size.   The step was, however, an improvement; there was less fraud in issuing light coins of purer metal than in issuing coins of full weight, most of which consisted of alloy.[1]   At the worst, Somerset checked the rapid process of debasement; he left the coinage better than he found it, but after his fall it sank to even lower depths.[2]

---

[1] *Cf.* Hawkins, *Silver Coins of England*, ed. R. L. Kenyon, 1887, p. 289 : "The propriety and necessity of re-establishing a currency of standard metal seems to have been perceived at an early period of his [Edward VI.'s] reign, and endeavours were made to accomplish so desirable an end.   The principles, however, were not well understood, the expense of doing it honestly was more than the state of the treasury could conveniently bear, and the reformation of the coinage was therefore marked by vacillation and injustice. The ultimate object of the Government was correct and good, but the mode of arriving at it was irregular and dishonest.   As their views were not clear, their proceedings were inconsistent."   This takes no account of the changes in Edward VI.'s Government, which explain much of the "vacillation."   See also on this subject Ruding's *Annals of the Coinage*, 3rd edition, by Akerman, 1840, the standard work.

[2] Warwick issued silver coins of which three quarters consisted of alloy ; he further "called down" the value of the testoons first to 9d. and then to 6d.   Mr. Oman says this first "calling down" was a base expedient which we owe to Somerset, but this is an instance of the failure to date accurately, which seems very com-

To this long list of sins of commission Henry Social distress. added a sin of omission which involved more danger to the commonwealth than all the others put together. Since Wolsey's fall he had taken no steps to check or remedy the incalculable evils wrought by the enclosure of common lands, the engrossing of holdings, the conversion of arable to pasture land, and the growing practice of dealing with land as an investment on commercial and competitive principles. The importance and effects of this complex movement must be considered later in connection with Somerset's remedial proposals, and here it is sufficient to suggest some of the problems which it thrust upon the Protector's Government. Employment became scarce, and prices rose while wages remained stationary; hundreds of thousands of labourers were expelled from their holdings, and vagabondage increased by leaps and bounds. The yeomanry decayed, and with it the only effective force for defence the realm possessed; the establishment of a mercenary army became a necessity, and

mon with writers dealing with Edward VI.'s reign. The proposal to call down the coin was first mooted in the Council in April 1551, two years after Somerset's fall. On the 30th of that month, a proclamation was signed calling down the testoon to 9d. and the groat to 3d. (*Acts of the Privy Council*); copies of this proclamation are in *Hatfield MS.*, vol. i. No. 355, in the Library of the Society of Antiquaries, *MS.* No. 116, and the substance is printed in Ruding, ii. 107. It was to take effect on 31st August following, but this date was anticipated, and the testoon was actually called down to 9d. on 9th July (Wriothesley, *Chron.*, ii. 50; *State Papers, Dom. Ser.*, vol. xiii. No. 29). And on 7th August following it was further called down to 6d., the proclamation to take effect on 17th August (Wriothesley, ii. 54; *State Papers, Dom.*, xiii. 33).

that involved a further drain on the impoverished exchequer. Schools and universities were affected and rapidly dwindled in numbers. The old feudal bond between the lord and all his tenants was destroyed; its place was taken by commercialism and ruthless competition. In one of their supplications the people adjured Henry to leave to his son a commonweal, and not an "iland of brute beasts, amongst whom the strongest devour the weaker." They appealed to ears that heard not, to a mind that did not understand. Henry was absorbed in foreign wars, in the spoliation of monasteries, and the subtleties of theological debate; and his successor was left to deal as he might with a land that had once "been famous throughout all Christendome by the name of Merrie England; but covetous inclosers have taken this joy and mirth away, so that it may be now called sighing or sorrowful England."[1]

Moral deterioration.

The economic and religious revolution was not accomplished without a notable deterioration of moral principle. Public virtue languished, and the ministers whom Henry trained were equally ready to abolish Catholic doctrine under Warwick, and to restore it under Mary, to deprive of their bishoprics Gardiner, Bonner, and Tunstall, and to burn Cranmer, Ridley, and Latimer. By offering them monastic wealth as a bribe for their support of religious changes, Henry debauched his courtiers as he had debased his coinage. As the desire for

[1] Francis Trigge, *The Humble Petition of Two Sisters: the Church and the Commonwealth.* London, 1604.

riches became the mainspring of action, scruples as to the means of attaining them disappeared. Public interests were sacrificed to private gain, and the welfare of the community counted for little against the temptation to double rents and enclose commons. Malversation became frequent, officials took bribes,[1] and offices were sold.[2] Corruption in high places made the task of government difficult, and rendered almost impossible a reformation in any direction.[3]

Such were the conditions with which Somerset had to deal, and to these manifold embarrassments were added the insecurity of his position and a circumscribed authority. It was enhanced by none of the "divinity that doth hedge a king." The Council which had set him up could, with the king's consent, remove him; and some among that Council watched with jealous eyes his rise to power. Seven only signed his patent as Protector, and among them was not found the name of Warwick.[4] This was not all; Henry might seem to have been animated by a desire to surround with as many

Difficulty of Somerset's position.

[1] Crowley, *Works* (Early English Tract Society), pp. 11, 12, 29.

[2] *Ibid.*, p. 98.

[3] By malversation in the court of first-fruits and tenths the king is said to have lost £10,000 a year (Tytler, i. 170; *cf.* Strype, *Eccles. Mem.*, II. i. 222–228).

[4] This circumstance has often been emphasised, but its significance is very doubtful. Lord Seymour's name is not among this list, and yet he admitted himself that he had agreed to his brother's Protectorate, and signed his agreement in writing. It is probable that all the others did the same. It is pointed out (pp. 78–9) that these signatures to the *Acts of the Council* are entirely untrustworthy (cf. *Hatfield MSS.*, *Acts of the Privy Council*, ii. 248).

difficulties as possible the Government during his son's minority. The composition of the body of executors had been such as to provoke administrative impotence, and the risk of civil war. The establishment of a Protectorate had removed this danger, but there remained the unprecedented statute, which empowered the king to repeal all Acts passed during his minority. This cast a shadow of doubt over the measures of Edward VI., and gave colour to the contention that the Protector and his Council had no authority to disturb Henry's settlement in Church and State, on which Gardiner and Bonner based their opposition to the Government. It was thus, invested with a crippled authority and assured of doubtful support, that the Protector entered on a task which would have taxed the power of Henry VIII., and set to work to effect a revolution not merely in the established beliefs of the people, but in the spirit of administration and in the laws upon which it was based.

CHAPTER III

PRINCIPLES AND METHODS OF GOVERNMENT

THE movement towards constitutional liberty which characterised Somerset's rule has been explained in various ways. The spirit of the hour was one of universal benevolence say some,[1] others that the ill-assorted body of councillors who exercised the functions of regency by Henry's testament were sensible that they had not sinews to wield his iron sceptre, and that some sacrifice must be made to a nation exasperated as well as overawed by the violent measures of his reign.[2] Universal benevolence is a singular sentiment to attribute to a generation which witnessed, apparently without any qualms, the burning of heretics and the hideous execution of priests as traitors; nor is it quite clear why, if Henry's executors felt themselves unequal to his task, they should voluntarily have deprived themselves of the weapons wherewith he imposed his authority. It is also a curious coincidence that the benevolent era should have closed so abruptly with Somerset's fall, and that the exasperation of the people should have so completely subsided as to enable Warwick thereupon to restore and augment the severity of the laws that oppressed them. Nor is

---

[1] Froude, iv. 305.　　　　[2] Hallam, i. 37.

it less remarkable that in spite of the universal benevolence these same executors, with one or two
exceptions, were strenuously hostile to the embodiment of this spirit in Acts of Parliament. "The
worst act," wrote Sir John Mason some years later,
"that ever was done in our time was the general
abolishing of the Act of Words by the Duke of
Somerset, whereof we have already had some experience." [1]   "What is the matter, then," echoed
Paget, "troweth your Grace?   By my faith, sir . . .
liberty, liberty.   And your Grace would have too
much gentleness, which might have been avoided
if your Grace would have followed my advice." [2]

The real
cause.

The only rational explanation of the experiment
in liberty that was now initiated is the obvious one
that the Protector was a believer in constitutional
freedom, and wielded for the time sufficient influence to put his ideas into force.   They were
a strange growth in one who had been nourished
and trained in the violence and oppression of
Henry's court; and there is nothing except Somerset's temperament to account for his adoption of
liberal views.   That he remained uncorrupted by
the spirit of his fellows argues something for his

---

[1] Mason to the Council, *State Papers, Foreign*, quoted by Froude,
iv. 306, *note*.   He refers of course to the statute 1 Edw. VI. c. 12.

[2] Paget to Somerset, 7th July 1549), printed in Strype, *Eccles.
Mem.*, II. ii. 429–436.   Bishop Ponet illustrates this community
of ideas between Paget and Mason: "Paget and Mason, albeit they
have not one father and mother, yet be they sworn brethren. . . .
Whatsoever Mason worketh, Paget uttereth, that the one inventeth
the other practiseth" (*Treatise of Politike Power*, 1556).   Paget was
Somerset's chief adherent: other councillors were even more
hostile to the Protector's "gentleness."

originality of ideas and tenacity of opinion. Ambition and a seeking after popularity may have sped his desire to give effect to his views, but they had been formed before power was within his reach, and from the letter already quoted [1] it appears that Paget on the night of Henry's death warned the future Protector against a too free indulgence in these sentiments. Somerset, however, was not a man to defer to the advice of others where he thought himself in the right, and with an authority enhanced by his victory over the Scots, he proceeded in his first Parliament, which met on 4th November 1547, to sweep away " the most miserable series of enactments that disgraces the statute-book." [2] He had not to wait for Parliament to begin the work on which he had set his heart, namely, to lift the weight of absolutism which the Tudors had imposed on England and which Cromwell had perfected. The executions for heresy and treason, the use of the pillory, and other incidents of arbitrary rule ceased with Henry's death, and the first Parliament of Edward VI. only ratified a practice the Protector had followed for nearly ten months.

The preamble of the great Act of Repeal [3] declares: Spirit of the new administration. " Nothing being more godly, more sure, more to be wished and desired betwixt a Prince, the Supream Head and Ruler, and the Subjects, whose Governor and Head he is, than on the Prince's Part great clemency and indulgency, and rather too much

[1] Strype, *Eccles. Mem.*, II. ii. 429–436.
[2] Canon Dixon, *Hist. Church of England*, i. 233.
[3] 1 Edward VI. c. 12.

Forgiveness and Remission of his Royal Power and just Punishment, than exact Severity and Justice to be shewed; and on the Subjects Behalf, that they should obey rather for Love, and for the Necessity and Love of a King and Prince, than for fear of his strait and severe Laws; yet such Times at some time cometh in the Commonwealth, that it is necessary and expedient for the Repressing the Insolency and Unruliness of Men, and for the foreseeing and providing of Remedies against Rebellion, Insurrection, or such Mischiefs, as God sometime with us displeased, for our Punishment doth inflict and lay upon us, or the Devil at God's Permission, to assay the good and God's elect, doth sow and set among us; the which Almighty God with his Help and Man's Policy, hath always been content and pleased to have stayed, that sharper Laws, as a harder Bridle should be made, to stay those Men and Facts that might else be Occasion, Cause and Authors of further Inconvenience; the which Thing caused the Prince of most famous Memory, King Henry the Eighth, Father to our said Sovereign Lord King, and other his Highness Progenitors, with the Assent of the Nobles and Commons, at divers Parliaments in their several Times holden, to make and enact certain Laws and Statutes, which might seem and appear to Men of exterior Realms, and many of the King's Majesty's Subjects, very strait, sore, extream, and terrible, although they were then, when they were made, not without great consideration and Policy moved and established, and for the Time, to the Avoidance of further Inconvenience, very ex-

pedient and necessary: But as in Tempest or
Winter, one Course and Garment is convenient, in
calm or warm weather a more liberal case or lighter
Garment, both may and ought to be followed and
used; so we have seen divers strait and sore laws
made in one Parliament (the Time so requiring) in
a more calm and quiet Reign of another Prince, by
the like Authority and Parliament, repealed and
taken away: The which most high clemency and
Royal Example of his Majesty's most noble Progenitors, the King's Highness of his tender and godly
Nature, most given to Mercy and Love of his Subjects, willing to follow, and perceiving the hearty
and sincere Love that his most loving Subjects, both
the Lords and Commons, do bear unto his Highness,
now in this his Majesty's tender age, willing also to
gratify the same therefore, and minding further to
provoke his said Subjects with great Indulgency and
Clemency shewed on his Highness Behalf, to more
Love and Kindness towards his Majesty (if it may
be) and upon Trust that they will not abuse the
same, but rather be encouraged thereby more faithfully and with more Diligence (if it may be) and
care for his Majesty, to serve his Highness now in
this his tender Age, is contented and pleased, that
the Severity of certain Laws here following be miti-
gated and remitted."

The statute then proceeded to enact "That from
henceforth no Act, Deed or Offence, being by Act of
Parliament or Statute made Treason or Petit Treason, by words, writing, ciphering, deeds, or otherwise
whatsoever, shall be taken, had, deemed, and ad-

Repeal of treason and heresy laws.

judged to be High Treason or Petit Treason, but only such as be Treason or Petit Treason, in or by the Act of Parliament or Statute made in the five and twentieth year of the reign of the most noble king of famous memory, King Edward the Third." A few exceptions to this wholesale abolition of treasons were made; those who coined false money, counterfeited the king's sign-manual,[1] or attempted to alter the succession as established by Henry's will, were to remain liable to the penalties of high treason, and servants who robbed their masters, to those of felony in accordance with statute 27 Henry VIII. c. 2 ; while the Act making the denial of the king's supremacy high treason was modified but not abolished. The modification was, however, all-important, and would have made impossible the execution of Fisher and More. It was, indeed, still high treason to affirm "by Writing, Printing, Overt deed or Act," that the king "is not or ought not to be Supream Head in Earth of the Church of England and Ireland"; but it was no longer treason to do so by "Open Preaching, Express Words or Sayings." Those who did so were to be punished, for the first offence, by loss of goods and chattels and imprisonment, and for the second offence, by perpetual imprisonment.

Other important relaxations of the law of treason were embodied in this statute. Benefit of clergy and right of sanctuary were again allowed, wives of attainted persons were permitted to recover their

[1] These two offences were, however, high treason under the Act of Edward III., 1352.

dower, and it was enacted that all accusations of
treason must be preferred within thirty days if
committed in England, and within six months if
committed abroad. But the most important modification was that contained in the last clause, which
was to the effect that no one was to be "indicted,
arraigned, condemned, or convicted for any offence
of Treason, Petit Treason, Misprision of Treason . . ."
unless he "be accused by two sufficient and lawful
witnesses, or shall willingly, without violence, confess the same." This clause, which has been
unaccountably overlooked, is really entitled to the
praise of being "one of the most important constitutional provisions which the annals of the Tudor
family afford," which has been bestowed on a clause
embodied in a later Act in the reign.[1]

Another reform effected in the fifth section of
the Act was the repeal of the statutes giving to
proclamations the force of law, but it has been much
criticised on the ground that proclamations were
issued exactly the same as before, and that some of
them exceeded all precedents[2] in the severity of the
penalties they inflicted. This clause, however, was

Proclamations.

---

[1] Hallam, i. 40; Froude, v. 61, 62. The clause referred to is
No. 12 in statute 5 and 6 Edward VI., c. xi. It did indeed extend
the former clause by enacting that the two witnesses were to be
confronted with the person they accused, which was an important
addition, but otherwise the clause is a verbal repetition of that enacted in 1547, which first required that there should be two lawful
and sufficient witnesses.

[2] Hallam, i. 37, 38; the proclamation especially objected to is
that mentioned in Strype, *Eccles. Mem.*, II. i. 233, which ordered
that the sowers of false rumours should be sent to the galleys.
Strype does not give this among his collection of proclamations

never intended to abolish the use of proclamations, which, indeed, would have in these days rendered government almost impossible, but merely to secure subjects from suffering pains and penalties for their infraction in the same way as if they were statutes. In Mary's reign the opinion of the judges was taken on the subject, and they pronounced proclamations legal *quoad terrorem populi*. There is no evidence that Somerset used them beyond this extent, or that subjects were fined or imprisoned for infraction of his proclamations, and, indeed, Warwick soon after Somerset's death found it necessary for his purposes to appoint a commission to see to their due execution.[1]

Religious freedom.

The last and one of the most significant of the clauses of this Act which call for attention is the third, which repealed "all Acts of Parliament and Statutes touching, mentioning or in anywise concerning

and I have not been able to verify the fact or date (29th April 1549) of this proclamation. In any case it is pretty certain that it was never acted on, for Somerset, in a communication to the French ambassador, made it almost a matter of complaint that he could not retaliate on the French king's treatment of English prisoners in sending them to the galleys, because the English had no galleys to send them to. So he threatened to hang the French prisoners if any more English were sent to the galleys (Odet de Selve, p. 187).

[1] Hallam also says that many of the religious changes effected during the reign were first ordered by proclamation, though afterwards confirmed by statute. So far as Somerset is concerned, however, the Acts of Parliament preceded the proclamations; *e.g.* the proclamation, 27th December 1547, for administration of communion in both kinds was preceded by an Act of the Parliament prorogued on 24th December. The case was similar with the proclamation against eating flesh in Lent.

Religion or Opinions." The Acts so repealed included Richard II. and Henry IV.'s statutes *de hæretico comburendo*, Henry VIII.'s "concerning the Punishment and Reformation of Heretics and Lollards, and every Provision therein contained," the Act of Six Articles, "and also the Act of Parliament . . . touching, mentioning or in any wise concerning Books of the Old and New Testament in English, and the printing, uttering, selling, giving or delivering of Books or Writings, and retaining of English Books or Writings, and Reading, Preaching, Teaching or Expounding of Scripture . . . and all and every other Act or Acts of Parliament concerning Doctrine or Matters of Religion; and all and every branch Article, Sentence and Matter, Pains and Forfeitures contained, mentioned or in any wise declared in any of the same Acts of Parliament or Estatutes." It would have been enough to entitle Somerset to a claim on the gratitude of posterity had he done nothing but remove the restrictions on printing the Bible in English, but the above clause did much more than that. It relieved not merely the men of his own religion from the penalties of the Six Articles, but the adherents of the Roman Faith. Save in the matter of the royal supremacy it established for the time religious liberty, and even the exception, which was justified then and afterwards by political rather than theological reasons, was enforced by milder penalties than obtained before or afterwards for many generations.

The Act was not, however, passed without some

opposition and alteration. The meagre entries in
the journals of both Houses of Parliament afford
no solution of the interesting question as to what
changes were made during its passage, or who were
responsible for them. It is possible that Parliament
endeavoured to extend the liberty it bestowed, but
it is more probable that some of the limitations
it contained were introduced in deference to protests from men of less liberal cast of mind than
Somerset. The bill was introduced into the House
of Lords on November 10, 1547, and was the first
measure in the session of which the journals make
mention. It was read a second time on the 12th
and a third on the 15th; it was then committed
to Lord Chancellor Rich, a provision, the nature of
which is not known, was added to it, and on the
16th it was read a fourth[1] time and sent down to
the Commons. There it met with scant respect,
and so much mutilated was it that on the 22nd a
new bill was introduced into the House of Commons.
It passed its first reading on the 22nd, its second
on the 30th, and its third not until the 12th of
December. This new bill was introduced into the
House of Lords on the 16th, but the peers objected
to accepting the extensive alterations that had been
made in the Commons, and a strong deputation—consisting of the Archbishop of Canterbury, the Lord

---

[1] The limit of three readings was not then in force, and there are
frequent references in the journals of both Houses to bills being
read five and even six times ; they were also on occasion committed
more than once, but it was to select bodies—sometimes to one
member. A committee of the whole House was apparently unknown.

Chancellor, the President of the Council (St. John), the Marquis of Dorset, the Earls of Shrewsbury and Southampton, the Bishops of Ely, Worcester, and Lincoln, and four barons—was appointed to confer with the representatives of the Commons. A satisfactory agreement was no doubt arrived at, for the bill had passed all its stages five days later.[1] An easier passage befell a bill for repealing the Act of Henry VIII. enabling a king when he came of age to annul all acts passed during his minority, which was not only a perpetual menace to the young king's Government, but one of the most arbitrary extensions the royal prerogative in England ever received. The act of repeal was introduced into the House of Commons on 19th December, and passed its third reading on the following day; on that same day it was read for a first time in the House of Lords, and on the 21st was read a second and a third time.

The importance of these enactments has seemed to justify a full description, for they effected a more abrupt constitutional, as distinguished from a religious, change in the spirit of the laws than occurred at any other period in English history except during the great rebellion and the Revolution. To sweep away almost the entire system of treason laws and heresy laws—an inveterate growth of two centuries —was nothing less than a revolution; but the

---

[1] There is, however, a curious entry in the *Commons' Journal* of a "new" bill of the same description introduced on December 21, which made no further progress. There is nothing to elucidate the significance of the entry.

temper which it illustrated is equally apparent in the treatment which Parliament itself received at the Protector's hands. His administration was marked by a fuller recognition of the powers of Parliament than had been accorded to it since the early days of the Lancastrian kings, and the history of Parliament during that brief period is notable for freedom of debate, immunity of its members from molestation on account of their words or actions, and total absence of attempts on the part of Government to influence either elections to, or proceedings in, Parliament. The prevailing freedom of debate is amply exemplified in the journals of the two Houses, and it is perhaps not entirely without significance that the journals of the Lower House commence with the first session of the Parliament summoned by Somerset. In the Lords' Journals there is frequent mention of prolonged discussions, close divisions, and measures defeated. Half the bills at least were carried only after divisions, and those included every measure of religious change. The bill for the administration of the Sacrament in both kinds was voted against by the Bishops of London, Norwich, Hereford, Worcester, and Chichester; that for granting chantries to the king by all these prelates reinforced by Cranmer, Tunstall, and Goodrich, and the Act of Uniformity by eight bishops, an earl, and two barons. Lord Seymour and the Marquis of Dorset voted against the bill for confirming letters patent issued since the beginning of the reign,[1] a vote that was

---

[1] *Lords' Journals*, 10th, 14th, and 15th December 1547.

a direct act of hostility to the Government, and yet in none of these cases did Somerset show any signs of resentment or attempt in any way to deprive his opponents of offices which they held under his authority. The freedom with which opinions were expressed in these debates can be judged from the interesting account—the earliest perhaps of a debate in either House—which has survived of the proceedings on the bill for uniformity of service in the church.[1] The journals of the House of Commons are more meagre, but it is recorded that the bill for uniting Trinity and Clare Colleges was defeated on a vote (February 1, 1548–49), as was a bill for " putting down parks " (March 11, 1548–49), while the divisions of opinion about the repeal of treason laws have already been indicated.

The absence of attempts on the part of the Government to influence indirectly the composition of Parliament during Edward VI.'s reign has been denied on the strength of the creation of new, and restoration of old, boroughs, and of a remarkable letter sent round to the constituencies urging them to return members recommended by the Council. This letter, which will be referred to later on, dates from three years after Somerset's fall, and does not affect the question of his action. The creation of new boroughs requires more attention. It is asserted[2] that twenty-two new boroughs were

Alleged interference in elections.

---

[1] See pp. 98, 99.

[2] Hallam, i. 45. He does not state his authority, but it is obviously Browne Willis's *Notitia Parliamentaria*, iii. 93 *et seq.* Bishop

created or restored under Edward VI., and that
though some of them were no doubt entitled to
send representatives to Parliament, the majority,
and notably those in the Duchy of Cornwall, which
was especially subject to Crown influence, were
erected to furnish seats for nominees of the Government.   The number should apparently be twenty-
four, but of these six were created in Henry VIII.'s
time, or not until Mary's reign.[1]   Of the remaining
eighteen seven were made boroughs by Somerset,
and eleven by Northumberland.   Of the former,
five—Wigan, Liverpool, Peterborough, Retford, and
Westminster—were certainly entitled by their growing population and importance to elect members
to Parliament, and their creation, so far from being
evidence of a design to pack the House of Commons, really indicates the adoption of a liberal
policy which had to wait three centuries for its
consummation.   The remaining two boroughs,
Hedon in Yorkshire and Brackley in Northamp-
tonshire, may have been in a similar condition, but
there is not sufficient evidence to decide.   They
may, moreover, have sent representatives to the
Parliament of 1545, no returns for which are
extant.   The whole of the Cornish boroughs on

Stubbs, in a note to vol. iii. p. 487, gives the list from Willis.   The
results given in the text have been obtained from an examination
of the Official Return of Members of Parliament, 1878, which is,
however, very incomplete,

[1] The six erroneously stated to have been created or restored in
Edward VI.'s reign are St. Albans, Preston, Ripon, Newport (Corn-
wall), and Boston.   Mr. W. P. Courtney, in his *Parliamentary
Representation of Cornwall*, follows Browne Willis's statements.

which the case against Somerset rests appear for the first time in the official return of 1553, when there is every reason to believe they were created by Northumberland to give him more control over Parliament, in view of the schemes he had probably already formed.

There is thus a total lack of evidence to prove that Somerset interfered in any way with the freedom of elections to Parliament.[1] The absence of unconstitutional interference on his part in the debates in the Lower House is aptly illustrated by the proceedings on the bill for granting chantries to the king. That bill contained a clause confiscating the lands of all guilds and brotherhoods, and with a laudable regard for the interests of

Freedom of speech in Parliament. The case of the members for Coventry and Lynn.

---

[1] There is, however, one instance of interference in Parliamentary elections during Somerset's Government. On 28th August 1547, after Somerset's departure for Scotland, the Council directed Sir Thomas Cheyney, warden of the Cinque Ports, "to recomende Sir John Baker so to those that have the namynge of knights of the Shire as at the nexte Parliamente he maye be made knighte of the Shire accordinglie" (*Acts of the Privy Council*, 1547–50, p. 516). The electors, however, objected, and on 28th September still in Somerset's absence—the Council wrote to the Sheriff that " understandinge that he did abuse towards those of the Shire their requeste into a comandemente, theire Lordshipes advertice him that as they ment not nor meane to deprive the Shire by any theire comandemente of their libertye of ellection whom they should thinke meete," nevertheless they "would take it thankfully " if they would " grant their voices to Mr. Baker." The warden was also advised "to use thinges in such soarte as the Shire might have the free ellection " (*ibid.*, pp. 518, 519). The attempt, however, proved fatal to Baker's candidature, and he was elected not for Kent but for Huntingdonshire. So that this solitary attempt, with which Somerset had nothing to do, ended in a signal vindication of the right of electors to choose their own representative.

their constituents the members for Coventry, Christopher Warenne and Henry Porter, and the members for King's Lynn, Thomas Gawdy and William Overend, offered it a strenuous resistance. They " dyd not only reason and argue" against it, " but also incensed many others to hold with them." " In respect of which their allegacions and great labour made herin unto the Hous, sich of Highnes counsaile as were of the same Hous there present thought it very likely and apparaunt that not only that article for the guildable landes shuld be dasshed, but also that the holl body of thact might eyther susteyn perill or hindrance, being already ingrossed, and the tyme of the Parliament Prorogacion hard at hand, onles by sume goode polecy the principall Speakers against the passing of that article might be stayed ; whereuppon they did perticipat this mattier with the Lord Protectour's Grace and others of the Lordes of his Highnes' Counsaile, who, pondering on thone part howe the guildable landes throughout this realme amounted to no small yerly value, which by tharticle aforesaid were to be acrewed to his Majestes possessions of the Crown ; and on thother part wayeng in a multitude of fre voyces what moment the labour of a fewe setters on had bene of heretofore in like cases, thought it better to staye and content them of Lynne and Coventre by graunting to them to have and injoye their guyld landes, etc., as they did before, then through their meanes, on whose importune labour and suggestion the great part of the Lower Hous rested, to have the article defaced."[1] Accordingly those Privy Councillors who were also members of the Lower House interviewed the members for Coventry and Lynn, and undertook on behalf of the Government that their guild lands should be regranted them by letters patent if they would cease their opposition to the measure. This they did, and the stipulation was faithfully carried out. It is hard to imagine an instance more closely parallel to modern Parliamentary tactics in cases of friction between Government and the House, but there can be little doubt that Henry or Elizabeth would have dealt in a very different way with members who obstructed and incited others to obstruct a Government bill. They would have been summoned before the Council, and probably committed to the Tower. Two other circumstances may perhaps be noted: one is that during Somerset's rule the royal assent seems never to have been refused to a bill passed by Parliament, and the other is his recognition of the right of Parliament to be consulted in the management of foreign affairs; writing to Paget, who was then ambassador at the Emperor's court, on 4th July 1549, the Council mention that "the treaty on the king's part must be ratified by Parliament";[2] and Somerset, in discussing with the French ambassador a negotiation for the restitution of Boulogne, stated that to carry it through he must win over several members of the Council, and that with their help he was confident of obtain-

---

[1] *Acts of the Privy Council*, ed. Dasent, ii. 193–195.
[2] *State Papers, Foreign Series*, Edw. VI., vol. i. No. 180.

ing from Parliament not merely power to conclude the treaty, but express direction to do so in the way he thought fit.[1]

It would, however, be a great mistake to assume that Government exercised no influence or control over Parliament. It has been said that in the House of Lords, owing to the large proportion of peers who held offices, Government in Tudor times could always reckon on a majority in its favour.[2] In the House of Commons the connection was no less close. Of the hundred and eighty-nine members of Edward VI.'s first Parliament whose names occur in the returns, at least a third either held some office about court, or were closely related to ministers for the time being. Nearly every member of his Council who was not a peer or a judge had a seat in his first House of Commons, and probably if the returns were complete the exceptions would be still fewer. The Speaker was Sir John Baker, who was both a Privy Councillor and Chancellor of the Court of

---

[1] *Corr. Politique de Odet de Selve*, p. 229. I mention this latter point with some hesitation, because I have been unable to find any satisfactory history of the control of Parliament over foreign affairs; but I believe any such claim on the part of Parliament as Somerset recognised would have been scorned by Henry VIII., Elizabeth, or the early Stuarts. It might indeed be doubted whether Parliamentary control over foreign affairs has advanced much since Somerset's time.

[2] The circumstances were somewhat different during the Protectorate, when opposition arose chiefly from members of the Privy Council itself. The House of Lords was far more hostile to Somerset than the House of Commons, from the fact that scarcely any peers were his personal adherents, or in favour of his social policy.

Augmentations,[1] and among other officials who were also members of Parliament were the two secretaries, Sir William Paget and Sir William Petre; William Cecil, who was Master of the Court of Requests which Somerset established in his own house; Armagil Wade, Clerk to the Privy Council; Sir John Williams, Treasurer of First-fruits; Sir Edward North; Sir Anthony Wingfield; Sir Anthony Browne; John Cheke, the young king's tutor; Sir William Sharington, Master of the Mint at Bristol, and many gentlemen of the king's chamber, and others who held important posts in what would now be called the Civil Service, the Foreign Office, or the War Office. The members of the Privy Council who sat in the House of Commons were indeed the recognised means of communication between it and the Protector, and various instances are recorded in which the House instructed them to convey its wishes to Somerset. This circumstance is of course capable of a twofold interpretation, but the same twofold interpretation applies equally to Parliamentary Government to-day. The presence of between

---

[1] The statement which Bishop Stubbs adopts from Sir T. Smith (*De Angl. Republ.*) that the Speaker was freely elected scarcely holds good for Tudor times. He was almost always a court official, and some years later than this Northumberland reminded Cecil of the necessity of selecting some one to be Speaker before Parliament met, in order that he might be ready with his speech for the occasion. Smith's book was written largely while he was ambassador in France, and is influenced by a desire to extol the English over the French Constitution. Thus he boasts that the English did not, like the French, use torture, yet a few years later he was himself called upon to examine prisoners under torture (*Hatfield MSS.*, i. 503, 508, 509, 520).

thirty and forty ministers in the House of Commons may be taken to show either that the Government controls Parliament or that Parliament controls the Government. Both interpretations are true, and both were true in Edward VI.'s time, then and now within certain limits. The inference is that there was no great divorce of opinion between the Government and the constituencies; when such a divorce of opinion arose under the Stuarts the court found it impossible to force its nominees on the constituencies. No such difficulty was experienced under Somerset, and the men who carried on the Government were also enabled, by the confidence of the constituencies, to exert a powerful influence on Parliament.

The Privy Council.

But if Parliament assumed under the Protectorate a more important part than it had been accustomed to play since the Wars of the Roses, the Privy Council still remained the pivot of the administration. It has been seen that the patent which gave Somerset the Protectorship also created a new Privy Council, which was identical with Henry VIII.'s Council, with the three exceptions of Gardiner, Thirlby, and Wriothesley, and the three additions of Thomas Seymour, Baron Seymour of Sudeley, Sir Richard Southwell, and Sir Edmund Peckham. In other words, it was composed of the executors and assistant-executors acting as one body, but neither they nor the Protector now derived their authority from, or were bound by the limitations of, Henry VIII.'s will, and the same patent empowered the Protector to summon what councillors he pleased. This authorisation afforded Attend-ances. him the opportunity of surrounding himself with personal adherents, and excluding all who ·showed any hesitation in obeying his will, and it is of some importance to discover what use Somerset made of this power. It has been remarked that only seven of the Council in addition to Somerset signed his patent as Protector, and from that time the number of signatures to the " Acts of the Privy Council" dwindle to an average of eight. From 6th June 1547 to 3rd January 1547–8 only seven, and always the same seven, without variation, sign; they are Somerset, Cranmer, St. John, Northampton, Sir Anthony Browne, Sir Anthony Wingfield, and Sir Edward North. From the 3rd of January 1547–8 until 17th January 1548–9, with one exception, there are no signatures at all. During the proceedings against Lord Seymour [1] nearly all the councillors sign, but again there is a total absence of signatures [2] from March till October 1549, when the councillors assembled to depose the Protector. It seems an obvious inference that Somerset governed by means of a camarilla which he selected from his personal supporters.

Such a deduction is, however, totally unwarranted, The "Acts of the Privy Council." and the signatures to the " Acts of the Privy

[1] January–February 1548–9.

[2] On 27th July 1549 St. John, Russell, Arundel, Shrewsbury, Southampton, Wentworth, Herbert, Wingfield, North, and Baker signed an entry in the Council-book as printed by Mr. Dasent, but this entry was struck out on 1st November following, and the signatures really refer to the cancelling of the order on 1st November, not to the original entry of 27th July.

Council" will bear no such interpretation. They
have indeed little or no significance, and became a
mere official convention, similar to the phrase " Given
at Westminster," which was inserted in mediæval
documents wherever the king might be when he
signed them. The most casual examination is
sufficient to establish this fact. Thus, with the
exception of the occasions mentioned, the signatures of the two secretaries, both of whom were
members of the Council, never appear, though one
of them was Paget, the Protector's most intimate
counsellor. The French ambassador constantly records official audiences with ministers whose names
do not at the same time appear in the Council-book,[1]
and State Papers throughout the period are signed
by councillors who never sign the " Acts."[2]   But not
only do these records omit the signatures of those
who were present at the Council meetings; they
also contain signatures of those who were not present
at the proceedings they sign.   Somerset's signature
appears on the 4th, 20th, and 25th of September
and the 2nd of October 1547, and yet during the
whole of this period he was absent on his Scottish
campaign.[3]   His signature indeed seems to have

---

[1] Cf. Selve, p. 193, and compare Acts of the Privy Council for
same date.   Russell and Seymour were present at this interview,
though their names practically never occur in the Council-book.

[2] See State Papers, passim, and Pocock's Troubles connected with the
Prayer Book, Camden Soc., throughout.

[3] Somerset left London on 24th August, or the day before, and
arrived at Newcastle on the 27th.   He remained in Scotland until
29th September.   He arrived in London again on 8th October.
See Patten, Expedition into Scotland, in Arber's English Garner, iii.

been considered indispensable, and is affixed to every minute that is signed at all, whether he was present or not. The "Acts of the Privy Council" is, in short, an authority of comparatively little value, and throws but a dim and fitful light on the secret history of the time. The record was kept by a clerk, who would be informed only of such decisions of the Council as there was no reason for keeping secret, while its really important deliberations were no more committed to writing than are those of a Cabinet to-day. Nor was the record kept with much care; it was frequently entered several weeks after the events described, with the result that the dates are sometimes wrong and the entries misplaced.[1]

As a matter of fact Somerset made practically no change in the composition of the Council. A comparison of the list of councillors at the granting of his patent with the number existing at his fall reveals only three additions: Southampton had been admitted to the place he would originally have held, had it not been for his illegal action; the addition of his name and those of Shrewsbury and Sir Thomas Smith, who had been made Secretary of

Changes in its composition.

77, 149; Selve, pp. 193–195; *State Papers, Domestic*, Addenda, Edw. VI., i. 28, 32; Wriothesley, *Chron.*, i. 186. A careful examination of the Council Register reveals what really happened; blanks were left for the Protector's signature, which he filled in on his return to London.

[1] Thus, vol. ii. p. 34, Wednesday the xvth of February, should be Wednesday the xvith, and on pp. 125–127 proceedings of the 11th and 12th of August are entered after those of 15th August to 10th September.

State,[1] was no doubt designed to supply the places of the three who had meanwhile deceased, Lord Seymour, Sir Anthony Browne, and Sir Anthony Denny.   The signature of seven councillors was meant to satisfy the requirements of an instruction drawn up at the commencement of the Protectorate, which laid down the rule that, without a quorum of six, no important business could be transacted;[2] and the suggestion that Somerset ruled through a junto of personal adherents is refuted by his constant employment in matters of the greatest importance of those who were really his bitterest enemies.   Those seven councillors, moreover, were not by any means thoroughgoing supporters of the Protector; four of them, St. John, Northampton, Wingfield, and North, shared in the intrigues which led to his downfall.   Two of those whose names were added to the Council took similar action, and only the third, Sir Thomas Smith, was in any sense a partisan of Somerset.

Exclusion of bishops and old nobility.   There was thus little change in the *personnel* of the Council.[3]   The body which administered the Government under Edward VI. was practically the same as that which had administered it under Henry VIII.   The exclusion of Gardiner and Thirlby had indeed given it a more distinctively

[1] In 1546 it had been settled that the two secretaries were *ex officio* members of the Council.

[2] *State Papers, Dom.*, Edw. VI., vol. i. No. 15.

[3] *i.e.* the Privy Council, but there was still an important distinction between the Privy Council and the king's ordinary Council. Members of the latter were not necessarily members of the former (cf. *Letters and Papers*, Henry VIII., vii. 1525, viii. 225).

secular tinge than had been the case since the
Privy Council came into existence, and explains
to some extent the anti-sacerdotal and Erastian
character of Edward's legislation.   Two bishops
only, Cranmer and Tunstall, remained on the
Council, and Tunstall soon withdrew to his northern
diocese and limited his secular activity to attendance at the Council of the North, and providing
for the defence of the borders.   Under Warwick
the process went still further, for Cranmer took
little part in civil affairs after the Protector's fall,
and though Goodrich, Bishop of Ely, held for a time
the Great Seal, he had little weight in the Council.
The separation from Rome was followed by a
gradual banishment of ecclesiastical influence from
the sphere of civil government, and an increasing
subjection of Church to State.   The Tudor policy
of neglecting the old nobility, and depending for
support on new men who owed their rise to Tudor
rule, comes out in a still more singular feature of
the Council's composition.   Of its twenty-six members, no less than seventeen were commoners; two
being prelates, and only seven temporal peers.   And
of these peers one only, Henry Fitzalan, twelfth
Earl of Arundel, could claim a noble ancestry.   The
remaining six were all born commoners, and not one
held a peerage of more than eleven years' standing.
The senior peer, except Arundel, was Somerset, who
had been created Viscount Beauchamp in 1536;
the peerages of Russell, St. John, and Northampton
dated from March 1539, that of Warwick from
1542, while Rich and Baron Seymour were created

in the first year of Edward VI. Never before or after was England governed by such an assembly of *parvenus*, and if the anti-sacerdotal character of Edward's reign is due to the absence of prelates from his Council, the era of social oppression which set in after Somerset's fall may not less surely be attributed to the rule of men who had inherited none of the instincts of mutual relationship which, even in the darkest of feudal days, had softened and humanised the treatment of their tenants by the lords of the soil.[1]

The Council's powers.

The authority wielded by this body embraced not only every department of administration proper, but also comprised what would now be considered exclusively legislative or judicial functions. It provided for the defence of the kingdom, regulated trade and the coinage, and retained under Edward VI. the sole right of issuing warrants and the partial management of foreign affairs. Its executive capacity had been greatly developed by the erection of the courts of augmentations and of first-fruits and tenths, and by the creation of the Councils of the North and of Wales.[2] These courts and councils were not strictly committees of the Privy Council, though the chief officials were generally Privy

[1] Somerset himself bitterly denounced the harshness of these new "lords sprung from the dunghill," as he termed them (Tytler, i. 208–21). He was a "new" lord himself, but he had a distinguished ancestry, and was not tainted by the oppression which roused his anger.

[2] The first two had been erected by Henry VIII. to deal with his newly acquired ecclesiastical revenues; the latter two were also erected during his reign.

Councillors; the less important members were
probably members of the king's ordinary Council.
They acted under the immediate supervision of
the Privy Council.   To all these functions was
added that of regulating religious beliefs and ob-
servances; in other words, of exercising that ecclesiastical supremacy which the Council claimed during
the young king's minority.   At the same time the
right of issuing proclamations gave it powers which
were difficult to define, and might easily encroach
upon the prerogative of Parliament.   It was by
proclamations and injunctions that some of the
ecclesiastical charges of Edward VI. were instituted,
though they were afterwards confirmed by Acts
of Parliament.   Nor is it easy to prove, in view of
the powers conferred on the Supreme Head of the
Church,[1] that these methods were illegal, though
they were certainly arbitrary.

It was, however, its functions as a court of jus- The Star
tice that gave the Council its most marked impress Chamber.
of authority.   These functions were civil, ecclesiastical, and criminal.   Civil jurisdiction was exercised
by the Court of Requests,[2] but ecclesiastical and
criminal cases were tried by the Council as a whole,
though criminal cases had formerly been entrusted

---

[1] Statute 26 Henry VIII. c. 1 gave the king full authority to
visit, repress, redress, reform, order, correct, restrain, and amend all
errors, heresies, abuses, &c.   Apparently it was left to him to determine the all-important question, what was heresy and what was
not, and this Act might be interpreted to cover almost any exercise
of power in ecclesiastical matters.

[2] See Mr. I. S. Leadam's *Select Cases from the Court of Requests*
(Selden Society, 1897).

to a committee by 3 Henry VII. c. 1, which had
since fallen into abeyance, and ecclesiastical cases
were afterwards deputed to the Court of High
Commission. The use to which the criminal jurisdiction of the Court of Star Chamber was subsequently put rendered its name a byword and a
synonym for tyranny, and led men to challenge
Its legality. both its legality and usefulness. Both are nevertheless tenable propositions. The sovereign is in
theory at any rate the fountain of justice and the
supreme judge, and the theory is still put into
practice, when, on the advice of the Secretary of
State for Home Affairs, criminals are pardoned or
sentences reduced. In judicial as in other matters
the presumption was always in favour of the royal
prerogative, unless there were statute or ancient
custom to the contrary, and probably in cases where
the law was not explicit the doubt would be interpreted in favour of the Crown, in much the same
way as, in default of sufficient title, an estate would
revert to the king. No Act of Parliament before
1640 asserted the illegality of the jurisdiction of
the Court of the Star Chamber; it was the court
in which the king administered justice without the
intermediation of the judges, and bills of complaint
which came before it were addressed, not to any
judge, but to the king himself.[1] Had it been illegal,
Coke could hardly have described it as, next to Parliament, the most honourable court in Christendom.
Usefulness. 　　The necessity, under the conditions of Govern-

---

[1] See any of the numerous bills of complaint extant in the Record
Office.

ment in the sixteenth century, for some such court as that of the Star Chamber is even less disputable. The capacity and opportunities of breaking the peace enjoyed by a powerful subject, who often controlled a considerable armed force, were far more extensive than they are at present, and at the same time the Government had no standing army or body of police to provide for its maintenance. The criminal jurisdiction of the courts leet of the hundred and manor had largely broken down, and were at all times liable to intimidation from local magnates. The Star Chamber was subject to no such influence, and afforded poor suitors the further invaluable boon of a speedy procedure. The composition of this court has been a matter of some variance of opinion, but it is evident that in Edward VI.'s time it consisted of the Council as a whole. When exercising its criminal jurisdiction, the Council sat in the Star Chamber, which was next to the Council's dining-chamber,[1] but it would be a mistake to suppose that the Council never transacted any but judicial business in the Star Chamber. It was in that chamber, for instance, that Lord Chancellor Wriothesley administered the oath of allegiance to the lords temporal and spiritual at the beginning of Edward's reign.[2] In the Star Chamber the Council transacted ordinary business on 31st January 1549–50, and again on the 7th of February.[3] Occasionally also the Council gave judicial

---

[1] *Acts of the Privy Council*, ii. 385.

[2] *Ibid.*, ii. 8.

[3] *Ibid.*, ii. 376, 385.

decisions in other chambers of the Palace, but as a rule it sat for this purpose in the Star Chamber, and in its judicial capacity it was known to suitors as the Court of the Star Chamber, to which they addressed their bills of complaint.[1]

Jurisdiction.

Its activity, however, in dealing with powerful offenders, has been emphasised to the neglect of the court's energy in other directions.   As a matter of fact only an infinitesimal proportion of the cases which came before it concerned men whose position was in any way a danger to the Government.   Its voluminous records are still extant, and offer virgin

Records.

soil to the historical investigator.[2]   They consist of bills of complaint, depositions, answers, and other documents, and deal with all manner of crimes and misdemeanours; with riots, unlawful assemblies and assaults, engrossing, forestalling, and regrating, and even with petty local cases like trespass.   The court was, in fact, a centralised police court, exercising jurisdiction over every part of the kingdom, and it is not therefore a matter of surprise that the existing records for Edward VI.'s brief reign deal with at least two thousand five hundred cases.   It

[1] The expression Court of the Star Chamber occurs twice in the first bill of complaint in Edward VI.'s reign, "Hartgill v. Symes."

[2] These records are contained in seven huge portfolios dealing solely with Edward's reign.   They have never been calendared, indexed, or arranged, and to all appearance never examined.   They comprise ample material for an authoritative history of the Court of Star Chamber, which would probably clear away many doubts as to its composition and functions.

Since the above words were written, Miss Cora Scofield of Chicago University has utilised these materials in her admirable *Study of the Court of Star Chamber*, Chicago, 1900.

could inflict any penalty short of death, including imprisonment, fines, and forfeiture of goods. It *Procedure.* proceeded either by bill or *ex ore*, and it could also employ torture. It controlled the press, and under its shadow the law of libel grew up. It could evoke cases from inferior courts, and put pressure on jurors to return verdicts in favour of the Crown. But above all the Council sitting in the Court of the Star Chamber could enforce its own proclamations, the legality of which might have been questioned in any other court of law. In short, as Coke declared, it kept the whole realm in order, and, as a means of coercion, supplied to some extent the want of a police force and standing army.

It is impossible to determine, from a cursory *Its activity under Somerset.* examination of these records, whether Somerset's rule had any influence in moderating the arbitrary exercise of these powers ; but his influence is very apparent in the number of fines entered in the Acts of the Privy Council. In the thirty-six months [1] of Henry's reign covered by these "Acts" one hundred and fifty-eight cases are recorded, in the thirty-two months [2] of Somerset's administration thirty-six, and in the first six months [3] after his fall sixty-seven. The average of four and a half per month in Henry's reign was reduced to one per month by Somerset, and increased by Warwick to the unprecedented number of more than eleven.

---

[1] The series of Acts of the Privy Council, edited by Mr. Dasent, begin in 1542, but there is a gap of more than two years, 1543–5.

[2] January 1546–7 to October 1549.

[3] October 1549 to April 1550.

The number of trials for treason was comparatively small, being limited to some half-dozen Cornish rebels, Baron Seymour and Sir William Sharington, whose cases must be more fully treated hereafter; and no instances have been found of the intimidation of juries such as occurred under Henry and were renewed under Warwick.[1]   Even more striking is the absence of the use of torture and the pillory, which distinguishes Somerset's administration from every other Government in the sixteenth and seventeenth centuries.[2]

The Council's work.   The multifarious character of these functions imposed on the Council an enormous amount of work, which was not relieved as it is now by its delegation to the heads of departments. The collective control of the Council was exercised in the most minute details ; no payments, for instance, could be made without a warrant from a quorum of the Council, and these warrants occupy the greater part of its records. The result was that instead of meeting once a week and not at all for several months of the year, like Cabinets of the present time, the Privy Council met almost every day, and was compelled to map out its time in a most methodical way. To each day in the week was

[1] *State Papers, Dom.*, Addenda, Edw. VI., iii. 78.
[2] This remarkable fact was noticed long ago, though it has been somewhat forgotten. In a transcript written about 1710, of the Privy Council Register (British Museum, *Harleian MSS.*, 6195, No. 7), after some entries recording some such penalties occurs the note, "that severities were not used till the Duke of Somerset was in disgrace, and the Earl of Warwick had got the power in his hands."

assigned its own particular business.[1]   No resolution
could be taken unless six councillors at least were
present; if there were not less than four they
might discuss matters, but come to no determination ; and when such discussions were held, note
was taken of how far they had proceeded and of
the arguments on both sides.   Letters addressed
to the Council might be opened by less than four
councillors, and in cases of special urgency might
be deliberated upon, the previous injunctions notwithstanding.   No councillor was to depart from
court for more than two days unless at least eight
of the Council remained in attendance.

The industry of the Council, however, was trifling
compared with that of the Protector, and whatever
charges lie against him, he was guiltless of neglecting his public duties or of preferring his own ease
to the demands of the State.   That he might be
more free to devote his whole time and energy to
public affairs, he entrusted the management of his
estates to Sir John Thynne,[2] the builder of Longleat and ancestor of the Marquis of Bath.   His
own reputation suffered thereby, for, as Paget wrote
to Petre, " there is no one thing of which his Grace
hath need to take such heed as of that man's pro-

Somerset's labours.

---

[1] *State Papers, Dom.*, Edw. VI., i. 15.   The memorandum, "Sunday to attend the affairs of the realm and answer letters, and be at
the common prayer," shows that Somerset had not imbibed any
sabbatical views on the Sunday, though probably an order to be
"at common prayer" would sound oddly to a Cabinet to-day.

[2] This relationship between Thynne and Somerset explains the
presence at Longleat of a number of MSS. relating to the Seymours,
some of them very valuable historically.

ceedings."[1]   Somerset held in his hands all the
threads of Government; except when away on his
Scottish campaign or on tours of inspection he
never missed a meeting of the Council, and he
seems to have been present at every sitting of
Parliament.   The management of foreign affairs
he retained in his own hands, assisted only by the
two secretaries, who were almost exclusively secretaries for foreign affairs.   All diplomatic correspondence was submitted to him, and he dictated or
directed the tenor of all communications to foreign
states.   It was with him, sometimes alone, at others
with Paget, that the ambassadors in London had
their interviews.   To give effect to his sympathies
with those he thought were oppressed he erected
a Court of Requests in his own house, and at all
times he encouraged the presentation to himself of
all suits and complaints.   "To receive poor men's
complaints that findeth themselves injured or
grieved," he wrote to his brother, "it is our duty
and office so to do."[2]   At the same time he super-
intended and directed all measures for the defence
of the kingdom and war against Scotland, and afterwards against France.   To these he added far-
reaching schemes of religious change and projects for
the reform of social ills.   Well might Paget warn him
against having "so many irons in the fire"; but the
amount of work, destructive and constructive, which
Somerset accomplished during his brief authority
remains a monument to his industry and zeal.

[1] 22nd July 1549, quoted in Tytler, i. 190.
[2] 1st September 1548.   Tytler, i. 121.

CHAPTER IV

SOMERSET AND THE RELIGIOUS REVOLUTION

THE Reformation of the sixteenth century, so far Character of the English Reforma- tion. as it affected the doctrine of the Church of Eng- land, has been interpreted in as many ways as there are shades of theological opinion. Even to-day men ask each other what really happened at the Reformation, and give each a very different answer.[1] For there was no such break with the past, no such doctrinal revolution in the religious history of the English people as there was in that of the Teutonic nations on the Continent. The movement in England came from above, was directed by sovereigns, statesmen, and prelates, and was influenced by political considerations ; the settle- ment arrived at breathes more of the spirit of compromise essential to every political institution, than of the hard and logical consistency of a creed. It was, moreover, the result of no sudden change, but of modifications spread over more than a cen- tury and a quarter. The formularies of the Church passed through the hands of men with divers temperaments and beliefs, and developed a flexi-

[1] See, for instance, Messrs. Augustine Birrell, J. H. Round, and G. W. E. Russell in *Nineteenth Century*, 1896.

bility which gives the Church its chief strength and vitality, and enables men to subscribe her articles who hold contradictory views on many not unimportant points of faith.

Of the men who helped to mould the English Church there is no one whose precise attitude is more difficult to determine than that of Protector Somerset.   There are scanty indications of what opinions he held during Henry VIII.'s reign, or how he came to adopt them.   When Henry's marriage with Anne of Cleves was arranged, he wrote that nothing had pleased him so much since the birth of the young prince.[1]   During Anne Askew's trial in 1545 she was asked whether Lady Hertford had not supplied her with money and support, and on January 26, 1546–7, Richard Hilles wrote from Strasburg that Hertford was well disposed to pious doctrine and abominated the fond inventions of the Papists.[2] A month later he wrote that the new Protector was not very favourable to priests, and a great enemy to the Bishop of Rome.[3]   Nor is there any reason to doubt the substantial truth of the assertion made in the dedications of various works to Somerset, that he had protected the Reformers in days when, by so doing, he incurred some danger.[4] These hints are vague enough.   But probably Somerset was too cautious to offend his master in giving open expression to views which are said to have nearly cost Catherine Parr her life.[5]

[1] *Letters and Papers of Henry VIII.*, vol. xiv. Part I. No. 1275.
[2] *Original Letters*, Parker Soc., i. 256.   [3] *Ibid.*, i. 258.
[4] See Peter Martyr's dedication of his *Sacrament of Thanksgiving;* Gasquet and Bishop, p. 158.   [5] See Mr. James Gairdner, in *Dict.*

There can, however, be no doubt that he had adopted what was known as the "new learning" before he became Protector. He has been forcibly but inaccurately described by an unsympathetic critic as a "rank Calvinist."[1] In most respects his tenets, so far as they can be inferred from a few indefinite phrases, more nearly resembled those of Zwingli, but the influence of the Genevan Reformer with whom he corresponded may possibly be traced in some of Somerset's public and private utterances. From these somewhat doubtful premises it may be inferred that he inclined to a belief in predestination, and regarded himself as one of the "elect." The phrase itself occurs somewhat incongruously in the preamble to the statute repealing treasons and heresies,[2] and in a prayer which the Protector used he spoke of himself as recorded in the book of life and called by Providence to rule.[3] Nor was he free from the more trivial manifestations of the Puritanic spirit, for in a proclamation[4] which he issued he warned "parents to keep their children from the evil and pernicious games of dising, carding, bowling, tenys, coytes, closshes, and the like." That these expressions represented genuine religious convictions can be doubted by no one who has perused Somerset's devotional writings, his private

<hr>

Nat. Biogr., s.v. Catherine ; he thinks there is considerable truth in the well-known story about Henry VIII. and his last wife.

[1] The late Rev. Nicholas Pocock, in *English Hist. Review*, x. 418. For Calvin's overtures to Somerset see *Stow MS.*, 155, *f.* 9.

[2] 1 Edward VI., c. 13.

[3] Printed in Strype, *Eccles. Mem.*, II. ii. 311, 312

[4] Cal., *Hatfield MSS.*, vol. i. No. 234.

prayers, reflections on the day before his execution,[1] and speech on the scaffold; hypocrites do not play their parts in their closets, and generally break down in the last act.

Their influ-
ence. The question how far the religious revolution embodied Somerset's personal views is rendered more difficult by the absence of direct and positive evidence. In his letters to the Protector [2] Gardiner implies that Somerset was led on by Cranmer, but this may only be "Winchester's wiliness." There was, however, some divergence between Cranmer's homilies and the Council's injunctions; Gardiner attacked the archbishop for separating charity from salvation, while the injunction maintained that giving to the poor would be rewarded with everlasting life, and there are other indications that Cranmer was ready to go further than Somerset in the direction of doctrinal change. On the other hand, the archbishop is said to have been a mere tool in the hands of the Protector, who wielded in ecclesiastical affairs the same arbitrary authority as Henry VIII. had done when he forced through Parliament the Act of the Six Articles. The latter statement, with all due deference to the writer [3] who makes it, must be regarded as highly disputable, for reasons that will be more fully explained hereafter.

---

[1] Some of these are written in his own hand, in a calendar he used in the Tower, and are dated "the day before my death." Inside the cover is inscribed the name of Somerset's daughter-in-law, Lady Catherine Grey, who also used it in the Tower. It is now *Stow MS.* 1066 in the British Museum.

[2] Printed in Foxe, *Acts and Monuments*, ed. Townsend, vol. vi.

[3] Pocock, in *Church Quarterly Review*, October 1892, pp. 38, 41, 42, 56.

Moreover, if Somerset was a " rank Calvinist," he was—what almost seems a contradiction in terms— a Calvinistic Erastian.   If he believed in anything he believed in the supremacy of State over Church. And he would have repudiated the domination of the presbyter as vigorously as he did that of the priest.   His religion was for himself purely a matter of private judgment, for others apparently it was a matter for the State to decide; in neither case did the priest enter much into the scheme. He would have reduced the Church to the position of a well-disciplined branch of the civil service, and the central point of his struggle with Gardiner and Bonner was his attempt to force on them a recognition of the authority of the Privy Council in ecclesiastical affairs—a controversy that is not yet extinct.   In the first month of the reign he induced the bishops to take out new commissions just like any other servant of the Crown,[1] and in his first Parliament an Act was passed directing that the election of bishops should be by letters patent.[2]   So, too, ecclesiastical commissions were composed largely of laymen, and heresy cases were sometimes—but very rarely—tried before the Council; religious changes were made by proclamations issued by a body consisting almost exclusively of laymen, or by Acts of a Parliament in one House of which the Church as a church had no representation, while in the other the bishops were outnumbered by secular peers.[3]

A Cal-
vinistic
Erastian.

[1] *Acts of the Privy Council*, ii. 13, 14.   [2] 1 Edward VI., c. 2.
[3] The bishops were, however, a powerful voting body; there were

These are,it may be said,legitimate deductions from the theory of a State Church. It is inconsistent to depend on State support and at the same time to repudiate State control, at once to claim independence in formulating doctrines and State aid in forcing them on others. Very possibly the inconvenience of State control in matters of faith outweighed the advantages of State support, but legally and logically the Church had given up its case for autonomy in recognising Henry VIII. as its supreme head. Nor could any Government with any respect for its own security afford to admit that its powers were limited by a royal minority. Such views, however, could not be expected to commend themselves to men like Gardiner and Bonner, who honestly abhorred the doctrines of those who for the time wielded the authority of the State, and they naturally seized upon the young king's minority as a justification for the plea of illegality which they urged against Somerset's proceedings.

Did Somerset force on the Revolution? But, Erastian though the Protector's views may have been, he was opposed by temperament and principle to coercion, and the assumption that he forced religious change upon a reluctant people

twenty-seven of them in the House of Lords, against forty-eight lay peers. The journals of the House of Lords are misleading to the unwary in the matter of attendances. At the head of each day's entry it is stated that those were present whose names are subscribed; but then follows a list of all peers, and really only those were present whose names are marked "p"; at other times the practice was varied, "a" being marked opposite the names of those who were absent. Another illustration of this Erastian tendency was the proposed Court of Chancery for ecclesiastical causes (*cf.* Stubbs's *Lectures on Mediæval History*, p. 368).

appears to arise not so much from a survey of the evidence as from a humane desire to fix upon a few rather than·upon the many the guilt of heresy. It is not denied that there was a very large proportion of the community opposed to religious innovations, or that Government used its influence in furtherance of the same; but in precisely the same way there is always a considerable body of opinion opposed to most legislative changes of to-day which Government promotes, without incurring any particular charge of tyranny. Nor is it at all clear that the religious changes effected during Somerset's Protectorate were distasteful to the clergy as a whole, and it might even be maintained that they were more advanced in their views than the laity. If such was not the case, convocation must have been more subservient than Parliament, for convocation approved without a dissentient voice the administration of the Sacrament in both kinds, and by a large majority sanctioned the marriage of priests, before Parliament touched these questions. So far from the Protector straining his authority to hasten on a religious revolution, it would appear that his endeavour was to steer a middle course and follow the line of least resistance.

His attitude is aptly illustrated by the remarkable debate on the Sacrament in the House of Lords in December 1548. Edward VI. remarks in his journal that there was a notable disputation of the Sacrament in the Parliament House,[1] and Traheron,

---

[1] *Literary Remains of Edward VI.*, ed. John Gough Nichols, for the Roxburghe Club, p. 224.

writing to Bullinger,[1] on 31st Deceember, says, " On the 14th of December, if I mistake not, a disputation was held at London • concerning the Eucharist in the presence of almost all the nobility of England." By a fortunate chance a detailed report of this debate has survived.[2]   Convocation had in the previous year sanctioned, without one dissentient voice, the administration of the Communion in both kinds,[3] a fact which is hard to explain on the theory of secular coercion of the Church ; equally inexplicable is the circumstance that the discussion of this question was now left almost exclusively to the bishops, who spoke and voted with absolute freedom.   Three laymen only took part in the debate, Somerset, Warwick, and Sir Thomas Smith, who had conducted the bill through the House of Commons,[4] and as secretary had also a seat in the House of Lords.[5]   Warwick was overbearing as usual, but Somerset, in the words of two hostile writers, " assumed, as moderator, a calmness and dignity which was only once disturbed by a sudden

The debate on the Sacrament.

[1] *Original Letters*, Parker Society, i. 322, 323.   There had been a debate on the same subject in December of the previous year, when the bill for administering the Sacraments in both kinds was brought up (Selve, p. 258).   He says the great men wished to abolish the Sacrament of the Altar altogether, but the others resisted.   Selve's statements must be accepted with caution on English affairs ; he was only two and a half years in the country, and, on his own admission, he did not understand a word of the language.

[2] British Museum, *Royal MS.*, 17 *B.* xxxix. ; it is printed in the appendix to Gasquet and Bishop's *Edward VI. and the Book of Common Prayer*, pp. 397–443.

[3] Wilkins's *Concilia*, iv. 16.

[4] *Commons' Journals*, under date 19th December 1548.

[5] See *Stow MSS.*, 141, *f.* 78.

gust of passion. . . . His observations had evidently been carefully considered, and were marked by studious self-control." [1] He seems to have intervened three times in the debate, once to rebuke Thirlby, Bishop of Westminster,[2] once to quote St. Paul and the gospels, and once to rule out the citation of the opinion of Erasmus " on the ground that he was ' but a new writer,' and it had been agreed to prove the arguments first from the Scriptures and ' old writers.'" The Catholic cause was maintained by the Bishops of London, Norwich, Hereford, Worcester, Westminster, and Chichester; while the Reformers were represented by the Archbishop of Canterbury, the Bishops of Coventry and Lichfield, Rochester, and Ely, and by Sir Thomas Smith, who spoke frequently. The third reading of the bill was taken on 15th January 1548–9.

[1] Gasquet and Bishop, pp. 160–164.
[2] The same authors unintentionally misrepresent their authority in describing this incident. The words of the reporter, in summarising the Protector's remarks in reference to Thirlby, are : " These vehement sayings sheweth rather a wilfulness and an obstinacy to say he will die in it. To say he will prove it by old doctors, and thereby would persuade men to believe his sayings, when he bringeth no authority in deed." Somerset obviously accuses Thirlby of pretending to base his views on old doctors without actually quoting them. Father Gasquet and Mr. Bishop, however, print in their text (p. 166) the following: " By this time Somerset had made up his mind how to act. He spoke in anger which he did not attempt to conceal. ' These vehement sayings,' he declared, ' show rather a wilfulness and an obstinacy to say he will die in it.' He would persuade men that he could prove his doctrine by ancient doctors, while in fact he brings no authority forward." The placing of the inverted commas makes the last passage read as if it were Somerset who failed to quote the old doctors.

There were enough bishops present on that occasion to have outvoted the temporal peers, had they been united. They were, however, divided, and even among the bishops the preponderance of opinion was in favour of the bill; twelve voted in its favour and eight against it, while all the temporal peers voted for it except three.[1] In a similar way there was a majority of the bishops in favour of all Somerset's religious measures. On the first bill for the abolition of chantries there was indeed a majority of eight to seven against it, Cranmer himself being a dissentient;[2] but this bill was dropped and a new one introduced, against which five bishops only voted.[3] It must be remembered, too, that these prelates were not Somerset's creatures; they had, on the contrary, all been appointed by Henry VIII., and it argues criminal time-serving on their part if they placed their convictions at the service of Government, without even the pretence of compulsion to justify them. For the bishops who voted against these measures, like Durham, Norwich, Carlisle, Hereford, Worcester, Westminster, and Chichester,[4] underwent no penalties for this exercise of their conscience.

Was the Church coerced?

So far, indeed, were the clergy from feeling particularly oppressed by the Protector that they

---

[1] *Lords' Journals*, 15th January 1548-9 ; these debates took place on the bill for uniformity, and not on that for the administration of the Sacrament in both kinds, which of course was passed in December 1547.

[2] *Ibid.*, 15th December 1547.   [3] *Ibid.*, 23rd December 1547.

[4] They were Tunstall, Rugge, Aldrich, Skip, Heath, Thirlby, and Day.

considered the first year of his rule a suitable
opportunity for an attempt to recover their lost
position as an estate of the realm. In convocation,
which met in November 1547, the clergy presented
four remarkable petitions to the bench of bishops:
first, that ecclesiastical laws might be settled by the
thirty-two commissioners (apparently in preference
to Parliament or the Council); secondly, that the
clergy might sit in the House of Commons, or else
have Church laws brought before them; thirdly,
that the work of the commission appointed by the
late king for altering the public services might be
laid before them; and lastly, that the exaction of
first-fruits might be modified.[1] It was not likely
that a man of Somerset's Erastian views would
entertain for a moment such proposals, but the
very fact that they were made indicates that even
the clergy felt the relief afforded by Somerset from
Henry VIII.'s oppressive rule. Such repression as
Somerset employed seems to have been directed
rather towards checking the excessive zeal of the
Reformers than to forcing upon Catholics changes
of which they disapproved. The first statute of
the reign was directed against such as should
" speak unreverently against the Sacrament of the
Altar." A proclamation was issued with a like
object on 27th December 1547 ;[2] another followed
in February 1547–8 against unlicensed preaching

---

[1] Wilkins's *Concilia*, iv. 15 ; *cf.* Cardwell, *Synodalia*, ii. 419 ; Atter-
bury, *Rights*, Addenda, 616–626 ; and Makower, *Const. Hist. of the
Church of England*, English translation, p. 207.

[2] Strype, *Eccles. Mem.*, II. ii. 340.

and unauthorised innovations,[1]   In the previous
November the Council had sought by proclamation [2]
to protect priests from the rough usage they met
with at the hands of "serving-men and other yonge
and light persons and apprenteses of London," and
on one or two occasions Anabaptists were made to
carry faggots and recant.[3]

Religious
changes.
The various measures of religious change carried
out during Edward VI.'s reign have been described so frequently, and with so much detail,
that it would be a work of supererogation to do
more than briefly mention them, and attempt to
mark as clearly as possible the limits which the
revolution reached under Somerset's direction.
Somerset's changes consisted largely of projects
which had been formed during the previous reign.
They had been laid aside in deference to Henry's
doctrinal orthodoxy, but some literary preparation
for them had gone on, and this was continued in
the new reign to pave the way for the change in
outward forms.   The first book of homilies was
issued to replace the "Necessary Doctrine and
Erudition of any Christian Man," the last and most
retrograde of the formularies issued under Henry.
There followed almost immediately the Paraphrases
of Erasmus, translated by Nicholas Udall, under
the patronage of Queen Catherine Parr, which may
have been designed to smooth the way for an
authorised edition of the Bible in English, and

---

[1] Strype, *Eccles. Mem.*, II. ii. 346.
[2] *Acts of the Privy Council*, i. 521.
[3] Wriothesley's *Chronicle*, ii. 12, 13.

also as an antidote to the extreme Protestant ver-
sions then in use.   In August 1547 began a general
visitation of the kingdom.   The injunctions which
regulated its proceedings were mainly a reproduc-
tion of the injunctions of Cromwell and Henry VIII.
They enjoined the use of the English Litany, the
reading of the lessons in English, the abolition of
processions and of images that were abused, and
made other minor changes in the English service;
but the vast majority of these injunctions dealt with
a reformation of Church practice, and not with
changes in Church doctrine.   The Parliament that
met in November sanctioned the administration of
the Sacrament in both kinds, and directed the
election of bishops to be by letters patent.   It also
bestowed all chantries and free chapels on the king.
In the following year the use of ashes, palms, and
candles on Candlemas Day, as well as of holy bread
and holy water, was forbidden.   Then came the
first English Order of Communion, which is more
remarkable for what it retained than for what it
abolished; and a few months later the first English
Book of Common Prayer was undertaken by Cranmer,
with the assistance of such bishops and divines as
he chose to call in.[1]   The first Act of Uniformity and
Parliamentary authorisation of the prayer-book was
the work of the second session of Edward's first
Parliament, which lasted from November 1548 to
March 1549.   The same session saw a grudging
permission granted to the marriage of priests.   Early

[1] It is difficult to believe in the so-called " Windsor Commission "
after Gasquet and Bishop's examination of its claims to existence.

in 1549 a new visitation followed, and a heresy commission, but the rebellions in the summer caused an interruption in ecclesiastical reform, and they had scarcely been disposed of when the Protector fell.

Their moderation under Somerset. It is possible that this did not represent the sum of what the Protector desired to accomplish.   He is said to have encouraged in secret the writings of those whose views went far beyond the reforms he was able to effect,[1] and it has been maintained that, had he continued Protector he would have reduced the ceremonial and doctrine of the Church of England to the level of the Zwinglian congregations on the Continent.   But assertions of what might have been are as easy to make as they are impossible to disprove, and this particular assertion of what might have been rests on a peculiarly weak chain of argument.   It is maintained that because extensive doctrinal changes were effected by the end of the reign they were intended from the beginning, and the basis of the contention is merely that the men who procured the first Act of Uniformity and the first prayer-book were the same as those who procured the second.   This is an entire mistake; the first Act of Uniformity and the first prayer-book were drawn up under the influence of Somerset, the second under that of Warwick.   Cranmer, indeed, was archbishop under both, but Cranmer was also archbishop under Henry VIII.; and to make

---

[1] The Rev. N. Pocock, in *English Historical Review*, 1886, and July 1895, and in the *Church Quarterly Review* for October 1892 and October 1893,

Somerset responsible for the religious revolution after October 1549 is no more reasonable than it would be to attribute either prayer-book and either Act of Uniformity to the influence of Henry VIII. It is more pertinent to point out the somewhat neglected fact that the doctrinal changes which Somerset actually carried out—as apart from his assumed intentions—were of an exceedingly moderate character, and certainly involved no risk to that "catholicity" which is reckoned the most important feature of the Church. It comes almost as a shock, after the denunciations of Somerset as a "rank Calvinist," to hear from the lips of one of the highest of High Churchmen [1] that Edward VI.'s first prayer-book, the tenor of which was determined more by Somerset than by any other, had only to be known to be appreciated, and to hear its use advocated as a preferable alternative to the present service-book of the Church of England. The customary method of treating Edward's reign as one uniform period has, indeed, led to a gross exaggeration of the anti-Catholic and anti-sacerdotal character of Somerset's legislation.[2] In matters of doctrine the service-book, as the Protector left it, is a striking testimony to the moderation of his public reforms; it assumed the real presence, allowed prayers for the dead and auricular confession, while abstinence from flesh during Lent was en-

---

[1] Lord Halifax at the Church Congress, 28th September 1897. The sanction of the use in St. Paul's Cathedral of this burial service, at the funeral of Archdeacon Denison, was also a concession to High Church views.

[2] Cf. Pocock, in *English Historical Review*, July 1895, p. 438.

joined both by proclamation and by Act of Parliament.   Such an ordinal was not a very Calvinistic
document, nor did it constitute so very violent a
break with the doctrinal traditions of the reign of
Henry VIII.

One more remark is perhaps worth making.
To discuss foreign influence on the English Reformation does not come within the scope of
this essay, because, except in so far as Cranmer
and a few other divines were influenced by their
sojourn abroad, the Reformation, so far as Somerset
carried it, was almost entirely the product of
English ideas.   Englishmen are little subject to
the domination of abstract thought, and the English Reformation did not begin with the enunciation
of any cardinal dogma or new truth.   No one
doctrine plays the same part in the English Reformation that justification by faith played among
Lutherans or predestination among Calvinists.   The
English Reformation began with an attack upon
the abuses of the spiritual courts, and down to
the end of Somerset's rule it was more concerned
to reform practice than to revolutionise doctrine.
Neither the abuses nor the reforms were particularly new.   There is little in the English
Reformation that was not anticipated by Wycliffe.
Wycliffe had called upon the State to reform a
corrupt Church, and the Tudors did but act upon
his precept; he attacked Church property by his
writings, they by the more practical method of
appropriation;   and even in its rejection of the
Roman doctrine of the Eucharist the Reformation

only followed a process that had gone on in Wycliffe's mind.

The evidences of moderation were no less marked in Somerset's treatment of ecclesiastical laws and jurisdiction. As an Erastian he insisted on the supremacy of the State in ecclesiastical matters, but even in the matter of jurisdiction the Protector entrusted the clergy with a large share of the power which the early gospellers had most bitterly denounced. The motive force might be the State, but the machinery remained ecclesiastical. The clergy were empowered to carry out the penal jurisdiction of the new Act of Uniformity, and they retained and used the right of condemning heretics. The proceedings against Gardiner and Bonner, whoever inspired them, were left mainly in Cranmer's hands, and, as we have seen, the bishops participated almost to the exclusion of laymen in the theological debates in the House of Lords. The right of the clergy to tithes was confirmed by a fresh Act of Parliament,[1] and when Sir Philip Hoby suggested that prebends might usefully be devoted to the defence of the kingdom,[2] Somerset left the proposal severely alone. No change was more strenuously urged by the Reformers than the marriage of priests, but even on this point Somerset—the feeling cannot be ascribed to Cranmer, who was already married—showed a singular reluctance to break with ancient custom. The only Act[3] during his sway that touched the question declared

Elements of the old ecclesiastical system retained.

[1] 2 & 3 Edw. VI. c. 13.
[2] Dixon, *Hist. Church of England*, ii. 503. [3] 2 & 3 Edw. VI. c. 21.

that it was better for the estimation of priests and other ministers in the Church of God to live chaste, sole, and separate from the company of women and the bond of marriage, whereby they might better intend to the administration of the Gospel, and that it was much to be wished " that they would willingly and of their selves endeavour themselves to a perpetual chastity." It proceeded to take away all positive laws against the marriage of priests, not as recognising a principle, but merely as a concession to human frailty for the avoiding of the practical results of a theoretical celibacy.

Marriage laws.

In other details of the marriage laws Somerset insisted upon the ancient use. By a statute (32 Henry VIII. c. 38) the invalidation of marriage by a pre-contract had been abolished. This statute was now repealed, and the old canon law restored. Similarly the view had gained ground that divorce *a mensa et thoro* destroyed the bond of marriage, and many men, having obtained this limited divorce from one woman, had gone through the marriage ceremony with another. Among these was the Marquis of Northampton, who had married Elizabeth Cobham while his first wife, who had been divorced *a mensa et thoro* for adultery, was still living. The fact came to Somerset's ears, and on 28th January 1547–8 Northampton was summoned before the Council.[1]   He pleaded justifica-

[1] *Acts of the Privy Council*, ii. 164, 165. Northampton's and other cases like it have been the test for very sweeping assertions as to the decay of morality under Edward VI., based on the sermons of

tion by the "word of God," and his view was strenuously supported by Hooper, who advocated equal liberty of divorce to both husband and wife in case of adultery.[1] The canon law, however, recognised no divorce except on account of some canonical disability which voided the marriage *ab initio;* separation *a mensa et thoro* did not in any sense destroy the marriage bond.[2] Somerset took his stand on this law, and Northampton was commanded to separate from his so-called second wife.   Three months later, on 24th April 1548, a proclamation was issued ordering such as had spiritual jurisdiction to proceed against all who put away one wife and married another, and to punish them according to the ecclesiastical laws, that others might be afraid to fall into such insolent and unlawful acts.[3]   Here again the result was due to Somerset, for soon after his fall Northampton procured an Act of Parliament legalising his second marriage.[4]   Somerset's view was, however, upheld

Latimer, Lever, Gilpin, and others, and on various Acts of Parliament for the reformation of morals.   But it is the business of reformers to make out as bad a case as they can against the state they wish to reform.   The existence of a Church of England Temperance Society does not prove that drunkenness is more rife than ever before ; nor do recent Acts of Parliament against seduction under a certain age prove that those offences are more numerous than before, but that the public conscience is more sensitive about them.   The denunciations of Latimer and various Acts of Edward's Parliament, *e.g.* 2 & 3 Edw. VI. c. 29, must be considered in the same light.

[1] *Original Letters.*   Parker Soc. i. 64.   Hooper to Bullinger.

[2] *Law Quarterly Review,* October 1897, pp. 397–399.

[3] Strype, *Eccles. Mem.,* II. i. 142.

[4] 5 & 6 Edw. VI.   Private Acts No. 4 ; it was repealed in the first year of Queen Mary.

by a declaration of the Court of Star Chamber in 1609, that marriage with a second wife while the first was still alive was invalid, and this remained the law until the present century.

Was there religious persecution?

The assertion that Somerset was a " rank Calvinist " stands thus in need of serious modification. There remains the important question how far he was a Calvinist in his intolerance of other men's opinions and readiness to resort to persecution to produce a hidebound uniformity. The break with Rome had indeed imposed upon reforming states the necessity of some compulsion in religious matters, and had started the perplexing problem how to reconcile the rights of private judgment with any religious unity. In England the theory of private judgment obtained a very limited assent, and the authority of the Pope was seized by the State. This almost inevitably led to the idea of uniformity in religion based upon the authority of the State, and hence political liberty and religious liberty became very much bound up together. Arbitrary rulers would be as eager to enforce their authority in the Church as in the State; Charles I. and Laud had a common object, and it is difficult to say whether political or religious freedom was the more powerful motive in their opponents. For a ruler in Somerset's position the only tolerable solution of the problem was a system of uniformity under which formularies should be so drawn up as to enable the greatest number to subscribe to them, and the penalties for nonconformity made as light as possible. The vagueness of the first Book of

Common Prayer has already been pointed out, and
it has received many practical illustrations in recent
years. That Somerset avoided excessive rigour in
his treatment of religious dissidents is sufficiently
clear. Any discussion of the question would be
superfluous, if the comprehensive anathema which
it is now customary to pronounce on the Protector
and all his works were based on any adequate
examination of the evidence. Three names at once
occur of prominent sufferers for their religion in
the reign of Edward VI.—the Princess Mary and The Prin-
Bishops Gardiner and Bonner. The first need not cess Mary.
detain us long. On 16th June 1549 information
was laid before the Council that Mary was infringing
the recent Act of Uniformity by having mass said
in her household.[1] Mary made no pretence at
concealment, and frankly announced her intention
of defying the law. The Council wrote her a letter
of advice, urging her to discontinue the use of the
mass, but when she refused Somerset granted her
a private license, much to the disgust of the Reformers, as whose mouthpiece Warwick denounced
the Protector for being "unwilling to restrain her
(Mary) in any way." Somerset's fall was attributed
by John ab Ulmis to "this especial reason that he
was of a more gentle and pliant nature in religious
matters than was befitting a nobleman possessed of
so much authority. Warwick, therefore, as soon as
he had succeeded to his office, immediately took care
that the mass priests of Mary should be thrown into
prison, while he himself entirely interdicted the use

[1] *Acts of the Privy Council*, ii. 291, 292.

of the mass and popish books." [1]   Her persecution was subsequent to the Protector's overthrow.

Bonner.

Gardiner and Bonner based their opposition to the Government on the same ground as Mary, namely, that neither Council nor Parliament had any authority to make religious changes during the young king's minority.   It was perhaps natural that they should take up this position, but it was quite untenable, and as they were men in authority and public positions, Somerset could not afford to ignore their contumacy as he had done Mary's.   But it was rather a question of enforcing political authority than of persecution for religious opinion.   Bonner was the first to be dealt with.   On 12th August 1547 he was summoned before the Council for his resistance to the ecclesiastical visitation, and for receiving the injunctions and homilies with the salvo "if they be not contrary to God's law and the statutes and ordinances of the Church."   He gave little trouble and made a full submission, but for the sake of example he was committed for a time

---

[1] John ab Ulmis to Bullinger, in *Original Letters*, Parker Soc., ii. 439 ; *cf.* Hallam, i. 95, *note*. " Somerset had always allowed her to exercise her religion, although censured for this by Warwick, who died himself a papist, but had pretended to fall in with the young king's prejudices.   Her ill-treatment was subsequent to the Protector's overthrow."   There is an interesting contemporary account of the treatment of the Princess, written by Sir Richard Morison, ambassador to the emperor, in *Harleian MS.* 353 *ff.* 130 *et seqq.*   Mary always entertained somewhat kindly feelings towards the Protector, and she was on intimate terms of friendship with his wife, whom she addressed in her letters as " My good Nan."   Mary and Gardiner are said to have desired to restore Somerset's sons to their titles and estates, but were dissuaded by other advisers.

to the Fleet.   He was released, however, before
Parliament met, and he took a constant and prominent part in the deliberations of the House of
Lords, in that and the following sessions.   Two
years later, his neglect to use the new prayer-book
again brought him under the notice of the Council,
and he was ordered to preach a sermon at St. Paul's
Cross on 8th September 1549, setting forth certain
points of doctrine.   In this he obeyed; but he was
also required to declare that the king's authority
was as great as if he were thirty or forty years old,
and this question he passed over in silence.   An
information was laid against him by William Latimer [1] and Hooper, and on seven different days he
was examined by Cranmer.   Finally he was by
Cranmer deprived of his bishopric on 1st October
and sent to the Marshalsea. [2]   It was not, however,
until 7th February 1549–50, four months after
Somerset's fall, that Bonner's appeal to the Council
against Cranmer's decision was rejected; he was
then sentenced to imprisonment during the king's
pleasure, and Ridley was appointed to his see two
months later. [3]

In the same way Somerset's responsibility for the proceedings against Gardiner was much less than that of Cranmer.   On 21st September 1547, while the Protector was absent in Scotland, the Council

Gardiner.

---

[1] " Parson of Saint Lawrence, Pountney " (Stow, *Annals*, 1631,
p. 597), not the famous Hugh Latimer ; for William see Hennessy,
Novum Repertorium Eccles. Londinense.

[2] *Acts of the Privy Council*, ii. 125, 517.

[3] *Ibid.*, ii. 385 ; Wriothesley, *Chronicle*, ii. 34 ; Le Neve, *Fasti Eccles.
Angl.*, ed. Hardy, ii. 300.

summoned Gardiner to appear before it on the following Sunday, the 25th.[1] He was then accused of having spoken impertinent things of the visitation, of having refused to set forth and receive the injunctions and homilies, and was promptly sent to the Fleet. On 8th January 1547–8 his imprisonment, during which, according to the Council Acts, he had been " as much at his ease as if he had been in his own house," came to an end and he was included in the king's general pardon.[2] Incarceration had, however, nothing daunted Gardiner, and as soon as he was at liberty he resumed his opposition to the Protector's ecclesiastical policy. He was accordingly on 29th June 1548 ordered to preach a sermon at St. Paul's Cross asserting the authority of the Government. He was also directed to maintain silence on the doctrine of the Sacrament, which was under discussion at the moment. Gardiner neglected both injunctions. On the 30th he was brought before the Council and sent to the Tower.[3] His confinement was not, however, harsh ; Somerset sent him his own physician to look after his health, and the personal relations between the two retained a friendly character. After his fall

[1] *Acts of the Privy Council*, ii. 517, 131, 132. Somerset's name is attached to the Council minute, but, as explained previously, that means nothing ; cf. *State Papers, Domestic*, viii. 57, 58.

[2] There was also a rumour that he was to be sent ambassador to the Emperor (Selve, p. 274).

[3] *Acts of the Privy Council*, ii. 208–210. Wriothesley, ii. 3 ; Selve, p. 397 ; *State Papers, Domestic*, Edw. VI., iv. 17–20. *Narratives of the Reformation* (Camden Soc.), p. 56 ; *Hatfield MSS.*, i. 236. Selve says that Gardiner told the king he could not and ought not to assume the title Supreme Head.

Somerset made strenuous efforts to procure the
bishop's release and prevent his deprivation, treatment which Gardiner repaid by the kindly interest
he subsequently took in Somerset's children.[1] Indeed the moderation with which Somerset used
his power comes out in striking contrast with
the conduct of Henry, Northumberland, Mary, and
Elizabeth. As we have seen, Somerset sanctioned
the deprivation of not a single bishop, and even
when Parliament proposed the deprivation of the
Bishop of Worcester he refused to carry out the
suggestion.[2] Yet before and after his rule bishops
were deprived almost by the score. The practice
was enforced against the non-jurors at the Revolution, the boasted beginning of the era of toleration,
and indeed it is difficult to see what other fate
would befall a bishop to-day who refused to carry
out any doctrinal or liturgical changes that Parliament might make.

His treatment of the bishops is, however, but one Other cases.
count in the charge of persecution against Somerset.
Roman Catholic martyrologies have, as a rule, an
unfortunate, but easily explained, habit of passing at
a bound from the reign of Henry VIII. to that of
Elizabeth, leaving out of account the two inter-

---

[1] Gasquet and Bishop (p. 62) remark : "Nor did Somerset and
Cranmer rest until he (Gardiner) was deposed from the See of
Winchester and was safe within the walls of the Tower."
Gardiner was deprived on 15th February 1550-1, sixteen
months after Somerset's fall, and one of the causes of his
death was the efforts he made to get Gardiner released from the
Tower.

[2] Dixon, iii. 9.

mediate reigns of Edward and Mary.[1]   There is thus a gap in the lists of those who suffered for the Roman Catholic faith, but it has been filled up by the zeal of Anglican divines, *Romanis ipsis Romaniores*. With the help of these and of Nicholas Sanders, it is possible to examine the evidence and form some idea of the persecution which Somerset employed. Sanders was an undergraduate at New College at the time, and the authority of his *De Visibili Monarchia* and *De Origine ac Progressu Schismatis*, somewhat impaired by the explosion of the " Nag's Head " story of Parker's consecration, has been to some extent rehabilitated by the confirmation of his account of Bishop Ponet's scandalous marriage.[2] He gives a somewhat meagre list[3] of ten sufferers for religion under Edward VI.; they were Drs. Crispin and Moreman, Henry Cole, Thomas Watson, John Seton, John Story, John Boxall, William Rastell, Cardinal Pole, and Richard Smith. The first two had been accused of stirring up insurrection in Cornwall, and imprisoned in the Tower; their release was made one of the demands of the Cornish rebels in 1549, which was naturally not

---

[1] *Cf.* Bridgewater (Aquepontanus) *Concertatio Ecclesiæ Catholicæ in Anglia*, 1594; Diego de Yepes, *Historia Particular de la Persecucion de Inglaterra*, Madrid, 1599; Circignano's *Ecclesiæ Anglicanæ Trophæa*, Rome, 1584; Charles Butler's *Memoirs of English Catholics*, 1819–21, 4 vols.; Challoner's *Modern British Martyrology*, 1836.

[2] *i.e.* with a butcher's wife while her husband was still alive; the bishop was consequently divorced from her. The story was always considered one of Sanders's inventions, until the publication of *Machyn's Diary* and the *Greyfriars' Chronicle* by the Camden Society placed it beyond doubt.

[3] *De Origine*, ed. Lewis, 1877, pp. 200 *et seq.*

complied with, and Moreman was still a prisoner in the Tower in 1552.[1] Henry Cole was warden of New College, Oxford, and in November 1550 the University visitors were directed to examine, and if they found sufficient cause, to depose him;[2] but this was more than a year after Somerset's fall. Thomas Watson was chaplain to Gardiner, and is said to have been imprisoned with the bishop in 1547, but of this there is no record. He was, however, summoned before the Privy Council on 4th December 1550, and was in prison in the Fleet in 1551, but this again was after Somerset's fall. He became Bishop of Lincoln under Mary, and was deprived by Elizabeth, surviving to be the last of the old Catholic bishops. John Seton was chaplain to Fisher and then to Gardiner; he was certainly at large as late as 1550, nor is there any record of any proceedings against him.[3]   Dr. John Story was notable as the first Regius Professor of Civil Law at Oxford, and afterwards the most bitter of the persecutors under Mary.   He was Queen's Proctor at Cranmer's trial, served on a commission in 1556 for discovering a severer method of dealing with heretics, and regretted afterwards that he had not done more towards their suppression.[4]   It is said to have been at his instigation that Alva established the Inquisition at Antwerp; finally he was kidnapped and

Cole, Watson, and Seton.

Dr. John Story.

[1] *Harleian MSS.*, 249 f. 40.
[2] *Hatfield MSS.*, i. 338.
[3] *Dict. Nat. Biogr.*, li. 271.
[4] *Acts of the Privy Council*, iv. 182; Strype's *Cranmer* and *Annals of the Reformation*, and Foxe, *Acts and Mon.*, passim; Wood, *Athenæ Oxon.*, ed. Bliss, i. 386–389.

executed for treason in 1571.[1] He would have
deserved little sympathy had Somerset meted out
to him the measure Story meted out to others, but
in reality the Protector had nothing to do with
Story's troubles. On the contrary, he continued to
Story his salary as Professor of Civil Law on 19th
November 1548 ;[2] on the 21st of January following,[3]
however, Story made a violent speech in Parliament; he was given to this method of procedure,
and got into similar trouble with the House of
Commons both under Mary and Elizabeth. On
this occasion he went so far as to quote from
Ecclesiastes, "Woe unto thee, O land, when thy
king is a child." Story was at once imprisoned by
order of the House. He made his submission, and
was released by the same authority on 2nd March
following; soon afterwards he voluntarily removed
to Louvain, where he remained until Mary's accession. This is the first recorded case of the House
of Commons punishing a member for his conduct
within its walls, but it is no evidence against the
Protector. There is a similar absence of evidence
to prove acts of persecution towards John Boxall,[4]
afterwards Secretary to Queen Mary, and William
Rastell,[5] the nephew of Sir Thomas More, and
editor of his works. Both withdrew to the Continent during Edward VI.'s reign, but there is nothing

---

[1] *Cal. Papers preserved at Simancas*, vols. i. and ii. *passim; Cal.
State Papers, Domestic*, vol. i.

[2] *Acts of the Privy Council*, ii. 229.

[3] *Commons' Journals*, i. 5 ; Hallam, *Const. Hist.*, i. 271.

[4] *Dict. Nat. Biogr.*, vol. vi.

[5] *Ibid.*, vol. xlvii.

to show that their retirement was other than volun-
tary, and due to a desire to avoid conforming with
the new order of things. Nor is the instance of
Cardinal Pole any more convincing as a proof of Cardinal
Somerset's persecution. He had, of course, been Pole.
an exile under Henry VIII., and on his death had
endeavoured to persuade the Pope and the Emperor
to invade England,[1] and assert Mary's claim to the
throne. It therefore argued some forbearance on
the Protector's part when he offered Pole a pardon
if he would return to England and conform to the
new religion.[2] Richard Smith, who was described Richard
as the greatest pillar of the Roman Catholic cause,[3] Smith.
had written a book upholding the mass in Henry's
reign; he recanted in 1547, first in London, then in
Oxford,[4] and according to Bishop Jewell he repeated
the performance on three subsequent occasions.[5]
In 1549 he had a great disputation at Oxford,
where he had been Professor of Theology, with
Peter Martyr.[6] He got into trouble with the University authorities, and is reported to have been
imprisoned for a few weeks by them. After his
release he fled abroad, to return with Mary only to
be again deprived of his professorship at Elizabeth's

[1] State Papers, Foreign, vol. i. No. 30.

[2] Somerset's letter to Pole is printed in Pocock's Troubles connected with a Prayer-Book (Cambridge), pp. vi-xiv. The Protector signs himself "Your loving friend if ye acknowledge your
dutie to the king's majesty."

[3] Wood, Athenæ Oxon., ed. Bliss, i. 333.

[4] Strype, Cranmer and Memorials: Lit. Remains of Edward VI.,
i. 214.

[5] Zurich Letters, Parker Soc., ii. 12, 45.

[6] Original Letters, Parker Soc., ii. 478, 479.

accession, because of his faith say his apologists, but according to Jewell because he was guilty of gross immorality.[1]

Such is the evidence for the assertion of the persecution of Catholics by the Protector. There was another class of men whose religious, or perhaps rather social, tenets laid them open to persecution at the hands of Catholic and Reformer alike. The Anabaptists, owing no doubt to social oppression, grew rapidly in numbers during Edward's reign. " England is at this day," wrote Chamberlain in 1551, " the harbour for all infidelity," and he urged the Council to forbid the immigration of Anabaptists.[2] In the spring of 1549 the ecclesiastical courts began to be active in repressing this form of heresy, and several Anabaptists were compelled to bear a faggot at St. Paul's Cross.[3] This was a comparatively trivial punishment, but in April 1549 Cranmer condemned for heresy and excommunicated the unfortunate Joan Bocher.[4] He then handed her over to the secular arm for execution, and sent a statement of his proceedings to the king. Lord Chancellor Rich had been particularly active in procuring this sentence, but Somerset's toleration extended even to Anabaptists, and so long as he remained in power he did nothing to carry out the ecclesiastical sentence. His successors were actuated by no such sentiments; on 27th April

[1] *Zurich Letters*, ii. 45 ; Dodd, *Church Hist.*, ii. 101.
[2] Tytler, i. 380.
[3] Wriothesley, ii. 34, 35.
[4] *Dict. Nat. Biogr.*, vol. x. 287 ; Hutchinson's *Works*, Parker Soc., p. v.

1550, six months after Somerset's fall, Rich issued an order for Joan's execution to the Sheriff of London, and she was burned on 2nd May.

This somewhat lengthy examination is perhaps justified by the importance of the facts it establishes. During Somerset's administration there was not a single execution for any kind of religious opinion;[1] there was no torture, and the severest penalties which Somerset tolerated were the bearing of faggots by Anabaptists, and the temporary imprisonment of two bishops for refusing to acknowledge the authority of his Government. It is only necessary to look before and after; to remember Fisher and More, Barnes and Lambert, Fetherstone, Abel, and Powell under Henry VIII.; Joan Bocher and George van Paris under Northumberland; Cranmer, Latimer, Ridley, and a noble army of martyrs under Mary; Campion, Robert Southwell, and the two hundred victims of Elizabeth's reign, to realise that the rule of Catholic sovereigns is not an unmixed blessing, and that the sway of a "rank Calvinist" may not be without its compensations.

A subject of hardly less importance than Somerset's share in the religious revolution, and a subject which is naturally associated with it, is his treatment of education. It would require many years

Education.

---

[1] There were, of course, some priests executed for their share in the Western rebellion, but that can no more be called religious persecution than can Queen Mary's execution of Sir Thomas Wyatt, Northumberland, or Lady Jane Grey. They were, moreover, executed under martial law by the military commanders; for the most part the regular Government executions did not take place till after Somerset's fall.

of study, and at least one volume to itself, to deal
at all adequately with the question, but it cannot
be passed over in silence, and one or two suggestions offered with much hesitation, may not be
out of place.   The traditional view of Edward VI.
and his advisers, as great educational benefactors,
has been largely discredited, and a recent writer [1]
has gone so far as to maintain that Edward VI.
did not found a single school, and deserves the
appellation "spoiler of schools." His educational
policy arose out of the abolition of chantries, which
has itself been the subject of much vague and not

The Chan-
tries Act.
Its objects

very intelligent abuse.   Despite the use which has
been made of the Chantries Act [2] as a weapon for
attacking the statesmen of Edward's reign, there was
little difference of opinion at the time on the waste-
fulness of hiring priests to pray for the souls of
the departed.   Even Gardiner, the stoutest champion of the Catholic faith, expressed his approval
of the Chantries Act.   "I that allow Mass so well,"
he said, "and I that allow praying for the dead (as
indeed the Dead are of Christian charity to be prayed
for), yet can agree with the realm in the matter of
putting down. chantries." [3]   Gardiner's approval was
no doubt partly due to the fact that the chantries
had already been abolished in the reign of Henry, on
whose authority he always took his stand.   But a
comparison between the statute of Henry [4] and that

[1] Mr. A. F. Leach, *English Schools at the Reformation*, 1897.
[2] 1 Edw. VI. c. 14.
[3] Foxe, *Acts and Mon.*, vi. 87–93.
[4] 37 Hen. VIII. c. 4.

of Edward illustrates the difference in spirit between
the former monarch and Somerset. The one
abolished chantries, the other devoted the proceeds
to education; Henry's reason, as expressed in his
statute, was that certain men "of their avaricious
and covetous minds" had misappropriated to their
own use chantry lands and revenues, and if appropriation, it was implied, was the order of the day
the king might as well do it as any other, and
with vastly more effect. Somerset's reason, also
expressed in the statute, was that chantries fostered superstition and errors in Christian religion.
Henry's object was declared to be the maintenance of the war with France, and the preservation and defence of the kingdom; Somerset's was
to convert chantries " to good and Godly uses, as
in erecting of Grammar Schools to the Education
of Youth in Vertue and Godliness, the further
Augmenting of the Universities, and better Provision for the Poor and Needy."

These excellent sentiments are, however, repre- and execu-
sented as a hypocritical cloak to conceal the real ^{tion.}
object of the measure, which was the aggrandise-
ment of the "gang of harpies" who constituted
Edward's court, and it is assumed that the bulk
of the chantry lands was diverted to this purpose.
This theory is a deduction from the instances [1]
which are known of chantries, colleges, &c., being
granted to private persons, but the number of these
instances is totally inadequate to justify so sweeping

[1] Canon Dixon gives a list, vol. ii. pp. 502, 503, but does not draw
the important distinction between grants and sales.

an assertion. There is no satisfactory statement of the annual values of the revenues that thus accrued to the Crown, but a large proportion of it can easily be accounted for without resorting to the theory that the bulk was swallowed up by the courtiers. The first charge on these revenues was to pension

Priests pensioned.

the disendowed priests. Their pensions were fixed on a fairly liberal scale. The chantry priest whose income had been £5 or under received the full £5 as pension, which might be anything between £60 and £100 of our present money; for incomes between £6, 13s. 4d. and £10 the pension was £6; and between £10 and £20 it was £6, 13s. 4d.[1] The total amount paid in pensions in 1549 was £11,147, 14s. 1d.,[2] which would make the number of chantry priests pensioned to be about 2000, or about one in every thousand inhabitants of the people. Reckoning the male adults at a quarter of the population—an excessively high computation —it would appear that out of every 250 male adults one was an ex-chantry priest in receipt of a pension. This leaves little room for the assertion[3] that few of the chantry priests received the pensions that had been promised them. The next charge on these revenues was the maintenance of the schools previously attached to the chantries, and the order for this purpose was that the same sum

[1] Leach, p. 77.

[2] This valuable piece of information is found in *Hatfield MSS.*, vol. i. No. 316, which contains the official list of such pensions drawn up for the Court of Augmentations. Somerset caused an act to be passed (3 Edw. VI. c. 7) securing to the priests the due payment of their pensions (*cf.* Gasquet, ii. 466). [3] Dixon, ii. 500.

should be paid for the maintenance of the schools as had been paid before the dissolution of the chantries. A third object swallowed up another portion of this wealth. The bankrupt state of the exchequer and crippled revenue which Henry had left to Somerset rendered absolutely necessary the appropriation of a further sum to the necessities of the realm. On 17th April 1548 a commission was appointed, with power to sell chantry lands to the value of £5000 [1]—not annual value, but market price for the freehold. This was an infinitesimal part of the whole, and the uses to which it was devoted were quite legitimate. Among them were payment of old debts of the Admiralty, the provision of arms and armour, victuals for the army, the payment of foreign soldiers, Irish captains, and the envoy to Denmark; the supply of clothing for soldiers, provisions and "lanskenets" for the war in Scotland, and provision for the conveyance of letters, arms, and ammunition.[2] The persons to whom these chantry lands were sold were, however, under no such obligation as the Government to provide out of them for the maintenance of schools and schoolmasters, and probably it was their neglect to do so that gave rise to denunciations like Lever's against the practice of suffering schools to decay.

Sale of chantry lands.

Of Somerset's intention to refound such schools as had been previously maintained out of the chantry funds there can be no reasonable doubt,

Somerset's intention.

---

[1] *Acts of the Privy Council*, ii. 184–186.
[2] These details are all collected from various entries in the *Acts of the Privy Council*, but there were many others of a similar description.

and his failure to do so is sufficiently explained by the pressure of other matters ; wars abroad and at home, an impoverished exchequer, and his own speedy fall. But one piece of evidence has been neglected. On 23rd January 1548–9 a bill was read for the first time in the House of Commons " for making of schools and giving lands thereto."[1] It was read a second time on 31st January, and a third on 9th February. It was introduced into the House of Lords on 16th February and read a first time on the 18th, but it got no further, and no light is thrown on its failure. Parliament was not prorogued until 14th March, so there would have been ample time for it to become law.

Were any schools founded under Edward VI. ? The statement, however, that no new schools were founded by Edward VI., or in his reign, is far too sweeping. It is made on the strength of the fact that all the schools, on which Edward's claim as an educational benefactor has been hitherto based, were in existence long before his time, and that all he did was to continue these schools, substituting a fixed pension to the schoolmaster for the potentially much more valuable chantry endowments which he appropriated. The mistake originated in Strype, who, finding the new patents for these schools but not the returns of the Chantry Commissioners, assumed that the foundations were new, and attributed the credit to Edward VI.[2] **Strype's erroneous list.** Strype's error was pointed out some time ago,[3] but the discovery does not entirely dispose of Edward's

[1] *Commons' Journals.*   [2] Strype, *Eccles. Mem.*, II. ii. 502, 503.
[3] Nicholas Carlisle, *Endowed Grammar Schools*, 1818.

case, or rather the case for the men of his reign. For, curiously enough, though Strype's list is disposed of, the assertion takes no account of any schools that may have been founded subsequent to the dissolution of the chantries, and are not mentioned by Strype.[1] All it does is to prove that the schools given in Strype's list were merely continuations of schools previously existing in connection with the chantries, and were therefore not founded by Edward VI. or in his reign. But it is evident that other schools were founded during this period. In the session of Parliament which followed the dissolution of the chantries two bills were passed for the foundation of new schools, and another for the confirmation and increased endowment of a third. On 9th February 1548–9 a bill was introduced into the House of Commons "for Richard Boreman,[2] clerk, to erect a free school in St. Albans, in the county of Hertford." It was read a second time on the 16th, and a third on the 2nd of March. It was read a first time in the House of Lords on the 7th of March, a second on the 8th, and a third on the 9th. A "saving" seems to have been then introduced, and with this addition it was read three times in the Commons on the 9th. It is entered

Other schools.

---

[1] Mr. Leach's researches are confined to the proceedings of the Chantry Commissioners, the certificates and continuation warrants. If a school occurred in these documents it was obviously not founded by Edward VI. If it does not occur it does not come within Mr. Leach's ken; so naturally he comes to the conclusion that no new schools were founded during the reign.

[2] He was last abbot of St. Albans (Gasquet, ii. 306, 308, 484). A Richard "Bowreman" said mass at Northumberland's execution (*Chron. Queen Jane*, p. 19).

as No. 14 among the private Acts passed during the session. A similar measure passed all its stages in the same session for the erection of a free school at Berkhampstead,[1] and a third for the confirmation of a free school at Stamford.[2]

[1] This Act for the foundation of a school at Berkhampstead causes some difficulty, for a school at Berkhampstead is mentioned in the chantry certificates printed by Mr. Leach, p. 112. It was founded by Dr. Incent, and the date Mr. Leach gives is 1545. Yet if the school founded by this Act of Parliament were merely a continuation of Dr. Incent's school, there seems no reason for the Act of Parliament at all; the school would have been continued, as the others were, on the authority of a mere warrant. Nor does the phraseology of the Act lend itself to the theory that it was a mere continuation or further endowment of the school, for when such was the case an Act was passed for the "confirmation" of the school, as at Stamford. There is no difficulty about the school at St. Albans, as it is one that is not mentioned by the Chantry Commissioners, and therefore is outside Mr. Leach's scope.

[2] This school had been founded in 1532 by one William Ratcliffe, who had left certain lands, &c., for the purpose of endowing a priest to pray for his soul and teach grammar. These lands were sold, and the Chantry Commissioners (Leach, pp. 133, 134) returned the endowment as worth £9, 5s. 8d. The history of this Act of Parliament is given in *Hatfield MSS.* i. 444, and as this document has been omitted by Mr. Leach, and throws some light on the subject, it may be worth while to quote the abridgment of it as given in the *Calendar* (Historical MSS. Commission), Part I. pp. 119, 120. The document is a letter dated 28th April 1553, from "John Fenton, Alderman of Stamford, and his bredern comburges of the same Town" to Sir William Cecil, afterwards Lord Burghley. The résumé begins by thanking Cecil for his goodness, and proceeds, "Where, by the common consent of the parishioners of Stamford, such plate and jewels, as were in the churches there, were sold toward the purchase of divers decayed houses and tenements in Stamford, that late were of divers guilds there, which plate and jewels, together with great sums of money, by the inhabitants of the said town were laid forth and disbursed to the intent that the issues and profits thereof should be employed to 'the exhibition and finding of an honest learned man continually to teach Grammar' within the said town of Stamford, and forasmuch

These instances, however, prove little beyond the particular cases, and the only credit the Government or Parliament can claim is that all these bills passed unanimously. But probably they could be supplemented by further search, and they are only cited to show that the question has not yet been settled, and that the claim of Edward VI.'s reign as an era of educational endowment is not disposed of by the assumption that chantry lands were swallowed up by courtiers, or the assertion that no new schools were founded during the reign.

as such lands and tenements; as late were master William Radcliffe's, deceased, in Stamford, by Cecil's furtherance and help, by Act of Parliament, were given and established for like intent and purpose, be not at this present of the clear yearly value of £6, besides charges, 'not able to find an honest learned man,' unless the other Guild lands now purchased may be applied and occupied for the same intent ; and now they are informed that the plate and jewels above-mentioned are now called for, to be answered to the King's Majesty ; if this should so chance, then, of necessity, the said Guild lands purchased must needs be sold again, to their great hindrance and loss ; 'and then this godly intent begun should take none effect, and that were great pity. In consideration whereof our most humble suit is unto you that, for the love of God and in the way of charity, it may please you to make suit to the King's Majesty for us, that, by your means, this godly act begun may have a perpetual continuance.'"

There were probably other instances of similar endeavours to supplement endowments during the reign ; the case above, in which Northumberland endeavoured to appropriate funds devoted to education under his predecessor, is an odd commentary on Mr. Leach's statement (p. 81) that Northumberland "is entitled to what credit there is in Edward VI.'s school foundations."

There is one other item connected with education which is interesting, in view of the controversy about the preservation of local records which took place in 1894, when the Parish Councils Bill was before Parliament, and of Professor York Powell's recent plea (*Trans. Roy. Hist. Soc.*, New Ser., vol. xi.) for local Record Offices. On 15th November 1547 a bill was introduced into the House of Commons "for a Treasure house in every Shire, for keeping of the records." Unfortunately it did not even reach a first reading.

CHAPTER V

FOREIGN RELATIONS DURING THE PROTECTORATE

Condition at Henry's death. IT has been already pointed out that the state in which Henry VIII. had left England's foreign relations was critical in the extreme. Neither Pope nor Emperor had recognised Edward VI.'s title to the crown, and they might at any moment unite to enforce the claims of his sister Mary. A war with France had just been concluded by an unsatisfactory peace, and the eyesore of Boulogne in English hands was a perpetual incitement to the French to renew the contest whenever a favourable opportunity arose. A union with the Protestant princes of Germany had been rendered impossible by Henry's latter-day zeal for orthodoxy, and his desire to stand well with Charles V. The king of Denmark and Norway, so far as he interfered at all with English affairs, did so only to render **Foreign affairs dominated by the designs on Scotland.** aid to Scotland against English attacks. It was indeed the pursuance of the English designs on Scotland, planned in the previous reign, that determined Edward VI.'s foreign policy. The aim which Somerset set before himself was to eliminate, if possible, all risk of foreign attack while he was dealing with Scotland. Such attack was mostly

130

to be feared from France, and the only means of
neutralising this danger was by embroiling France
with the Emperor.   There were sufficient causes
of quarrel between them, and the alliance between
France and the Papacy, and the passing of the
Council of Trent out of Charles V.'s control, added
to the latter's irritation.   For the present, however,
Charles had enough to do in reducing the German
Protestants to submission, and so long as this
task remained undone, he was not likely to seek a
quarrel with France.   It thus became the interest
of France to keep alive the struggle in Germany,
not by open alliance with the Protestants, for that
would have at once involved open war with Charles,
but by secret promises and support.   The same
circumstance rendered the continued struggle in
Germany prejudicial to English interests, though
Somerset sympathised with the religious objects of
the Protestant princes.   Hence the Protector persistently refused to form an open league with them,
and as constantly urged the French king to do
so, in order that he might become involved in
war with Charles.   This policy was sound enough
according to the principles of the age.   And war
eventually did break out between Charles V. and
France; but it only came in time to save England
from foreign invasion under Warwick, and not in
time to promote the success of Somerset's Scottish
enterprises.

At Henry's death the more immediate danger Attitude
seemed to threaten from Charles V.   At Pole's of the
Emperor.
instigation the Pope wrote to the Emperor urging

him to vindicate his cousin's claim to the English throne, and it is quite possible that had Charles's hands been free, and had there been any signs of discontent with the Protector's assumption of power, some such attempts would have been made, but the moment was not opportune; the Protector's *coup d'état* had been received without a murmur, and the princes of Germany were still unsubdued. This did not remove the necessity for providing against the danger, and the first two months of the Protectorate were marked ˙ by an approach towards a closer understanding with France. A defensive league between the two countries had been proposed in the previous January, and two days before Henry VIII.'s death Paget suggested to the French ambassador an offensive and defensive alliance; he also proposed a defensive league with the German Protestants, on condition that Francis I. would join it. Immediately after Henry's death Odet de Selve reported that England was more eager than ever for peace with France, and at his first audience under the new régime a proposal was made for the marriage of Edward VI. with Elizabeth de Valois, and of the Princess Mary with Antoine de Bourbon.[1] Somerset was not likely

---

[1] *Correspondance Politique de Odet de Selve, 1546-8*, 1888, is the chief authority on this subject. Some of the materials for the diplomatic history of the period, including the Calais Papers, are calendared in the *Calendar of State Papers, Foreign Series*, vol. i. But as much, if not more, exists uncalendared and unprinted among the MSS. in the British Museum, and among the most important of these are Bergenroth's transcripts of the Simancas Papers (*Addit. MSS.* 28595-7.) For diplomatic relations with Germany see *Die*

to fall in with this suggestion, which would have put an end to the project of Edward VI.'s marriage with Mary Stuart, but the negotiations for a defensive league proceeded rapidly. On 15th February the Baron de la Garde was commissioned by Francis I. to act with Selve for that purpose, and on 4th March the English commissioners, Russell, Warwick, Seymour, and Paget, were appointed. On 11th March the terms of the league were agreed upon, and on the following day the Council notified to Dr. Wotton, the ambassador in Paris, the conclusion of the treaty. About the same time an agreement was arrived at regarding the boundaries of the English Pale in the Boulonnais.

The growth of friendly feelings between the two kingdoms was proceeding apace when, on 31st March 1547, Francis I. died. There was at once a revolution in the diplomatic situation. The new king, Henry II., had been while dauphin the leader of the Anti-English party in France, and he came to the throne imbued with grandiose ideas of foreign conquest.[1] The Baron de la Garde was at once recalled, and his revocation convinced the English that the new king wanted war;[2] ratification was refused to the defensive treaty which had already been concluded,[3] and a similar fate befell

Change produced by the accession of Henry II. in the friendly relations between England and France.

Englische Diplomatie in Deutschland zur Zeit Edward VI. and Mariens, by Arnold Oskar Meyer, Breslau, 1900.

[1] *Cf.* Michelet, *Histoire de France,* ed. 1879, tom. xi. chaps. i.–vii. ; *Calais Papers,* No. 99, i.

[2] Selve, p. 132 ; *Addit. MSS.* 28596, *ff.* 8, 9.

[3] On 1st April the English Government, in ignorance of Francis I.'s death, had appointed Wotton commissioner to receive the

the agreement about the limits of the English Pale.
Fortunately the Protector was not altogether un-
provided for this contingency; perhaps foreseeing it,
or perchance in deference to the strong Imperialist
party in England, he had insisted on inserting in
the defensive treaty with France an express provision that England was not to be bound to help
France if she invaded Flanders, and he had also
avoided giving offence to Charles V. by declining
the overtures of the envoy of the German Protestants, the Chancellor de Saxe, and had contented
himself with giving 50,000 crowns, with the stipulation that the gift was to remain a secret.   There
was thus nothing to prevent him from again turning to the Emperor as a counterpoise to the renewed
hostility of France.   Charles was too much occupied in Germany to give England any substantial
help even if he had wished to do so, but he warned
the French king that he, quite as much as his ally
of England, must be considered at war with the
Scots; he allowed the English to levy mercenaries
in his dominions, and forbade any French ships
going to Scotland to touch at his ports.

The Emperor's aid was not immediately required.
The King of France, hostile though he was to
England, hesitated to declare war without assured
prospect of success, and he had difficulties and
dangers of his own to reckon with.   Moreover, his
immediate object was the defence of Scotland and

French king's oath to observe the new treaty (*State Papers, Foreign*,
i. 48).   The next State Paper, No. 49, contained the news of
Francis I.'s death.

its conversion into a French province; and if he
could do this without war with England, so much the
better. The Scottish question must be left to the
following chapter, but it is necessary to give here a
brief sketch of the two years' bickerings which preceded the outbreak of war between England and
France, and the efforts which Somerset made to
avert it, the more so because the records of these
negotiations have but recently been made accessible.

It has been already pointed out that Henry The English
VIII.'s peace treaty with France had left the way Pale in
France.
open for all manner of disputes, and that Boulogne,
his sole foreign conquest, was a ruinous gain. In
addition to the ancient possessions of Calais and
Guisnes, there were now placed temporarily in
English hands the upper and lower town of Boulogne—with its outlying forts, Boulogneberg,[1] Tour
de l'Ordre, the Old Man and the Young Man—and
the smaller towns or fortresses of Ambleteuse or

---

[1] British Museum *Additional MS.* 5476 gives a schedule of the
forces at Newhaven, Blackness, and the forts called the Old and
Young Man, with the payments they received. It is printed as an
appendix to *Acts of the Privy Council*, ii. 437-442. Blackness was
on the coast close by Ambleteuse, and Selve mentions a plan the
English conceived of making it an island by cutting a canal. It has
been said (Introd. to Selve) that Newhaven, as the English called it,
was identical with Ambleteuse, and this is probably correct, as on the
English maps it appears as "Haven Etewe." No satisfactory map
has been published. There is a curious Venetian map, executed in
1546, in the British Museum collection of published maps, but it only
gives the immediate surroundings of Boulogne. There are, however, a dozen or more contemporary maps of various scope and
size among the unpublished maps and drawings in the British
Museum, and they are indispensable for the true understanding of
the negotiations between England and France.

Newhaven, and Blackness. The adjoining territory in English hands was ill defined; it did not include Ardres or Marquise, but extended to Fiennes, the possession of which was, however, disputed. A commission appointed to settle the boundary had completed its labours when Francis I. died, but the terms of settlement were never ratified. A new commission was indeed appointed in April, but the French commissioners were instructed to protract the negotiations, and care was taken that nothing should come of them. Similarly when a jetty [1] was begun at Boulogne to protect the shipping in the harbour, the French affected to believe it was meant to carry ordnance, and commenced a fort on the other side of the river which completely commanded the lower town. More legitimate were the complaints lodged by the French against the depredations of the Channel pirates, with whom Lord Seymour, the High Admiral, had established an understanding.

On the English side, Somerset denounced the issue of letters of marque to the inhabitants of Dieppe and other ports, and remonstrated with

[1] Mr. Froude, who had not the advantage of Odet de Selve's correspondence as an authority, accuses Somerset of a flagrant breach of the treaty of peace, but apparently he confuses this jetty with the mole Somerset began eighteen months later, to reply to the fort on Mount Bernard, which the French had constructed in open violation of the treaty. He also points out that the cession of Boulogne was a proposal Somerset ought to have made to buy off the hostility of France, without being aware that that was exactly what Somerset did, but in vain. For the fortification particularly in dispute see an elaborate representation of it among the unpublished maps in the British Museum, *Cotton Charters*, xiii. 43.

Henry II. on his treatment of John Knox and other
prisoners whom the French sent to the galleys, and
whose release the Protector repeatedly demanded.
The French were also continually providing the
Scots with help in the form of money, arms and
ammunition, ships and men, and for nearly two
years there was the curious spectacle of two nations
nominally at peace fighting one another on the
territory of a third. These proceedings did not Proposals
for ceding
Boulogne.
pass without frequent protests on the part of the Pro-
tector, but he was above all things anxious not to
come to a rupture with France while he had Scotland on his hands, and early in August he let drop
a hint that he might be willing to restore Boulogne
before the time stipulated in the treaty, if the
French would make it worth his while. Further
progress with this proposal was interrupted by the
Scottish expedition, and in the meantime the breaking off of the negotiations about the limits of the
Pale, coupled with the victory of Pinkie, caused the
English to take a higher tone. "Rumpez quand
vous voulez," said Paget to Selve, "nous sommes
prestz." The ambassador's reply was a hint to his
master to seize the English wool fleet, which he
estimated as being worth two or three hundred
thousand crowns. Nothing, however, came of these
amenities, and on Somerset's return from Scotland,
which Selve attributed to fear of war with France,
the negotiations took a more amiable turn. An
agreement was concluded for the mutual restoration
of captured ships and prisoners, and the suggested
cession of Boulogne was again discussed. Selve asked

the Protector for something more definite than words,
to which the Protector replied that if the French
king would submit some slight ground for negotiation, such as a verbal communication through his
ambassador as to the desirability of removing the
root of their daily differences, it would smooth his
path, since he had no hope of being able to carry
the proposal either in the Council or in Parliament
if it appeared that he had started the proposal for
cession on his own initiative.   On 10th November
Somerset inquired of Selve if the French king had
sufficient ready-money to buy back Boulogne, and
then suggested that it might be much more profit-
ably spent in recovering Milan from the Emperor.
Henry II., however, was not to be caught in that
trap, and on the 16th the Protector submitted his
first proposal for the restitution of Boulogne.   He
began in orthodox fashion by asking much more
than he expected to obtain.   After dilating on the
advantages which would accrue to the French king
by the proposed surrender, and hinting that perhaps
if his terms were not accepted Edward VI., when
he came of age, might not feel disposed to give
up Boulogne at all, or recognise the validity of a
treaty for which he had not himself been responsible, Somerset offered to give up Boulogne with
all its ports if England were allowed to retain
Ambleteuse and Guisnes, and to acquire Marquise
and Fiennes.   This he thought would satisfactorily
round off both the French and English possessions,
and obviate further cause of discord.   The revenue
from these acquisitions was only 3000 crowns a

year, and Somerset offered to pay ten times that
amount for them. The French king was also to
use his influence to procure the marriage between
Edward VI. and Mary Stuart.

This proposal, whereby the French king was to pay
for the anticipation of the restitution of Boulogne—
i.e. six years' occupation—by ceding in perpetuity a
considerable portion of territory, naturally met with
little acceptance. Odet de Selve pointed out that if
the French king used his influence in favour of the
Scottish marriage it would mean the acquisition of
a new realm for England, to which Somerset replied
that he would have Scotland in any case in the
following year. While the French Government was
concocting a reply to this proposal, it seized and
fortified Fiennes, to which the English responded by
seizing and fortifying Hardinghem, near Boulogne.
When the French answer arrived, on 5th December,
it was found to be conceived in the same spirit as
Somerset's proposal. Dismissing the Protector's proposal as unreasonable, Henry offered to support the
Scottish marriage if Somerset would restore not
only Boulogne, but Calais, Guisnes, and Hames-
Boucres. With reference to Somerset's boast about
Scotland, the French king somewhat maliciously
reminded him of Robert Bruce and Bannockburn,
to which the Protector replied that Bruce's case was
not to the point, for in those days everything depended upon the chance of a single battle, whereas
he hoped to make his position quite secure by the
fortification of towns and strong places. The French
king's proposal he at once rejected, saying that he

would not advise Edward to surrender Calais for ten million crowns, and would rather die than listen to such a suggestion. After these preliminaries, Somerset came down to the reasonable and statesmanlike proposal to restore Boulogne at once if Henry would pay the original sum stipulated in the treaty, and promote the Scottish marriage. These terms met with no more consideration than the others, and late in December Chastillon, the French commander, made an incursion into the Boulonnais, and killed some thirty or forty Englishmen. Somerset, in his anxiety to preserve peace, strictly forbade reprisals, but early in 1548 the aggressive attitude of France, and the aid she persisted in rendering Scotland, had convinced him that war was inevitable, and in February he set out for Portsmouth, to see that it was secure against a possible French attack.

Both sides, however, hesitated to make open declaration of war: Somerset because he wished at all costs to avoid it, and Henry II. because Charles V.'s success in Germany made him more ready to threaten war in Italy. It was also quite possible that Charles might take the English side and join in a war against France, and his ambassador had held language towards the Scots envoys that was by no means reassuring to France. The result was that for the time being Henry was more open to arguments in favour of an Anglo-French alliance, and discussions about the proposed cession of Boulogne were once more renewed. They finally fell through on 4th April 1548, and the diplomatic amenities

went on as before. The English were accused of
breaking down images at Fiennes ; both parties laid
ingenious schemes for burning each other's ships.
The soul of the French ambassador was vexed to
see so many French soldiers serving in the English
army, and so many French pilots in English ships,
but he had his revenge when Captain Hugh Luttrell
undertook to betray Boulogne. The plot failed, and
Somerset demanded Luttrell's surrender. The French
Government denied all knowledge of him, while the
English refused an exchange of prisoners unless
Luttrell were produced ; in the end both Governments stuck to their points and their prisoners.
Chastillon began a fort on Mount Bernard, which
commanded lower Boulogne, and said he would capture Boulogne in a month or six weeks. Somerset
replied that he would risk the kingdom rather than
yield, sent reinforcements to Boulogne, and fortified
the mole. The French then projected an attack on
Ambleteuse and Boulogneberg, which elicited from
Somerset the threat that rather than yield Boulogne
to the French he would hand it over to Charles V.,
who would be an even worse neighbour than the
English. On 31st August he told the French
ambassador that their continued aggressions in the
Boulonnais and their conduct in Scotland rendered
war inevitable, and a few weeks later that a despatch
from the king was practically a declaration of war.
An unusually large meeting of the Council was held
on 3rd October to consider what reply should be sent
to this despatch. Apparently it was decided to put up
with more aggression, and war remained undeclared.

During the autumn a faint gleam of hope encouraged Somerset. Six months before, the acute Dr. Wotton had reported from Paris that some French towns were so oppressed with taxation that they desired to be under English rule.[1] The rumour was correct, and in August 1548 the country round Bordeaux rose against the *gabelle*. The peasants and bourgeois had apparently some lingering tradition of English rule, and refused to submit unless they were granted the privileges they had enjoyed under the English kings.[2] The rebels were believed to have sought English help, but if any was sent the rebellion was suppressed before it arrived.

Though war was not yet declared, the hostility between the two countries amounted to little less. Somerset laid a secret embargo on all French ships in English ports, and sent an embassy to Denmark requesting help and offering the Princess Elizabeth's hand in marriage to the Danish prince. Henry II. on his part sought to turn to good advantage the arrest of the Lord High Admiral in January 1548-9. He sent an envoy to Selve to say that he thought it had happened very opportunely for the advancement of his affairs in Scotland, and that he would be very glad to find the means, if possible, of embroiling England in civil war. Odet was instructed to find out the nature and extent of the conspiracy, and to ascertain if any members of the Admiral's faction remained undiscovered who might be em-

[1] 27th March. *State Papers, Foreign,* i. 77.
[2] Selve, pp. 447, 448, 467 ; *cf.* Michelet, xi. 46.

ployed for that purpose.[1] This project came to nothing, for, with the exception of Northampton and perhaps Dorset and a few corrupt officials and pirates, the Lord High Admiral had no following. But the war which had threatened so long approached at last. Thirlby reported that the Pope had given the French king 120,000 crowns to prosecute his aims in Scotland, while at the same time the insurrections in England made it utterly impossible to provide for the adequate defence of the English places in the Boulonnais. In June 1549 Paget was sent to the Emperor to concert a joint invasion of France, but even then Somerset hung back, and when the news arrived that Henry II. had appointed fresh commissioners to treat on the boundary question, Paget was instructed to delay the proposal for invasion, though nothing was expected from the new commission. Paget was also to make an offer of Boulogne to the Emperor, but Charles declined it and abruptly broke off the negotiation.[2] In August Henry threw off all disguise, and on the 8th his ambassador " gave my Lord Protector defyance."[3] The English Government had no choice but to reply with a declaration of war.

[1] Selve, pp. 478 *et seq.*; *Hatfield MSS.*, i. 268; Haynes, *Burghley Papers*, p. 135.

[2] Strype, *Eccles. Mem.*, II. i. 242 *et. seq. ; State Papers, Foreign,* i. 180.

[3] Wriothesley, ii. 20; *State Papers, Foreign,* i. 200.

CHAPTER VI

THE ATTEMPTED UNION WITH SCOTLAND

The age of national consolidation.

THE sixteenth century was an age of national consolidation. It was then that most of the European states assumed their modern form. Spain grew out of the union of Castile and Aragon, France absorbed Brittany and a large portion of Burgundy, and the union of Poland with Lithuania in 1569 formed a state that then exceeded Russia in size. Marriage was the general method, and the matrimonial felicity proverbially attributed to Austria [1] was almost equally shared by other states. Henry VII. was influenced by the universal movement, and no doubt had the union of England and Scotland as his ultimate aim when he secured the marriage of his daughter Margaret with James IV. His son did his best to defeat that object when he postponed the claims of the Scottish line to the English throne, and France sought by a series of marriages to prevent the union of Scotland with England and to substitute its union with France. The marriage of James V. with Mary of Guise was intended to counteract that of James IV. with Margaret Tudor,

---

[1] "Bella gerant alii, tu, felix Austria, nube." Somerset himself quoted all these instances in support of his own policy (*Epistle*, ed. Early Engl. Text Soc., pp. 243, 244).

but the defeat at Solway Moss once more re-established English influence, and the treaty of marriage between the infant Mary, Queen of Scots, and Prince Edward, which was accepted by the Scots Parliament on 12th March 1543, seemed to place the union between England and Scotland within measurable distance of achievement.[1]

This hope was doomed to speedy disappointment.   The influence of that shifty Anglophile Arran waned before that of Cardinal Beaton and Mary of Guise.   On 3rd December 1543 the Scots Parliament accepted the French offer of alliance,[2] and Henry VIII. replied with a declaration of war.   In May 1544 Hertford burned Edinburgh, but was called away in the following year to defend Boulogne, and the danger from France prevented any serious attempt on Henry's part to compel Scotland to renew the marriage treaty.   Peace was made with France in 1546, and Henry died a few months later, leaving the union with Scotland as far off as ever.   There is, however, no doubt as to his intentions; in November 1546 Selve reported to his Government that the King of England refused to include the Scots in the peace with France, and the Scots envoy, David Paniter, confided to him his conviction that Henry intended to renew the war with Scotland.[3]   The French ambassador was even able to transmit details of the proposed expedition, which were very similar to those actually

---

[1] *Acts Parl. Scot.*, ii. 411.

[2] See *Diurnal of Occurrents* (Bannatyne Club); Teulet, *Papiers d'État d'Écosse* (Bannatyne Club), and Tytler, *Hist. Scotland.*

[3] Brit. Mus. *Addit. MSS.*, 28595 *f.* 276 *b.*

carried out by the Protector, but after Henry's death Selve declared that the chances of the expedition coming off were less than before.[1]

French
opposition.

Meanwhile the French had not been idle. They had, indeed, concluded a peace in which the Scots were not included,[2] but they had no intention of foregoing their designs on that kingdom, or of permitting without a struggle its union with England, and in November 1546 Francis, through his ambassador, promised the Scots his protection.[3] Protection, however, was not the limit of French desire, and their aims were not altogether altruistic. It is impossible to discover how long ideas have dwelt in the minds of rulers and statesmen before they appear in official or other documents, and the exact date when the notion of marrying Mary Stuart to the Dauphin's son occurred to the French must remain unknown. Probably it was suggested by the mere fact of her existence as Queen of Scotland, and almost certainly it must have occurred when her proposed marriage to Prince Edward became known.[4] At any rate before the death of Francis I.[5] the English ambassador at Paris got wind of a project for carrying off the young queen to France, the object of which could only have been her marriage with a French prince, and it was unlikely that the Government would allow so rich a prize

---

[1] Selve, *Corresp. Pol.*, pp. 50–120 *passim*.

[2] Froude says the Scots were included, but such was not Henry VIII.'s opinion; see Selve, pp. 66, 78, 86.   [3] *Ibid.*, p. 57.

[4] "There can be no doubt that Mary had by this time [1543] formed the design of marrying her daughter into France " (*Dict. Nat. Biogr.*, xxxvi. 392).

[5] *Calais Papers*, No. 67, i.   9th March 1546–7.

to fall to any one but the Dauphin's son. When Designs of Henry II.
the Dauphin became king, the danger became im-
minent.   The Queen-Regent of Scotland was a
Guise, and her daughter was half a Guise ; Henry II.
was her adopted brother, and under the ægis of
Diana of Poictiers the Guises became supreme at
Henry's court.   They already controlled the Scottish
Government ; they now came into possession of that
of France.   The protection of Scotland became not
merely a matter of policy but a family affair,[1] and
the Scottish question, no longer one between English
control and Scots independence, resolved itself into
a struggle between England and France as to which
was to rule in Scotland.   England was threatened
with a *pacte de famille* more serious than that of the A Guise
Bourbons ; the union of France and Spain under a *pacte de famille.*
grandson of Louis XIV. was a trifling danger com-
pared with that of France and Scotland under a
son of Mary Stuart and the future Francis II.
England's hereditary enemy threatened to make
Scotland a province, and extinguish for ever her
prospects of greatness.   The danger had to be
averted at all costs, and Somerset's invasion of
Scotland, which has been represented as an act of
wanton aggression, might with more justice be
described as an imperative measure of defence.   He
had no choice between criminal neglect of interests
vital to England and an endeavour to save Scotland
from the clutches of the house of Guise.[2]

---

[1] Michelet, *Hist. de France*, ed. 1879, vol. xi. chaps. iii. and vii. ;
Introduction to *Corresp. Pol. de Odet de Selve*, p. xvii.

[2] A writer in *Social England*, iii. 171, says the immediate effect of
the Battle of Pinkie was " to destroy at a blow all the work of

The Pro-
tector's
aims and
methods.

Henry VIII. is said to have enjoined upon Somerset with his latest breath the prosecution of the
war with Scotland; he had certainly begun extensive preparations for an invasion that was to
take place in the following April. The policy which
dominated the French Government from the accession of Henry II. in March added tenfold strength
to any arguments Henry VIII. may have used.
But when Somerset took up the question of the
union with Scotland he informed it with ideas that
were peculiar to himself, and raised him above the
level of the self-seeking courtiers with whom he
was surrounded. That union was to be no mere
union of the crowns, but a complete incorporation
of the two realms in one body politic, and the far-
reaching character of Somerset's aims is illustrated
by the remarkable propositions he laid before the
Earl of Huntly, the Scots Chancellor, whom Somerset had captured at Pinkie and brought to London
in the hope of inducing him to further the cause of
the union.   In addition to other details of the plan,
he proposed that the names England and English,
Scotland and Scottish, should be abolished, and the
united kingdom be called the Empire, and its sove-

Henry's years of firm but patient diplomacy, to lead to Mary's
being taken to France, married to the Dauphin, and set up as a
Catholic rival to Elizabeth. The ulterior effects of this fatal victory
were still more far-reaching," and he proceeds to attribute to it
the Ridolfi, Babington, and Throckmorton plots; the Armada, and
even the battles of Dunbar and Worcester. It is just possible to
attribute in a minor degree some of these events to the French
marriage; but that was projected long before the battle of Pinkie,
and Somerset's one endeavour was to prevent it.

reign the Emperor, of Great Britain.[1]   In making
this proposal, in which he was at least a century
in advance of his time, Somerset was actuated by
religious, even more than by political, motives.
Proselytising zeal was always one of his most powerful springs of action, and his desire to form a great
Protestant state, which under his direction should
become the protagonist of the Reformation, was
quickened by his eagerness to rescue a kingdom
from the dominion of Antichrist.   Throughout his
Protectorate the union with Scotland was com-
monly known as the "godly cause."

The Protector's other dominant idea—his dislike
of coercion—struggled in his mind with his determination to effect the Scottish union.   In this
resolve he never wavered ; through disaster and
adversity he clung to it tenaciously to the end, but
he was almost painfully anxious that it should be
accomplished if possible in peace.   "Most merciful
God," he prayed, before the hope of peace had
failed, "the Granter of all peace and quietness, the
Giver of all good gifts, the Defender of all nations,[2]

[1] These proposals were made to the Earl of Huntly, the Scots
Chancellor, while a prisoner in England in the autumn of 1547.
See Selve, p. 268, and compare Somerset's own *Epistle*, 1548
(reprinted by Early English Text Society, 1872) : "We have offerd
not onely to leaue thaucthorite, name, title, right or chalenge of
conquerours but to receiue that whiche is the shame of men ouer-
comed, to leaue the name of nacion and the glory of any victorie,
if any, wee haue had or should haue of you, and to take the in-
different old name of Britaynes again" (pp. 241, 242).

[2] This expression is a curious illustration of Somerset's enlightened ideas ; it takes nations a long while to get rid of the
idea that God is their own special defender, and the enemy of
their enemies.

who hast willed all men to be accounted as our
neighbours, and commanded us to love them as
ourselves, and not to hate our enemies, but rather
to wish them, yea, and also to do them good if we
can, bow down Thy holy and merciful eyes upon
us, and look upon the small portion of the earth
which professeth Thy Holy Name, and Thy Son
Jesus Christ. Give unto us all desire of peace,
unity, and quietness, and a speedy wearisomeness
of all war, hostility, and enmity to all them that be
our enemies, that we and they may in one heart
and charitable agreement praise Thy Holy Name
and reform our lives to Thy godly commandment.
And especially have an eye to this small Isle of
Britain; and that which was begun by Thy great
and infinite mercy and love to the unity and concord of both the nations; that the Scottishmen and
we might hereafter live in one love and amity, knit
into one nation by the most happy and godly marriage of the King's Majesty, our Sovereign Lord, and
the young Scottish Queen, whereunto provision and
agreement hath been heretofore most firmly made
by human order. Grant, O Lord, that the same
might go forward, and that our sons' sons and all
our posterity hereafter may feel the benefit and
commodity thereof. Thy great gift of unity grant
in our days. Confound all those that worketh
against it. Let not their counsel prevail. Diminish
their strength. Lay Thy sword of punishment upon
them that interrupteth this godly peace; or rather,
convert their hearts to the better way, and make
them embrace that unity and peace which shall be

most for Thy glory and the profit of both the realms.   Put away from us all war and hostility; and if we be driven thereto, hold Thy holy and strong power and defence over us.   Be our garrison, our shield and buckler; and seeing we seek but a perpetual amity and concord, and performance of the quietness promised in Thy Name, pursue the same with us and send Thy holy angels to be our aid, that either none at all, or else so little loss and effusion of Christian blood as can, be made thereby. Look not, O Lord, upon our sins or the sins of our enemies what they deserve; but have regard to Thy most plenteous and abundant mercy, which passeth all Thy works, being so infinite and marvellous." [1]

The Protector was thus no advocate of war for the sake of war, for the purpose of exhibiting his powers, or of triumphing over a foe.   Indeed he refused to regard Scotland as a foe.   He took his stand upon the marriage treaty which had been ratified by the Scots Parliament in 1543, and regarded that as the expression of the true mind of Scotland.   He insisted that the advantages of the union would be not less for Scotland than they would be for England, and he attributed the repudiation of that treaty to the influence of Mary of Guise and Cardinal Beaton, who were as much traitors to the true interests of Scotland as they were instruments of the designs of the Guises. They and their adherents were the enemy.   The band of ruffians who then constituted the nobility of Scotland   Somerset   knew   to   be   amenable to

---

[1] *State Papers, Domestic*, Edw. VI., vol. ii. No. 6.

two arguments only, gold and steel, and it was indeed these two arguments that carried the day against him. For the present, interest and principle alike compelled him to rely upon the small but growing body of Scots Protestants. A personal union of the two kingdoms was not likely to be successful while one was Roman Catholic and the other Protestant, and the conversion of Scotland was an essential feature in the Protector's scheme.

Mutual hostilities.

This policy had been adopted to some extent by Henry VIII., and one of the first acts of the new Government was to continue the payment of pensions to the English party in Scotland.[1] Endeavours were also made with some success to win over new adherents, and several, including some noblemen, came in during the first few months of the reign,[2] signing articles of agreement to the marriage between Edward and Mary. The castle of St. Andrews was still held by the murderers of Cardinal Beaton, and in March some English ships were ordered to sail from Holy Island to its relief.[3] They appear, however, to have been captured and taken into Leith.[4] The French party in Scotland was now supreme, and any disposition there may have been to consider the terms offered by England was counteracted by the zeal with which

[1] *Acts of the Privy Council*, ii. 12, 13.
[2] *State Papers, Scotland*, Edw. VI., and *State Papers, Domestic*, Edw. VI., Addenda, vol. i.
[3] *State Papers, Scotland*, Edw. VI., vol. i. No. 12; Selve, p. 110. Mr. Froude has reproached Somerset with making no effort to save St. Andrews.
[4] *State Papers, Scotland*, Edw. VI., i. 16.

the new Government of France supported its adherents. David Paniter, afterwards Bishop of Ross, and Sir Adam Otterbourne, two of the most able of them, had apparently come to an understanding with France on Scotland's behalf,[1] and already, in March 1547, two French ships had arrived with munitions of war at Dumbarton.[2] They were but an advance-guard, and in May an expedition under the redoubtable Leo Strozzi, a kinsman of Mary of Guise, was preparing to sail for Scotland to capture St. Andrews, and, as the English believed, to carry off the young queen.[3] Precautions had already been taken by the English Government; on 27th February Andrew Dudley, Warwick's brother, had received directions to cruise in the North Sea,[4] and intercept the French fleet. An engagement had taken place in March[5] in which the English were victorious, but Dudley failed to stop Strozzi, who in July passed within sight of Berwick with twenty galleys.[6] It was then reported that the young queen would return to France in them, and though the French party was not strong enough to accomplish this at the time, St. Andrews was taken. Encouraged by this promise and performance, the Scots took the offensive and captured the castle of Langholm, which was then in English hands.[7] A more important

---

[1] Selve, p. 123.
[2] *State Papers, Scotland*, i. 10.
[3] Selve, pp. 158, 161, 167, 168, 172, 173; *State Papers, Domestic, Addenda*, i. 10–24.
[4] *Acts of the Privy Council*, ii. 44; *State Papers, Domestic*, i. 23.
[5] Selve, p. 118.
[6] *State Papers, Domestic, Addenda*, i. 24 (i.).
[7] *Ibid.*, Selve, p. 157.

result was the refusal of Somerset's proposal to discuss terms of peace, for which he appointed Tunstall and Bowes commissioners in July.[1]   Before the end of that month the Scots had collected a large force on the Borders, which, taken with the French king's despatch of ships, Somerset construed as a threat of invasion.[2]

The invasion of Scotland. The English army had meanwhile been assembling at Berwick.   A fleet under Edward, Lord Clinton, was to accompany the expedition.   On 21st August Thomas, Lord Seymour, was appointed Lieutenant and Captain-General of the "South parts" during the Protector's absence, and Cranmer, St. John, Russell, Northampton, Paget, and the rest of the Council were left to conduct the management of affairs in London.[3]   Warwick had already been sent to the Borders as lieutenant of the English forces. In vain had Somerset remonstrated with the Scots Government on its uncompromising attitude, and depicted to the French ambassador the evils that war would entail on Scotland.   In the commission he issued for the conduct of affairs during his absence, he complained that Arran and other Scots nobles had not only broken and repudiated treaties and engagements solemnly ratified by their Parliament, but had invaded Edward VI.'s dominions with an armed force and carried off prisoners.[4] Similar accusations, coupled with arguments advocating the union and appeals to the people of Scotland to declare in its favour, were set forth

---

[1] *State Papers, Scotland*, i. 29, 31.   [2] Selve, pp. 172, 173.
[3] *Acts of the Privy Council*, ii. 115-119.   [4] *Ibid.*

in proclamations printed in London and scattered
broadcast through Scotland by means of the English
adherents. The Protector made one last vain effort
to avoid bloodshed by inviting Scots envoys to
negotiate at Berwick.[1] The Scots army greatly
outnumbered that which the English were putting
into the field, and they were confident of victory.

Somerset left London on the 22nd or 23rd of
August; and arrived at Newcastle on Saturday the
27th.[2] On the following day a muster was held,
and forty Scots gentlemen came in from the Lowlands; an illustration of the Protector's temper was
given on the same day, when he erected a new pair
of gallows, and hanged a soldier for quarrelling and
fighting. On the morrow he started for the Border,
sleeping that night at Alnwick Castle. On the
30th, after an interview with Clinton at Bam-
borough, he reached Berwick. Norroy king of arms
was then sent on to Edinburgh to explain to the
Queen-Dowager and Council that the Protector's
invasion was only "to bring to good effect the
godly purpose of the marriage between Edward VI.
and Queen Mary, to show them the advantages
of the match, and to tell them that, in case they do
not yield to the Protector's amicable proceedings,
he will accomplish his purpose by force."[3] Their
reply was to speed the fiery cross through Scot-

---

[1] Selve, p. 180.

[2] Patten's *Expedicion into Scotland*, 1548 (reprinted in Arber's
English Garner, 1880); compare for the Scots account of the battle
the *Diurnal of Occurrents* (Bannatyne Club), pp. 44, 45; and
Lesley, *History* (Bannatyne Club), pp. 195–199.

[3] *State Papers, Scotland*, Edw. VI., i. 53.

land.   The nation was not, however, united in support of the French and Catholic cause; the Earl of Lennox, the Earl of Bothwell, the Earl of Glencairn, Patrick, Lord Gray, the laird of Langtown, and others besides the Protestants were in correspondence with Somerset, and a large portion of the Scottish forces consisted of raw Irish levies brought by the Earl of Argyll.   Disunion reigned in the Government; Mary of Guise and Arran distrusted each other; both were opposed by large sections of the nobility, and these divisions told fatally upon the conduct of the campaign.[1]

Pinkie.   The Protector crossed the Border on Sunday the 4th of September.   On Monday the castle of Dunglass, near Dunbar, surrendered; the garrison was allowed to go its way, but the fortifications were blown up.   The same fate befell Thornton, and on Tuesday the army marched past Dunbar without waiting to attack it.   Supported by the fleet, it continued its route along the coast, and on 9th September came in sight of the Scottish army. On that day Arran sent a message to Somerset, offering to allow him to return unmolested, as he had "not done much hurt in the country," and to discuss conditions of peace; to which the Protector replied that the Governor had refused better terms of peace than the English would ever give again. With the same envoy came a challenge from the Earl of Huntly, to decide the dispute by personal

---

[1] *Cf.* Huntly's statement to Selve ; he attributed the Scots defeat to Arran's resolve to attack in spite of the opposition of himself and others (Selve, p. 218).

combat, or with ten or twenty champions. This
challenge Somerset refused, having, he said, no
power to accept it, considering his office of Governor of the king and Protector of his realms. On
the morrow both sides prepared for battle. The
Scots were in an almost impregnable position; in
their front was the river Esk, with only one narrow
bridge over it; on their right was a marsh, and on
their left the sea. This was, indeed, commanded by
the English fleet, but the Scots were daily expect-
ing ships from France, which should take the
English in the rear, and complete their anticipated
rout. On land the Scots numbered twenty-three or
twenty-five thousand to the English twelve thousand
infantry and four thousand cavalry, and so confident
were the Scots of victory that the night before the
battle they played at games of chance with their
future prisoners' ransoms as the stakes. The same
assurance led them, as it did a century later at
Dunbar, to abandon their impregnable position, and
attack the English before daybreak on the 10th.
Crossing the Esk, they endeavoured to turn the
English left; Grey was ordered to charge, but his
cavalry broke against the Scottish lances. In
their flight they threw into confusion the English
infantry, and for the moment a Scottish victory
seemed assured. But the Scottish line, which stood
firm against Grey's horse, was broken by pursuit.
Their advance exposed their right, which was
turned by Warwick; at the same time the Protector restored order to the English cavalry, and
the field artillery came into play. The Scots became

confused and then panic-stricken, and, attacked in front and on the right, while the fire from the fleet annoyed their left, they broke and fled. Their rout was complete, and six thousand Scots or Irish strewed the field before five o'clock, when the Protector ordered a cessation of the pursuit. Fifteen hundred were taken prisoners, including the Earl of Huntly, the Scottish Chancellor.[1]

On the following day the English occupied Leith without opposition. The Protector then sailed up the Firth of Forth, and secured the island of Inchcolm and fortress of Blackness, about ten miles above Edinburgh. Some ships that were too old to be of any use were burnt in Leith harbour, and the town itself was fired without, Patten says,

---

[1] There are several contemporary accounts of the battle of Pinkie or Musselburgh. The most detailed is that of William Patten, which was printed by Richard Grafton in June 1548. There are two editions in the British Museum, and it was reprinted in 1798, and by Mr. Arber in 1880. It was largely incorporated in Holinshed, whence it filtered into the pages of Mr. Froude. Patten was present throughout the campaign as an official in the Provost Marshal's court, Cecil being his colleague, and contributing, it is said, to Patten's account. Another account by an eye-witness is that of the Sieur de Berteville, which was published by the Bannatyne Club in 1825. Berteville was one of the chief mercenaries in the English service; he owned some property in Alençon, which was seized by the French king, who also imprisoned his mother. But throughout he seems to have been playing a double game; he frequently gave information to the French ambassador, who entrusted him with money to bribe one of Paget's clerks. He pretended to be anxious to return to the French service, and claimed a pension, and the restoration of his property; but at the same time he was treated with great favour by the English Government : when he was wounded on 7th September Somerset allowed him the use of his own surgeon and carriage, and Paget

the Protector's authorisation.   Edinburgh, which
was defenceless, was spared, and no attempt was
made to occupy it, as the castle could only be
forced to surrender after a protracted siege.   On
Sunday the 18th the English army began its
retreat.   Home Castle was occupied on the way,
and both it and Roxburgh were fortified.   On the
28th Scots envoys arrived with a promise to treat
at Berwick within a week, and Warwick was left
there to negotiate.   On the following day Somerset
crossed the Border into England, and proceeded to
London, where he arrived on the 8th of October,
refusing the city's proposal for a triumphal entry.
His speedy departure has been variously interpreted; the French ambassador thought it was due

did him the honour of dining with him later.   He was afterwards
accused of being Somerset's instrument for the assassination of
Warwick, and was put in the Tower, but no further proceedings
were taken against him.   The accounts of two other eye-witnesses
are given in Selve's correspondence, namely, of the Earl of Huntly
and of Jean Ribauld, who is frequently mentioned by Patten ;
like Berteville, he also gave information to Selve, and attempted
to escape to France, but was arrested at Rye (Selve, pp. 220, 242,
288, 317, 324, 362, 368).   One or two deviations from Patten
have been adopted from these other accounts ; *e.g.* the number
of the Scots slain given at about 12,000 by Patten seems incre-
dible, seeing that the battle only began at one o'clock, and the
cessation of the pursuit was ordered at five.   Ribauld's number, 6000
or 7000, is much more probable, and the Scots loss was also fixed
at that figure by the Earl of Huntly.   Mr. Froude says, "Multi-
tudes of priests, at one time, it was said, as many as four thousand,
were among the slain."   As this report originated in Patten, it may
be as well to give his exact words : "Among them lay there many
priests and 'kirkmen,' as they call them ; of whom it was bruited
among us, that there was a whole band of a three or four thousand ;
but we were afterwards informed that it was not altogether so "
(Patten, in Arber's *English Garner*, iii. 127, 128).

to a fear of the declaration of war by France;[1] it is also said that rumours of conspiracies against his authority in London had reached his ears, and the attitude of the west was already causing anxiety.[2] Or it may only have been to arrange for the coming session of Parliament, writs for which had been issued in September.

Further successes.

From this time, either from choice or compulsion, Somerset adopted a different method of dealing with Scotland. Possibly he thought that he had already given sufficient proof of the hopelessness of Scotland attempting to resist England by force, and that the Scots would benefit by the lesson, and give ear to the proposals for peace he was willing to make. The victory of Pinkie was followed by the adhesion of many Scots to the English cause,[3] and the Protector brought back with him several prisoners among the nobles, of whom the Chancellor Huntly and the Earl of Bothwell were the most influential. These he treated with great consideration, in the hope that they would adopt as their own the cause of the English marriage. In case they refused, he thought he had hold enough over Scotland to enforce compliance with his will. Besides Inchcolm and Blackness,[4] which controlled the Firth of Forth, a detachment of Clinton's fleet had captured Broughty

---

[1] Selve, 213.

[2] Levies, which had been raised apparently for the Scottish invasion, had already been sent to the west ; perhaps this diversion of his forces partly accounted for the speedy return of the Protector.

[3] *State Papers, Scotland*, ii. 6, 13.

[4] This must, of course, be distinguished from the Blackness near Boulogne.

Castle, which commanded the entrance to the Firth of Tay,[1] and a simultaneous incursion by Wharton and Lennox from the west Borders had resulted in the capture and fortification of several castles in Dumfriesshire;[2] at the same time, the possession of Dunglass, Roxburgh, Home, and other castles made the eastern Lowlands almost English territory. Further strongholds were gradually acquired. Clinton's fleet, after reducing Broughty Castle, landed a force which occupied Arbroath and Dundee[3] in December 1547, and offers were made for the surrender of St. Andrews, St. John's (Perth), and even of Edinburgh.[4] In January Sir John Luttrell made some impression upon Aberdeen and Burntisland.[5] In February concerted action was arranged between Wharton on the west marches, Grey on the east, and Sir Andrew Dudley from the basis of Broughty Castle. Wharton captured Dumfries, and Grey the Castles of Hailes, Yester, and Waughton, but retreated precipitately on a false alarm of Wharton's total overthrow.[6] He renewed his incursions in March and April, when Dalkeith, Musselburgh, and Dunbar were seized, and their fortifications destroyed. Haddington was captured, and made an almost impregnable stronghold in the

---

[1] *State Papers, Scotland*, i. 56. Clinton wrote that in the neighbourhood of Dundee the people would be glad to submit to Edward VI. if it were not for the great men and the priests.

[2] *State Papers, Dom.*, Edw. VI., Addenda, i. 44–60.

[3] *State Papers, Scotland*, ii. 54, 57, 61, 67.

[4] *Ibid.*, ii. 47, iii. 7, 8. [5] *Ibid.*, iii. 5.

[6] *Ibid.*, iii. 51, 53; *State Papers, Dom.*, Edw. VI., Addenda, ii. 17, 42, 59.

English hands.[1]   Lauder and Newark Castles were
also taken.[2]

Progress of
the move-
ment for
union.
By the acquisition of these places Somerset sought
not merely to put pressure on the Scots Government.
Each was designed as a centre for missionary efforts
to convert Scotland to the virtues of Protestantism
and the benefits of the English marriage.   Wherever
the English armies went, they dissolved monasteries,
and set up Bibles in the churches.[3]   " Those friars
who have taken the oath and relinquished the Bishop
of Rome [are] to be cherished and advised to leave
off the habit and put themselves into secular weeds,
and conform to godly and Christian professions ;
and if any of them are able to preach, to do so, and
expose the abuses which have crept in among them." [4]
It was also suggested that if church lands were dis-
tributed among the nobility it would soon lead to
the eradication of *papismus* in Scotland ; [5] and the
oath administered to all who adopted the English
cause was that they would serve the King of England,
renounce the Bishop of Rome, do all in their power
to advance the king's marriage with the Queen of
Scotland, to take his part, and refrain from assisting
his enemies.[6]   Nor was this missionary enterprise
entirely without success.   The English captains frequently reported a desire from the common people

---

[1] *State Papers, Scotland*, iv. ii. 19 ; *Domestic*, Addenda, ii. 62, iii. 7 ;
British Museum *Addit. MSS.*, 32657 ; *Hamilton Papers*, vol. ii.

[2] *State Papers, Scotland*, Edw. VI., iii. 12, iv. 4.

[3] *State Papers, Dom.*, Edw. VI., Addenda, i. 49, 50, ii. 11.

[4] *Ibid*, 44 ; *cf.* Selve, p. 233.

[5] *State Papers, Foreign*, Edw. VI., i. 115.

[6] *State Papers, Dom.*, Edw. VI., Addenda, i. 45.

for good preachers " and Bibles and Testaments and
other good English books of Tyndale's and Frith's
translation." [1]   On the west marches there were said
to be daily suits to be allowed to serve the king,[2]
and Huntly told Odet de Selve that Grey could ride
in safety anywhere he liked throughout the Lowlands with but a small bodyguard, consisting mostly
of Scots.[3]

Political went with religious instruction, and in
January 1547–8 the Protector wrote an epistle to
the people of Scotland.[4]   He once more pointed out
the advantages to Scotland of the union, and the
dangers which would threaten their liberties if they
chose a Frenchman as husband to their queen.   His
object, he said, was " not to conquer, but to haue in
amitie ; not to wynne by force, but to conciliate by
loue ; not to spoyle and kil, but to saue and kepe ; not
to disseuer and diuorce, but to ioyne in marriage from
high to low, both the realmes, to make of one Isle
one realme in loue, amitie, concorde, peace, and chari-
tie. . . . We intend not to disherit your Queene,
but to make her heirs inheritors also to England.

---

[1] *State Papers, Scotland*, Edw. VI., ii. 26.
[2] *State Papers, Dom.*, Edw. VI., Addenda, i. 39.
[3] Selve, p. 251.
[4] " An Epistle or Exhortation to unitie and peace sent from the
Lorde Protector . . . to the Nobilitie . . . of Scotlande " (printed
simultaneously in English and Latin by Reynold Wolfe. London,
1548. 8vo. It was reprinted in 1872 for the Early English Text
Society under Dr. J. A. H. Murray's editorship). This epistle,
says Dr. Murray, " differs greatly from the manifestoes that had
preceded it in its moderation of tone, persuasive reasoning, and
omission of all claims to supremacy over Scotland " (E.E.T.S., 1872,
p. cxxi).

. . . These vain feares and phantasies of expulsion of your nacion, of chaungyng the lawes, of makyng a conquest, bee driuen into your heddes of those who indeede had rather you were all conquered, spoyled, and slain, then thei would lose any poynte of their will, of theyr desire of rule. If wee two being made one by amitie bee most hable to defend us against all nacions ; and hauyng the sea for wall, mutual loue for garrison, and God for defence, should make so noble and well agreeing a monarchy, that neither in peace we may be ashamed nor in warre afraid of any worldly or forrein power; why should not you be as desirous of the same, and haue as much cause to reioyse at it as we ? ''

He then proceeded to justify his invasion of Scotland on two grounds ; firstly, Mary had been solemnly promised in marriage to Edward, and secondly, his object was to prevent all possibility of war between the two realms in the future. War, he said, was " an extreme refuge, to atteigne right and reason emonges Christian men. If any man may rightfully make battaill for his espouse and wife ; the daughter of Scotland was by the greate seale of Scotland promised to the son and heire of England.[1] If it bee lawfull by God's lawe to fight in a good querrell, and for to make peace ; this is to make an ende of all warres, to conclude an eternall and perpetuall peace.''

No record has been discovered of the full details of the plan of union which Somerset had in his mind, but the indications that have survived suggest

---

[1] By the treaty of 12th March 1543. See p. 145.

that it embodied not a few of the conditions upon
which union was eventually accomplished, and upon
which alone it was possible.   It has been already
remarked that Somerset, realising the natural objection of Scots to the terms England and English,
proposed to abandon their use, and style the united
kingdom the Empire, and its sovereign the Emperor of Great Britain.   Scotland was to retain her
autonomy.   " For policy," he said—and the political
wisdom of the remark is worthy of Burke—" must in
sundry places of necessity require sundry laws," and
he quoted as an example the Emperor's dominions
which under one sovereign enjoyed separate legal
systems.   Free trade was to be established between
the two kingdoms, and all laws prohibiting the " in-
terchange of marriage" were to be abolished.

The only obstacle, wrote Wharton, to the accomplishment of the "godly purpose" was now the
nobility,[1] and many of them were influenced by the
successes of the English and the tendency among
the common people to adopt both Protestantism
and the cause of the union.   Lennox, Glencairn, and
Bothwell had been adherents of the English cause
before Pinkie, but towards the end of the year some
of its more pronounced opponents began to waver.
Argyll declared himself a favourer of the English,
and on the strength of his professions received a
liberal grant of money.[2]   John Hamilton, sheriff of
Clydesdale and brother of the Governor Arran, came
over to the same side, and also John Maxwell, who

---

[1] State Papers, Dom., Edw. VI., Addenda, i. 49.
[2] State Papers, Scotland, Edw. VI., iii. 53, 60, 77 ; Selve, p. 303.

took service under Wharton.   Even Angus, in reply
to a request that he would "set forward the godly
purpose," wrote that he trusted that Somerset would
consider it sufficient that he had sent his seal and
handwriting, which he had never broken or intended
to break,[1] while his brother Sir George Douglas
undertook to persuade Mary of Guise to entrust her
daughter to English hands.   Huntly, the most influential of all, offered to negotiate the marriage on
conditions, and was declared by Selve to have been
empowered by Arran to promise the same on his
behalf unless France would give Scotland ample aid
and declare war on England.[2]

The attitude
of France. The success of Somerset's policy, however, depended upon two circumstances over which he had
little or no control.   One was tranquillity at home,
and the other was absence of interference from
France.   On both of these he reckoned, but in
vain.   Tranquillity at home was perhaps beyond
any man's power, in the social crisis that was approaching, to command; and French abstention
could only be secured by purchase or compulsion.
Purchase Somerset had tried by the offer of Boulogne, but French terms were higher than any one
in the Protector's unstable position could afford to
pay.   On compulsory abstention Somerset counted,
because he was confident that before next summer
there would be war between France and the Pope
on one side, and the Emperor on the other.[3]   There

---

[1] *State Papers, Dom.*, Edw. VI., Addenda, i. 59; *Scotland*, iii. 53 (ii.).
[2] Selve, pp. 224, 247.
[3] *Ibid.*, pp. 219, 302.

was sufficient ground to justify this expectation, but though France and the Empire were on the brink of war, the outbreak was delayed long enough to enable Henry II. to interfere with decisive effect in the Protector's Scottish project.

Upon the French decision hung the issue of the day. Arran would accept the Protector's terms unless France would declare war or render Scotland efficient aid. The Scots nobles would do the same for the sake of what they could get out of it—unless France made a higher bid. Gold and steel were to them arguments more powerful than the welfare of Scotland, and the English sword would carry the day unless enough French gold was forthcoming to turn the balance. One and all they had made their adherence a matter of bargain.[1] Arran was to have a dukedom, and the hand of Mary or Elizabeth for his son. Huntly demanded one of the Protector's daughters, release from his ransom, and his appointment as Royal Lieutenant in his shire. Bothwell wanted to marry Mary, Elizabeth, or the Duchess of Suffolk, but was contented with a pension of three thousand crowns and the offer of Anne of Cleves.[2] Glencairn's desire was not a wife but lands, and John Maxwell, who had joined the English because his suit for Lord Herries' daughter had been refused,[3] became a patriot again when Arran yielded; and took the occasion of Wharton's raid in March 1547–8 to turn his arms

---

[1] Cf. Tytler, *Hist. of Scotland.*
[2] Selve, p. 230 ; cf. *State Papers, Scotland,* i. 59.
[3] *State Papers, Dom.,* Edw. VI., Addenda, ii. 59.

against his comrades and join the enemy.   One and
all the Scots nobles promised service to both kings at
once, and the English Government may have been
as perplexed as Selve confessed he was to know
which oath they meant to keep.   Probably, however, Somerset knew that the oath they would keep
would be the one they had sworn to him who
should prove to have the longest purse and heaviest
sword.   Arran became Duke of Châtelherault;
Bothwell claimed a pension of two thousand crowns
from Henry, and Huntly an even larger sum.   The
French Government grasped the situation, and when
in December 1547 some French ships arrived off
Dumbarton they brought "as much money as would
wage ten thousand Scots."[1]

Sends help to Scotland.   Ships and men, however, did more than gold.
Immediately after Pinkie, France gave the Scots
specific assurance of aid, and Warwick, with his
fellow-commissioners appointed to discuss the terms
of peace, waited in vain for the Scots envoys.[2]   On
29th December the French ships arrived off Dumbarton with Paniter, the Scots envoy, La Chapelle,
the French commander, sixty captains, and thirty
thousand crowns.[3]   La Chapelle apologised for his
delay, but excused himself on the ground that
"God was too much an English God, for He had
held them long from that realm after their appointment, by contrary winds."[4]   In January 1548 a con-

[1] *State Papers, Scotland*, ii. 68.
[2] *Ibid.*, i. 60.
[3] *State Papers, Dom.*, Edw. VI., Addenda, i. 61.
[4] *Ibid.*, ii. 2.

vention at Stirling suggested the marriage of Queen
Mary with the Dauphin.   On 20th February
Wharton was ordered to take the offensive against
Angus, whose estates had been spared, but who had
now made default.   Wharton obeyed, but at the
critical moment Maxwell played the traitor, and on
2nd March Dumfries surrendered to the Scots.[1]
Arrangements were made for the delivery of Dunbar,
Edinburgh, and Dumbarton into French hands, and
for the conveyance of Queen Mary to France.   The
English were compelled to abandon Inchcolm after
destroying the fortifications, and they had already
left Blackness.   At the end of January, Dundee was
regained by Argyll,[2] and the tide of success seemed
definitely to have turned against the English.   More
French aid was on the way.   Early in June another
French fleet, slipping by the English ships which
had been stationed at Newcastle in March to intercept their passage, landed some men at North
Berwick, and on 16th June disembarked the remainder, numbering some ten thousand, at Leith.
It then set sail for Broughty Castle, from which the
English still threatened Dundee.[3]

It was now an open struggle between England
on the one hand and France and Scotland on the
other, but it was not an uneven match.   England
had before then been victorious over the same com-
bination, and she still possessed able leaders and
excellent fighting men.   The successes during 1548

[1] *State Papers, Dom.*, Edw. VI., Addenda, ii. 11, 17, 22, 42, 59.
[2] *State Papers, Scotland*, iii. 27 (i.).
[3] *State Papers*, Addenda, iv. 36.

were not all on one side, and, granted peace at home
and tenacity of purpose, the English might yet have
carried the day.   Their enemies were by no means
united ; the Scots might hate English domination,
but they did not love the French, and the thought
of French soldiers holding Dumbarton and Edinburgh was bitter.   The Protector told Odet de
Selve that he did not care how many soldiers
the French king sent to Scotland, as they would
only eat up the country and incur the hatred of the
Scots,[1] while the English were well able to hold
what they possessed.   Nor had the French been
long in Edinburgh before a bloody affray between
them and the citizens bore out the truth of Somerset's words.[2]   The Parliament which on 7th July
agreed to the French marriage, and proposed the
immediate sending of Mary to France, was held in
the presence of the French army, and was scantily
attended.[3]   Angus, Somerville, and other lords held
aloof, and the declaration of the French king, that
he would come to Scotland with forty thousand
men and stay till it was either French or English,[4]
was not calculated to soothe the fears of such as
were anxious for the independence of their country.
The French help had not, moreover, been so successful as was hoped.   The ships that had gone off
to capture Broughty Castle were compelled to return without effecting their purpose.   The possession

[1] Selve, p. 325.
[2] Lesley, pp. 217, 218 ; Ellis, *Original Letters*, 3rd Series, iii.
292–300.
[3] Lesley, p. 209.
[4] *State Papers, Dom.*, Edw. VI., Addenda, iii. 8 (i.), 9.

of Haddington gave the English command of the
country right up to the gates of Edinburgh; the
whole available forces of Scots and French combined laid siege to it in June, but the French
refused to assault until the Parliament which was
held under its walls ratified the proposal of marriage
between Mary and the Dauphin. That did not
ensure the success of their attack, and a brilliant
defence was followed by an equally brilliant relief,
which enabled Haddington to hold out until the
advance of Lord Shrewsbury, the new Lord Warden,
compelled the raising of the siege.[1] Nor was this
all. In July an English fleet under Clinton arrived
at Holy Island, and on the 30th it started for the
Firth of Forth. In the first week in August it
burnt twelve French ships in the harbour of Leith,
and drove the rest to seek protection far up the
river. Proceeding northwards it recaptured Dundee,
attacked St. Ninian's and Montrose, and ravaged
Angus and Fife. It was little wonder that "the
Governor repented of his covenant with France,"
and was in the position of one "that holdeth a wolf by
the ears, in doubt to hold and in danger to let go."[2]

Meanwhile the young queen had been transported *Mary, Queen of Scots, transferred to France.*
to France. The French ambassador in London
had recommended this step in December 1547,
not indeed as a preliminary to the marriage, but

---

[1] See many letters about the siege from Sir Thomas Palmer and
other captains, in British Museum'*Addit. MSS.*, 32657 ; *State Papers,
Dom.*, Edw. VI., Addenda, ii. 62, iii. 3, 8, 9 ; *State Papers, Scotland,*
Edw. VI., iv. 20, 21, 22, 23, 35, 47, 49, 53, 54, 59–120 ; *Diurnal of
Occurrents*, pp. 47, 48 ; Lesley, p. 206.

[2] *State Papers, Scotland*, iv. 119.

in order that France might be able to exact a high
price when the English sought peace.   The designs
of the French Government, however, went further
than Odet imagined, and the conveyance of Queen
Mary to France had been the principal object of
the despatch of French ships to Scotland.   A month
earlier the Protector had learnt from his agents in
Scotland that preparations were being made for
her embarkation and the transference of the chief
strongholds to French hands.   The Governor's last
scruples were removed by the grant of the Duchy
of Châtelherault, and the thirty thousand crowns
the French ships brought salved the conscience
of many others.   Even Huntly was, according to
Selve, made a true Scot again by a French pension.
In February 1547–8 Mary was transferred from
Stirling to Dumbarton, and in July she embarked
on a French galley.   For some days it remained
at anchor in the Clyde, but on the 7th of August
it sailed for Brest, where it arrived on the 13th.
On the 11th of October Mary arrived at St. Ger-
mains, and negotiations were at once commenced
for her betrothal to the Dauphin.

Somerset's revival of the feudal claim.   In the presence of this immediate danger; Somerset took a step which has been always misdated
and given an entirely false significance.   The conventional account is that Somerset, not content
with Henry VIII.'s demands for a marriage union
between England and Scotland, revived Edward I.'s
obsolete claims to feudal suzerainty, and entered
upon his Scottish policy with these grandiose and
arbitrary ideas.   This view involves a twofold mis-

conception.   In the first place, it was not Somerset
but Henry VIII. who revived England's feudal claims
over Scotland, and he revived not merely Edward I.'s
claim to suzerainty, but Edward I.'s claim to sovereignty as well.   In statute 35 Henry VIII. cap.
27, James V. is described as "the late pretensed
king of Scotland," and Henry is declared to have
a "right and title to the crown and realm of Scotland."   In the same year (1543) the king's printer
issued a "Declaration . . . wherein appereth the
trewe and right title that the kinges most royall
majesty hath to the souerayntie of Scotland," and
the Scots lords taken at Solway Moss were forced
to take an oath upholding the same before they were
released.   Probably nothing did so much to set the
Scots against the English marriage as this implied
denial of the right of Mary to be their queen, for if
James V. was only a "pretensed king," his daughter
was in no better case.   The revival of the feudal
claim was thus the work of Henry VIII., and to
him belongs the opprobrium heaped upon the Protector for a policy which was not his.   Indeed,
when he began his Scottish enterprise he dropped
the feudal claim altogether, and based his case
upon the marriage treaty of 1543, and upon the
advantages which union would bring to both the
realms.   When he alludes to James V. he calls
him not a "pretensed king" but a "prince of much
excellence."   He would never have impugned Mary's
title had she merely refused Edward VI.'s offer, and
married a Scottish noble or a prince whose position
was not a menace to England.   But the immediate

prospect of her marriage to the heir of the French monarchy, the danger of France becoming supreme in Scotland, and through Scotland exercising a powerful influence over Ireland, and of thus encircling England with a hostile ring, created an entirely different situation. Such an eventuality must be prevented at all costs, and in the interests of both countries alike. There may have been no legal justification for the revival of this claim, but its justification on the grounds of political necessity was as conclusive as any plea of expediency could make it. That Somerset saw this danger and sought to prevent it is as creditable to him as its total neglect by his two successors is discreditable to them. Rather than submit to such an act of aggression the Protector was resolved either to set up an English claimant to the throne of Scotland or to assert Edward VI.'s sovereignty over the whole island, as Edward I. had done when Balliol failed to satisfy his conception of a vassal's duties. These were the motives that impelled him to revive the feudal claim. In September 1548 he directed Sir John Mason to search the records for this purpose,[1] and on 14th October he informed the French ambassador of what he had done, declaring at the same time that if the French marriage took place he would send aid to the rebels in Guienne—a province, he significantly hinted, which had once belonged to England.[2]

---

[1] *Acts of the Privy Council*, ii. 225 ; Mason's collections are extant in Brit. Mus. *Addit. MSS.* 6128 ; *cf.* also Brit. Mus. *Royal MSS.* 18, A. xxxvii, li, B. vi.

[2] Selve, pp. 457, 458; cf. *State Papers, Foreign*, Edw.VI., i. 712. At

Want of time, means, and opportunity, however, prevented the Protector from pursuing his enterprise against the union of Scotland with France. The English maintained their ground at Haddington, Broughty Castle, Roxburgh, Dunglass, and elsewhere throughout the spring and summer of 1549. The nobles of Scotland were still many of them wavering, and others renewing their allegiance to the English cause. Irritation against France was increasing, and Protestantism made slow and silent but steady progress among the lower orders.[1] Time was still on the side of the Protector's policy, if it could be pursued with tenacity and without interruption. But the rebellions at home rendered it impossible to prosecute the Scottish enterprise with any vigour. For the time the Protector had to content himself with defending what he held with what troops he could spare from the west and the east. Almost immediately after the danger in those quarters had passed away, the Protector was deposed. His successors were careless of everything except the maintenance of themselves in power, and they abandoned Scotland to France.

the same time there was published "An Epitome of the Title that the King's Maiestie of Englande hathe to the Soueraigntie of Scotlande" (reprinted with other tracts, E.E.T.S. 1872).

[1] For the progress of the English party in Scotland see the *Complaynt of Scotland*, 1549, written by an adherent of the French, to counteract the English influence (reprinted E.E.T.S., 1872). It is stated that from thirty to fifty thousand Scots had become adherents to the English cause. One of them was James Henryson or Harrison, whose work in favour of the union mentioned in the *State Papers* (Scotland, iv. 67, 68) as "The Godly and Golden Book for concorde of England and Scotland," is printed with the *Complaynt of Scotland* (E.E.T.S. 1872).

But though the Protector's policy was reversed, it does not follow that it was a wrong policy or that it eventually failed. It is a self-evident proposition that England's true interests lay in a marriage between Edward VI. and Mary, Queen of Scots, rather than in a marriage alliance with France, which Warwick proposed, or with Spain, which Mary effected. The conversion of Scotland to Protestantism and reliance on a Protestant party were no less indispensable. Union could only be established on a Protestant basis, and though, when Warwick made peace with Scotland and relinquished every object for which Somerset had striven, the Protector's efforts seemed to have been utterly vain, yet in reality they fostered the elements which eventually produced success. The English occupation sowed the seeds of the Reformation in Scotland, and though that cause seemed for the moment to be identified with an anti-national party, it forced the Roman Catholics into the arms of France; and then in turn the Roman Catholic cause became linked with that of French domination. National sentiment was evoked against it, the Protestant became the national party, and Knox, the protégé of Somerset, the national hero. When Northumberland and Mary had given place to Elizabeth, it was her support of this party which enabled it to expel the French and become the dominant religious party in Scotland; and thus was removed the difference of religion which was the most fatal obstacle to union between the two realms.

CHAPTER VII

THE PROTECTOR AND THE LORD HIGH ADMIRAL

OF all the events connected with Somerset's Protectorate, the attainder of his brother Thomas, Baron Seymour of Sudeley and Lord High Admiral of England, was the most tragic. It did more almost than anything else to weaken his position and undermine his popularity, and it has given occasion for the most reckless accusations against the Protector's character. Sympathy with the Admiral's fate has led to the assumption that the charges against him were false, and that they were concocted by the Protector to rid himself of a dangerous rival and inconvenient critic of his policy.

The Admiral was some two or three years younger than the Protector, and like him he had enjoyed considerable favour and held various employments under Henry VIII.[1] As early as 1530 he had been attached to the embassy of Sir Francis Bryan to the French court, but it was not until the marriage of one of his sisters to Henry VIII., and another to

(marginal note: Thomas Seymour's career.)

[1] These details are gathered from the *Letters and Papers of Henry VIII.*; see also a *Life of Seymour*, privately printed by Sir John Maclean in 1869, and Mrs. Dent's *Annals of Winchcombe and Sudeley.*

Cromwell's son, that he came into any prominence. In 1537 he became a Gentleman of the Privy Chamber to Henry VIII., and was enriched by numerous grants from the lands of dissolved monasteries.   In July 1538 the Duke of Norfolk proposed that he should marry his daughter Mary, widow of Henry's illegitimate son, the Duke of Richmond. The proposal was renewed towards the end of the reign, but Surrey's haughty spirit could ill brook the union of his sister with one whom he regarded as an upstart.   On the failure of these proposals Seymour sought the hand of Catherine Parr, then the widow of Lord Latimer, but his suit was soon balked by that of a more powerful rival, the king himself.   Meanwhile Seymour was gaining experience in diplomacy and war.   In 1538 he accompanied Sir Anthony Browne on an embassy to the French court, and in the following year he was one of the lords and gentlemen who went to Calais to meet Anne of Cleves and conduct her to her capricious spouse.[1]   In the summer of 1540, when Henry VIII. was on the brink of war with France and Scotland, Seymour was despatched to seek help from Ferdinand, King of Hungary and brother of Charles V., and to enlist mercenaries for the English service.   In this distant land he had the rare experience of seeing something of the war between the Turks and Hungary, which he described in his letters to the king.   He remained attached to Ferdinand's court for two years, and immediately after his return in October 1542 he was once more

[1] *Chronicle of Calais*, Camden Society, pp. 168, 17?

sent to levy mercenaries in Germany. Early in 1543 he was commissioned with Dr. Nicholas Wotton to the court of the Regent of the Netherlands,[1] but he soon exchanged this peaceful occupation for the pursuit of war, and when in June hostilities broke out between France and the allied powers, England and Charles V., Seymour was appointed second in command to Sir John Wallop in the English army in the Netherlands, which was to co-operate with Charles's forces in invading France. He acquitted himself with credit, and participated in the capture of several French strongholds. After a mission to the Regent of the Netherlands, the illness of Wallop placed the command of the division in Seymour's hands, and in this capacity he reduced Bohaine. In the April of 1544 Seymour was appointed Master Gunner of England, and throughout the following summer he served in France. In October he was made admiral of the fleet which was directed to revictual Boulogne, and then await the French ships in mid-channel. But the chance of distinguishing himself by a naval victory was frustrated by storms which compelled the French fleet to remain in harbour. During the year 1545 he was actively employed in the defence of England against the French invasion, but he saw little actual fighting. For the greater part of the time he was in charge of the fortifications along the Kentish coast; but in August he was present at Portsmouth at the review of the English fleet, which was disastrously signalised by the capsizing of the *Mary Rose*. In

[1] *State Papers*, 1830, vol. ix. *passim*.

September he was sent back to guard the Narrow Seas, but the French fleet never came into action, and finally dispersed. In October 1546 he was elected one of the commissioners for the difficult and abortive task of endeavouring to settle the limits of the English Pale in France, and the question of what fortifications were to be permitted at Boulogne.[1]   His services were amply rewarded with large grants of land, situated chiefly on the Welsh marches, but including also Sudeley Castle.   Five days before Henry's death he was sworn a member of the Privy Council.   Henry also left him £200, and directions that he should be made a baron, and appointed him one of the twelve assistant executors of his will.   On 16th February 1546–7 he was accordingly created Baron Seymour of Sudeley, and on the following day he became a Knight of the Garter and Lord High Admiral in place of Warwick, who succeeded Somerset as Lord Great Chamberlain.   At Edward's coronation he was ranked first of the six knights who challenged all comers on the king's behalf, and in the evening the court dined at his house, where the Council frequently met during the first two years of the reign.   When the executors and assistant executors were merged into one body, Seymour became an influential member of the new Privy Council, and when Somerset mentioned to Selve that before he could hope to carry the proposed cession of Boulogne he must gain the support of one or two members of the Council, St. John and

[1] Selve, pp. 47, 181.

Seymour were the two he particularly mentioned.[1] His position as Lord High Admiral was one of considerable importance, and during Somerset's absence in Scotland, his brother was appointed Lieutenant - General of the South, in preference to others like Russell, who had seen far more service.[2]

Nevertheless Seymour was profoundly discon- Discontent with his tented with his own and jealous of his brother's position. position, and from the beginning of the reign he set himself to undermine the Protector's authority, stopping short of nothing, however prejudicial it might be to the kingdom at large or perilous to himself. His first proceeding was to cast about for a wife whose position and property would further his designs. According to the French ambassador he tried Anne of Cleves, the Princess Mary, and then the Princess Elizabeth.[3] The first of these attempts would have been comparatively innocuous, but the last, had it succeeded, and had Seymour effected it without the Council's leave, would have deprived the princess, by the terms of Henry's will, of her claim to the succession. But if these intentions were real they came to nothing, and Seymour renewed his suit for the hand of Catherine Parr, now a widow for the third time. The marriage was His mar- riage with arranged so secretly that no record has survived of Catherine Parr. its exact date, but it was certainly accomplished before the end of May 1547; it followed, it was

---

[1] Selve, p. 200.   [2] *Acts of the Privy Council*, ii. 115–119.
[3] Selve, pp. 154, 155; Wood, *Letters of Royal and Illustrious Ladies*, iii. 191, 192.

alleged, so soon upon the king's death that a child born to Seymour might have been represented as Henry's issue and dissensions have arisen as to the future succession to the crown.   In any case it was an aggressive step to take without consulting the Council or the Protector, and Somerset was naturally much annoyed.[1]   It at once involved the Admiral in disputes with his brother and his brother's wife. The duchess, a proud and arrogant woman, could not tolerate the precedence of the wife of her husband's younger brother, and the quarrels between these two ladies were popularly believed to have been the original cause of the ill-feeling between the two brothers.   Seymour also made, on his wife's behalf, another claim which the Protector refused to acknowledge.   The Admiral maintained that the jewels his wife had possessed as queen were her personal property, and should remain in her possession; and after her death he even declared that they had become rightfully his.   The Protector held, on the other hand, that they were Crown property, and had descended on King Henry's death to his son, King Edward.

Attitude towards his brother's Government.   These trivial disputes were only one indication of Seymour's temper, and it soon manifested itself in a much more serious direction.   He searched the records of previous Protectorates, and came to the conclusion that when there had been two uncles of a king during his minority, authority had been shared between them: one had been Protector and the other Governor of the king's person.   He

---

[1] *Literary Remains of Edward VI.*, Roxburghe Club, p. 215.

therefore contended that he was entitled to the latter office, and that his brother had no right to monopolise both. This idea led him into a course of reckless opposition to his brother's Government. When the Protector offered him the command of the fleet which was to co-operate with the army in the invasion of Scotland, he refused it, and used his position as Lieutenant-General of the South, which Somerset then conferred upon him, to intrigue against his brother's authority while he was away. Similarly he again refused the command of the fleet for Scotland in July 1548,[1] and Clinton, the vice-admiral, was once more appointed to take his place. When Sir William Sharington asked why he did not go, he replied that " it was good abiding at home to make merry with one's friends in the country," [2] and Throckmorton gave him sound advice when he said that if he " were wise or politic he would now become a new manner of man both in heart and service, for the world began to talk very unfavourably of him, both for his slothfulness to serve and his greediness to get." [3] Again, when Somerset, with a view to providing for the king's necessities and checking the enormous extension of sheep-farming, proposed a tax of 2d. for every sheep, Seymour told the Marquis of Dorset he would never give in to it.[4]

This general factiousness soon crystallised into a His intrigues.

---

[1] Sir John Maclean erroneously states that Seymour was in command of the fleet on this occasion, but the Scottish State Papers prove beyond doubt that the commander was Clinton.

[2] *Hatfield MSS.*, i. 303.   [3] *Ibid.*, i. 257.   [4] *Ibid.*, i. 300.

systematic endeavour to upset his brother's authority.
He now began to insinuate himself into the boy-
king's favour, and this he endeavoured to accomplish by supplying him liberally with pocket-money,
and hinting that his uncle treated him badly in
"giving him nothing for play or to give his servants." He also bribed several of the attendants
about the king's person. When he thought he had
made sufficient progress in the king's graces to
counteract his brother's influence, Seymour formed
a plan for ousting him from power. The king was
to be declared old enough and able to rule by
himself without the intervention of a Protector.
Edward himself deposed that the Admiral had told
him "he must now take upon himself to rule, for
he was able enough as well as other kings," while
Sharington heard Seymour say that he would never
consent to the king's being kept a ward until he was
eighteen years of age. The Admiral himself confessed that he had once said to the king that he
trusted within three or four years he would "be
the ruler of his own things, and should by that time
help his men himself to such things as fell in his
gift." To render his influence over the king more
secure, Edward was to marry Lady Jane Grey, whom
the Marquis of Dorset "had given wholly to him
[the Lord Admiral] upon certain covenants that
were between them." The "covenant" was a bribe
of two thousand pounds which Seymour gave Dorset
to be allowed to retain Lady Jane in his own household, where she lived for some years.

But influence over the young king was of no avail

so long as the Protector's patent, which granted him that office until Edward was eighteen, remained in force, and the next object was to get that revoked. Seymour and Dorset voted in the Lords against its confirmation by Parliament, but they were the only peers who did so, and some other expedient had to be thought of. This was a fresh patent which limited the duration of the Protectorate to the boy-king's pleasure;[1] when once this was in force, Seymour thought he would have little difficulty in securing the speedy termination of that "pleasure." The patent, however, though drawn up and signed by many peers and Privy Councillors, never passed the Great Seal.

These proceedings, unjustifiable and mischievous though they were, were not actual infractions of the law, but Seymour also began to meditate the use of force. Catherine Parr died in childbed on 5th September 1548, but her husband only regarded her death as a stepping-stone for his ambition. He at once renewed his suit for Elizabeth's hand, though his brother frankly told him he would "clap him in the Tower" if he attempted such a marriage. The princess, then a girl of fifteen, had since Henry's death resided in Seymour's house under the protection of Catherine Parr, but the indelicate famili-

Relations with Elizabeth

---

[1] This is the interpretation put upon this curious patent by John Gough Nichols in *Archæologia*, xxx. 363-389, where it is printed; but the question is a difficult one. It is possible that Somerset himself advocated it, being willing to surrender the fixed term of office for the countervailing advantage of having his office confirmed by Parliament. In which case the Council would have been unable to depose him as they did without consulting Parliament.

arity with which the Admiral treated her[1] caused
Catherine to remove her elsewhere, and on her death-
bed Catherine is said to have accused her husband
of poisoning her in order to marry Elizabeth.   No
credence need be attached to this statement, but
the haste with which Seymour renewed his suit to
Elizabeth after Catherine's death argues ill for
the way in which he treated the Queen-Dowager.
Elizabeth could not be married out of hand, and
in the meanwhile. the Admiral sought to form a
party among the nobles.   Dorset he had already
won over, and he attempted to do the same with
his brother-in-law, Northampton, who had a grudge
against the Protector for his refusal to recognise the
legality of his second marriage.   He urged them to
strengthen their position in the country by increasing
their number of retainers, and ingratiating themselves with such as had no interest in the maintenance of the existing régime, though his own
conduct to his inferiors was so harsh that the Protector and others had frequent occasion to remonstrate with him.   At the same time he set to work
to get into his own hands as many manors and
stewardships as possible, especially on the Welsh
Marches.   There, in his castle in Cheshire, he began
to form a depôt for arms and ammunition, and he
boasted of having ten thousand men at his back.

**and with
Sir William
Sharington.** To provide for this numerous army of adherents,
he made a corrupt compact with Sir William Shar-

---

[1] See the depositions printed in full in Haynes's *Burghley State
Papers*, pp. 65-107. Dr. Lingard has quoted many of the most
improper details, in order to hint doubts as to Elizabeth's character.

ington, Treasurer of the Mint at Bristol.   Sharington
was an old acquaintance of Seymour's, both having
been in the service of Sir Francis Bryan.   In May
1546 Sharington had been appointed to the mint
at Bristol, and this position of trust he abused to
enrich himself and his friends.   In three years he
made £4000 by clipping and shearing the coin, but
his profits from its debasement must have been
even more extensive.   In April 1547, as a slight
remedial measure, the Protector forbade the coining
of any more " testoons " or shillings, of which 'two-
thirds were alloy.   Sharington disregarded this prohibition, and buying up large quantities of church
plate on easy terms from the Somersetshire villagers,
he coined it into shillings, of which probably even
less than a third was good metal.   To conceal these
frauds and defalcations he falsified the books of the
mint, destroyed the original accounts, and fabricated
others.   It was to this swindler that Seymour
applied for funds to carry on his seditious under-
takings;   he calculated that he would require
£10,000 a month, and asked Sharington if he could
" make " so much money,   In return he promised
to screen Sharington from the consequences if his
misdeeds were discovered.

Seymour used his position as Lord High Admiral Connives at piracy.
for the same disgraceful ends, and with even more
prejudicial effects to his country.   When he was
appointed to the post he said he was as glad of that
as of any, because it gave him command of ships
and men.   This influence he proceeded to employ
for the furtherance of his private ends to the com-

plete neglect of his public duties.   One of the most important of these was the suppression of the pirates who swarmed in the English, Irish, and Bristol Channels, but instead of doing so, Seymour entered into an agreement with the pirates to connive at their proceedings on condition of receiving their support and a portion of their stolen goods.   Early in 1547 Thompson of Calais, a notorious freebooter, who had been "wanted" more than once under Henry VIII,[1] and had always escaped, seized the Scilly Islands and intrenched himself in this advantageous position.[2]   The Protector sent Seymour with a much superior force to dislodge him, but the Admiral left him unmolested, having, it was believed, come to an understanding with Thompson to share his plunder and the control of the islands. Lundy Isle was used for the same purpose, and the Admiral pursued this policy even in the Admiralty Courts, protecting those who were accused of piracy, and denying redress to their accusers.   This brought him into collision with his brother's authority, but other effects were more serious.   Not the least of the causes of French irritation was the continual risks to which their merchants were thus liable. Odet de Selve admits that the Protector issued commissions for the seizure of the pirates, but complained that they had no effect, and he began to disbelieve the good faith of the English Government.

---

[1] *Acts of the Privy Council,* i. 364 *et seqq. passim.*
[2] Selve, pp. 130, 189 ; Oppenheim, *Administration of the Navy,* 1897, pp. 102, 104 ; *Spanish Chronicle of Henry VIII.*, ed. Hume, 1889, pp. 161, 162.

Others besides the French were offended. In 1549, the envoys sent to raise mercenaries in the Hanse and other towns attributed their ill-success to the irritation these towns felt on account of the piracy of English ships.[1] Dymock reported from Hamburg that he could have secured levies there but for the complaints the Hamburg merchants made against the proceedings in the English Admiralty Courts, and similar offences were alleged in Denmark. At Lübeck, an English agent, Robert St. Leger, was put in prison until the goods of its merchants were restored.[2] Charles V.'s ambassador made similar complaints, and the English Admiralty Courts became a byword among merchants of all nations. The Admiral not only received goods from the pirates, but imprisoned those who brought charges against them; he sent private letters to his officers directing them to pay no attention to the Council's orders for the restoration of goods, even when he had signed them himself. He seized and robbed weather-bound ships, and exacted extortionate blackmail from ships going to Iceland and elsewhere.[3]

This conduct was not unknown to the Protector His arrest. or to the Council. In the Parliament of 1547–8

[1] *State Papers, Foreign Series*, Edw. VI., i. 125–132, 134.

[2] *Ibid.*, No. 206. Seymour had begun his piratical pursuits in the previous reign, and on 20th September 1546 the Council had before it complaints of the piracy of his servants.

[3] It is not clear why Iceland was specially mentioned ; there was some importance attaching to it, for in the next session of Parliament an Act was passed specially forbidding the exaction by the Admiral of such fines from ships going to Iceland.

Seymour had obtained the king's signature to a bill of complaints he intended to present to one or other of the Houses, and had threatened in the hearing of several Privy Councillors to make that "the blackest Parliament that ever had sat in England" if his demands were refused. Throughout its course he had made himself conspicuous by opposing Government measures on every occasion. He had been repeatedly warned by his friends, ministers like Russell, and by the Protector himself, but to avoid scandal no open proceedings had been taken against him. Early in January 1548–9, however, Sharington's frauds became known; on the 6th his house, Lacock Abbey, was searched. Seymour's implication was too patent to be passed over, and the Protector privately summoned him to explain matters. The Admiral refused to come,[1] and on the 17th of January, at a Council meeting attended by nearly every councillor who was in England—including Warwick, Wriothesley, Earl of Southampton, Shrewsbury, Cranmer, and others—it was unanimously decided to send Seymour to the Tower. Sharington made three confessions, on the 2nd, 11th, and 16th of February, each fuller than the last, and on 11th February a Bill of Attainder against him was introduced into Parliament. Throughout the first three weeks of February witnesses were being examined by the Council. Among them were the king himself, the Marquises of Dorset and Northampton, the Princess Elizabeth,

---

[1] His letter conveying this refusal is among the *State Papers, Domestic*, Edw. VI., vi. 1, dated 11th January.

the Earl of Rutland, and many others.[1] Thirty-
three articles [2] which closely followed the wording
of the depositions were drawn up, and on the 23rd
of February the whole Council except the Protector,
the Archbishop of Canterbury, who was apparently
engaged in convocation, and Sir John Baker, who
was kept away by his duties as Speaker of the
House of Commons, waited on the Admiral in the
Tower to hear his defence Seymour, however,
resolutely refused to make any answer to the
charges "except he were brought in upon triall
of arraignement," and on the following day it was
decided to ask the king whether he "wolde be
content that his Majestes Lawes shuld procede
uppon him according to thorder of justice and
thaccustome of the realme in like cases, and specially
for so muche as thies thinges have chaunced to be
reveled in the tyme of his Majestes High Court
of Parliament, that the Parliament shuld have the
determinacion and ordre thereof." That afternoon
the Lord Chancellor declared to Edward the
Admiral's crimes and his opinion of them; each
member of the Council did the same; "lastly the
Lorde Protectour, declaring how sorrowfull a case
this was unto him, said that he did yet rather regarde it his bounden dewtie to the Kinges Majestie

The Protector's action.

---

[1] These examinations and confessions are mostly printed in full
in Haynes; abridgments of these and of some others are printed
in the first volume of the calendar of *Hatfield MSS.* The depositions among the *State Papers* (*Domestic*, Edw. VI., vol. vi. Nos. 6–22)
contain a few, *e.g.* Southampton's, not among the *Hatfield MSS.*

[2] These articles are printed in *Acts of the Privy Council*, ii. 248–
256.

and the Crowne of Englande than his owne sonne or brother, and did wey more his allegiaunce than his bloode, and therfore he coulde not resist nor wolde not be against the Lordes request, but as his Majestie wolde he wolde most obedyently be content."[1]   The king, as was to be expected, gave his consent, and it was resolved to introduce a Bill of Attainder into Parliament.   But " that neither excuse for him nor enformacion to the House shuld want if he wolde or coulde make any answer or defence," the Council made a concession unusual in the case of persons against whom a Bill of Attainder was drawn, and appointed some of their number being members of both Houses of Parliament to endeavour to extract some defence from the Admiral.   The Admiral now condescended to answer the first three articles charged against him ; he practically admitted the facts, but declared that their intention was innocent, and refused to reply

Bill of Attainder.

to the remaining thirty charges. " The next day, the xxvth of Februarie, the Bill was framid and put into the Parliament and there emonges the Lordes uppon mature deliberacion, hearing thexaminacions, deposicions and wytnesses, the Judges and all the Kinges Majestes learned cownsell declaryng playne the case to be manifest Treason, with one hole voice

[1] *Acts of the Privy Council*, ii. 257.   The substantial truth of the charges against Seymour is proved by much corroborative evidence. " Although some of the details of the complaints made against him may be inexact, there can be no doubt that the charges as a whole were well founded, and it is significant that the Council dealt with the trouble [piracy] more successfully after his execution " (Oppenheim, *Administration of the Navy*, 1897, i. 105).

of all and singuler the Lordes being there, the
Lorde Protectour only for naturall pities sake de-
siring license at the passing of the Bill to be away,
the said Bill was allowed and sent downe into the
nether Howse, where it was very muche debated
and argued ; and at the last the myndes of the
lawers axed and declared that the saide offences
of the Lorde Admirall for divers cawses were in
the compasse of Highe Treason ; whan no man
was able to say the contrary, being dyvers tymes
provoked therunto by the Speaker, the nether
Howse being marvailous full almost to the nomber of iiij^c persones [1] not x or xij at the most
giving their nays therunto, the Bill was there likewise passed and assented unto the vth of Marche
1548."

Such is the Council's record of the proceedings ;
the Journals of the two Houses supply further
details. The bill passed its second reading in the
House of Lords on the 26th of February, and its
third on the 27th. It was read a first time in
the Commons on Thursday the 28th of February.
On Saturday the 2nd of March the House resolved
that on the second reading it would hear the evidence " orderly as it was before the lords, and also
to require that the lords which affirm that evidence
may come hither and declare it *vivâ voce.*" The

---

[1] Such is the statement in the *Acts of the Privy Council*, and it
illustrates the incompleteness of the Official Return of Members of
Parliament, 1878. There only 193 members appear in the first
Parliament of Edward VI. The boroughs and counties from which
returns are noted as missing would supply 140 more, making a
total of 333.

reply to this resolution, which the Master of the
Rolls conveyed to the Commons, was that it was
not the king's pleasure that the Admiral should be
"present in this court," but "that if the House
would require to have the Lords to come to satisfy
the House for the evidence against the Admiral,
the Lords would come down." [1]   Whether this was
done or not is uncertain, but the bill passed its
third reading in the Commons on Monday the 4th
of March.

It now devolved upon the Protector and the
Council to decide whether the Admiral was to be
pardoned or executed, but it was not till six days
later that the Council took any further steps.   On
the 10th of March "forsomuch as thei did perceive
that the case was so hevy and lamentable to the
Lorde Protectour," the Council requested the king's
authority to make the final decision and take the
final steps "without further troubling or molesting
in this hevy case either his Highness or the Lorde
Protectour."   Five days later "the Lorde Chancellor
and the rest of the Cownsell" ordered Seymour to
prepai e for death, and on the 17th they directed
his execution to take place on Wednesday the
20th.

Question of
its justice.
The attainder of his brother lies heavy on the
Protector's   memory,   and   an   attempt   must   be
made to reach some conclusion as to the justice
and truth of the charges that it has occasioned.
It is impossible to feel much sympathy for the
Lord Admiral.   Latimer stated publicly that Sey-

[1] *Lords' and Commons' Journals*, February to March 1548-9.

mour was the man furthest from the fear of God
that he knew, and he added specific accusations of
moral profligacy which are rendered quite credible
by the details of Seymour's treatment of Elizabeth,
and a flat assertion that the last act of the Admiral
was to endeavour to persuade the two princesses
to conspire against his brother. It can hardly
be believed that Latimer was so utterly base as to
prostitute his conscience to the court and curry
favour by libelling a dead man's memory; but no
amount of vice or crime can palliate the denial
of justice to the criminal, and the condemnation of
the Admiral by Act of Attainder instead of by open
trial has been considered at least unjust, if not illegal.
Open trial is, of course, more consonant with modern
ideas, but whether it would actually have given
the Admiral a better chance of justice is reasonably
open to doubt. The only alternative to an Act of
Attainder was trial by his peers, and it is assumed
that Seymour would have been more fairly treated
by the House of Lords sitting as a court of justice
than by the House of Lords sitting as a branch
of the legislature. But it must be remembered
that when the peers tried a fellow-peer, the tribunal
could easily be, and was frequently, packed. It
was not considered necessary in such cases to
summon all the peers; sometimes there were less
than half present, sometimes only a quarter, and
as it rested with the Government to decide who
should be summoned and who not, it was simplicity
itself to exclude the accused's adherents. No such
packing was possible when the peers sat in their

legislative capacity.[1]   And in Seymour's case con-
cessions beyond what was usual were made to liberal
ideas.   The opinion of the judges and of the law
officers was taken in the House of Lords, the
examinations and depositions were heard and the
witnesses were summoned, heard, and possibly cross-
examined.   Moreover, the assent of another body,
the House of Commons, was necessary to an Act of
Attainder, and it is obvious from the protracted
debate in the Lower House, and from the division
which actually took place, that the one chance for
Seymour lay in the possible rejection of the bill by
the Commons, who would have had no voice in the
matter had the Admiral been tried by his peers.
Further, had Seymour been tried by his peers, the
Commons could not have heard or examined the
witnesses, and they were actually heard and examined by the peers before the passing of the Act,
just as they would have been had Seymour been
tried before them.   Undue stress has been laid
on the refusal of the Government to allow the
Admiral or the witnesses to appear before the
Commons, for it is almost certain that neither
course was constitutional.   The Admiral was a
peer, and the Commons had no power to summon
him before them without infringing the privileges of the other House.   Nor could they examine witnesses upon oath, not being a court
of justice; so that, whoever was responsible for

---

[1] Thus in Somerset's own case twenty-six peers tried him out of
seventy-four, twenty-seven of whom were spiritual peers, and so
were precluded from sitting as his judges.

the decision, it was taken on strictly constitutional lines.

The assumption that the Protector destroyed his brother, with the implication that the testimony against him was fabricated, is not supported by a particle of evidence. It is manifest, on the contrary, that Somerset felt considerable affection for the Admiral,[1] and keen grief at his execution. He was no Brutus, who could send his nearest of kin to the block without shedding a tear, and throughout the proceedings against Seymour he vacillated between his affection for his brother and what he conceived to be his duty to the State. He assented to the proceedings against him, but that was as far as he would go; he took no part in drawing up the articles against him, or in his examination.[2] Neither did he share in the deliberations of the Council as to whether the Admiral should be executed or not,[3] and he absented himself from the

Was the Protector responsible for his fall?

[1] See especially the affectionate letter he wrote the Admiral on the birth of his daughter, 25th August 1548, though on the same day he had to remonstrate with him on his illegal conduct. Both letters, dated 1st September 1548, are among the *State Papers* (*Domestic*, Edw. VI., vol. v. Nos. 1, 2), and have been printed in Tytler.

[2] See *Acts of the Privy Council*, ii. 236-263.

[3] This is proved by the phraseology of the minutes of the Council and warrant for the Admiral's execution. The ordinary phrase "the Lord Protector and the rest of the Council" becomes "the Lord Chancellor and the rest of the Council," which was quite an impossible phrase if the Protector were present. This is proved beyond doubt by an examination of the MS. Register. The Protector's signature has been filled in afterwards in quite a different ink from that in which the minute and other signatures are written.

House of Lords when the Bill of Attainder was passed.[1] It is true that he signed the warrant for the execution, though the signature is almost illegible; but he signed every such document during his Protectorate, and it is doubtful whether it would have been considered valid without his signature.

There remains one more question suggested by one or two contemporary references to this event. Some years afterwards Queen Elizabeth stated that if the two brothers had been allowed to meet after the attainder, the Admiral would not have been executed, but they were prevented by the designs of others.[2]   Bishop Ponet also speaks of those " who conspired the death of the two brethren . . . so as they might robbe the king, and spoile the Realme at their pleasure." [3]   This could only mean Warwick, but other hints seem to point at Wriothesley, Earl of Southampton.   It is impossible to unravel the truth behind these mysterious suggestions, but it is a singular fact that those who were most active in the proceedings against Seymour also took

[1] This is explicitly stated in the *Acts of the Privy Council*, ii. 260. It has been denied, on the ground that Somerset was present on the two days when the bill was debated in the Lords ; but that does not prove that he was present when the vote was taken, which is probably meant by "the passing of the bill."   Eighteen out of the twenty-seven bishops are also marked as present on these two days, and they could scarcely have voted on the bill.   If they did, they constituted another security for fair dealing towards the Admiral, as they could have taken no part had he been tried by his peers.

[2] Ellis, *Original Letters*, 2nd Ser. ii. 256.

[3] *Treatise of Politike Power*, 1556.

part against Somerset.[1] But again it must be remembered that practically the whole of the Council shared in them, that the attendance in both Houses of Parliament when the Bill of Attainder was passed was abnormally large, and that it passed in one House without any dissentients, and in the other with only ten or twelve.

In any case it was an act of weakness on the Protector's part to allow his brother to be executed. It may have been, and probably was nothing more than justice, but it was a serious blow to Somerset's authority. Possibly the vacillation he showed encouraged his enemies to intrigue against him, and certainly it alienated not a little of that popular favour which constituted Somerset's sole support.

[1] They were Southampton, Shrewsbury, and Rich ; cf. *Hatfield MSS.*, i. No. 295.

CHAPTER VIII

THE PROTECTOR AND THE SOCIAL DISCONTENT

The social revolution and its effects. SERIOUS as were the difficulties which beset the Protector in his dealings with Scotland and France, and in the maintenance of his authority, it was not any of these questions that finally caused his fall. The real cause of his overthrow was his attitude towards that social revolution which lay at the root of most of the internal difficulties of Tudor Governments. If the sixteenth century was the era of the birth of modern Europe in its external relations, it was no less the era of the birth of the social organisation of modern England. The foundations upon which society had been based for five hundred years were broken up, the ideas which dominated it passed away, and those which were to regulate the new society were still without form and void. The change was neither begun nor ended during the Tudor period, but that age felt more severely than any other the stress and the shock of the revolution.

The feudal state was in idea and in practice essentially conservative. Everything was based upon custom; custom was appealed to in defence of constitutional liberty; custom regulated justice, the assessment of taxes, the imposts on foreign trade, and rent paid for land. Of all mediæval expressions, the words " custom " and " customary " are the most distinctive. The idea implied in it determined the form of society, and the social organisation in its turn ensured the practice of the idea. A stationary society is only possible with a stationary population, and this was ensured by the rigidity of the feudal organisation, which fixed the number of holdings, and rendered marriage almost impossible without the possession of a holding. It checked the tendency of the population to increase, it almost eliminated the struggle for existence in the Darwinian sense, and left no room for competition, which is the mother of progress.

The feudal system had, however, suffered serious inroads long before the accession of Henry VII. The Black Death and the Peasants' Revolt, added to more silent and gradual causes, impaired the strength of conservative tendencies. Custom gave way to competition, and ancient usage to what is called free contract, though the term is singularly inapplicable to a condition in which one of the parties to the contract is almost always driven by necessity. The fixity of the social system was relaxed. Feudalism was eliminated from the sphere of government, and the title to rule was no longer based exclusively on the tenure of a certain amount of land on specific terms. Ministers began to be chosen from among men like the Poles,[1] who

---

[1] His connection with trade was one of the chief causes of complaint against Michael de la Pole, Earl of Suffolk (1330 ?-1389), Richard II.'s Lord Chancellor, and the first merchant to attain high office in England.

owed their influence not to the number of fees they held, but to wealth acquired in trade. Money became a path to power, and golden keys began to open the doors of office and social position. The desire for riches received a powerful stimulus, and competition followed in its train with its now familiar concomitants of good and evil. Increase in national wealth was purchased by the pauperisation of large sections of the community. It was marked by the "engrossing" of industry and commerce in the hands of the few, who used their power to control the market by "regrating" and "forestalling," to the injury of their smaller competitors, and enhancing of prices for the consumer at large. Another symptom of ill-regulated competition—the sale of fraudulent goods—is very apparent in the statutes of the Parliaments of Edward VI. These include an Act for the true currying of leather, another for the true tanning of leather, an Act for the true making of malt, an Act against the false forging of "gadds of steel," an Act for the true making of woollen cloths, an Act for the true stuffing of feather beds, mattresses, and cushions, an Act for the true "fulling and thicking" of caps, and other statutes with similar objects. New Acts were added to the long list of those against forestalling and regrating, and vain attempts were made to check by statutes and proclamations the rapid increase of prices.

Application of competitive principles to land.

The operation of this principle made itself felt in every department of production, but it was its application to the land that engendered the most

critical problems. The entire social fabric had
hitherto been based upon land, and his relation to
the land determined the rights, duties, and position
of almost every member of the community. The
feudal theory recognised no absolute ownership in
land; every one was a tenant in some degree of
relationship to the Crown, and his power over his
sub-tenants was strictly limited. Barons could only
be evicted by legal process, and Magna Carta. extended the same privilege to sub-tenants; even
villeins had security so long as they performed their
proper services. The reason was that land was
regarded not as a source of wealth but as a source
of men; on it was based the defensive forces of the
kingdom, and it was more important for the lord to
have men to defend him than for him to increase
his wealth by extracting as much rent as he could
from his tenants. The same tradition held good
when money payments were gradually substituted
for personal service, and for many generations these
payments remained fixed. The way in which this
system was broken down is a matter of dispute.[1]
The current theory is that the enormous decrease in
population caused by the Black Death enabled the
surviving labourers to demand double the wages
they had before received, that the lords resented
these claims and attempted by the various statutes
of labourers to reduce them to their former position,

---

[1] *Cf.* Rogers, *Economic Interpretation of History* ; Ashley, *Economic
History* ; and Leadam, in *English Hist. Rev.*, viii. 684 *sqq.*, in *Trans.
Royal Hist. Society*, 1892, and *Select Cases from the Court of Requests*,
1897 (Selden Soc.).

and that the peasants' revolt which was the result, though apparently a failure, ultimately gave the labourers the victory. It is said that the masters then learnt from the servants to raise their prices when occasion offered, but this process is scarcely perceptible until towards the later half of the fifteenth century, when the general substitution of competition for custom became as marked in the treatment of land as in the management of industry and commerce. Land then came to be regarded as an investment and a source of wealth; the lord claimed absolute ownership and the right to do what he liked with his own,[1] in order to make as much profit out of it as was possible. The process was probably accelerated by the growing practice of merchants seeking to become landowners, in order to make themselves gentlemen and obliterate the stigma attached to trade. They carried their commercial principles into their relations with their tenants; rack - rents were substituted for customary rents, and the object of the lord became not to support retainers but to raise revenue. " If merchants," exclaimed Crowley, " would only leave farms to such as must live thereby! But they take farms to let them out again, to levy fines and raise the rent ; "[2] and he complained especially of the London merchants who bought up farms near the city. " They take our houses over our heads, they buy our grounds out of our hands, they levy great (yea unreasonable) fines. . . . In the towns they

[1] Crowley, *Works* (Early English Text Society), pp. 47, 144.
[2] *Ibid.*, p. 41.

buy up whole rows and alleys of houses; yea, whole
streets and lanes, and raise the rents double, triple,
or even fourfold what they were twelve years past." [1]
Nine-tenths of the houses in London, he declared,
were let by those who had the lease and not by the
owners, and these leasemongers raised the rents and
oppressed the poor. The earliest symptom of the
application of competition to the relation between
landlord and tenant was the levying of fines upon
new leases. Tradition at first had been too strong
to enable the new landlords, who had none of the
hereditary feeling of relationship between the superior lord and his dependents, to do away with the
customary rent, but they really increased it by
levying these unreasonable fines. The raising of
rents soon followed, and the dissolution of the
monasteries gave fresh scope to this evil. When
the lords bought the lands of the monasteries,
complained the Commons in one of their "Supplications," they made the tenants believe that their
"copies" were void, and turned them out unless they
consented to take new leases on an increased rent. [2]

The institution of rack-rents was, however, but Enclosures.
one indication of the revolution in the ideas which
governed the system of land-tenure. A far more
important manifestation of the same spirit was seen
in the various movements which are somewhat
loosely and indiscriminately described as "enclosures." [3] The movement has been dated from

[1] Crowley, *Works* (Early English Text Society), p. 133.
[2] *Four Supplications* (Early English Text Society), p. 80.
[3] A great deal has been written on this subject, but a really
scientific treatment of it was first rendered possible by Mr.

various periods in the fifteenth and even sixteenth centuries; but as a matter of fact a kind of enclosing had been going on for at least four hundred years. Licenses to " empark " a certain number of acres were from the twelfth century among the commonest privileges granted to barons and others who were in favour with the Crown; but these no doubt referred only to waste lands, and at that time inflicted nothing but a potential harm on any one. Enclosures in the Tudor sense meant some thing or things very different. The word is used to describe three distinct movements—firstly, " engrossing," that is, the concentration of many holdings in one hand; secondly, the enclosure of common lands for purposes of either arable farming or of pasture; and thirdly, the conversion of arable into pasture land. The first of these movements was a change from *la petite* to *la grande culture*, and may in the first instance have been a movement

Leadam's discovery in 1894 of the returns of Wolsey's commissioners appointed in 1517. A portion of these was printed by Mr. Leadam in the *Domesday of Inclosures*, 2 vols., 1897 (Royal Historical Society), with an introduction. A good bibliography of the subject is given in Ashley's *Economic History;* see also Cheyney, *Social Changes in England in the Sixteenth Century*, 1895; and Miss Lamond's edition of *A Discourse of the Common Weal of England*, 1893. The *Discourse* and Fitzherbert's *Book of Husbandry* are the most valuable contemporary works; but the subject is illustrated by numerous other books of the time, the best of which are Starkey's *England under Henry VIII.*, Brynkelow's *Complaynt of Roderick Mors*, Crowley's *Works*, *Four Supplications* (all published by the Early English Text Society), Sir Thomas More's *Utopia*, Latimer's *Sermons* (Parker Soc.), Lever's *Sermons* (ed. Arber, 1871), Gilpin's *Sermons* (in Gilpin's *Life*, 1753), *Ballads from MSS.* (Ballad Society), and Tusser's *Five Hundred Points of Husbandry*.

for the better cultivation of land. The method of its accomplishment was that a comparatively wealthy farmer obtained several holdings, and, instead of leasing them out to different yeomen, kept them all in his own hands, and "decayed" all but one holding; that is to say, he occupied one homestead himself and suffered all the others to fall into ruin, whereby the place of the independent yeoman, with his own holding, homestead, and family, was taken by hired labourers who generally boarded for the time of their service with their masters, and consequently had neither homestead nor family. This *Measures to check them.* process was the earliest of the three; in the sermon or speech delivered by the Lord Chancellor, John Russell, Bishop of Lincoln, in January 1484, at the opening of Parliament, he declared that "this body falleth in decay as we daily see it doth by closures and emparking, by driving away of tenants and letting down of tenantries."[1] It was part of the Yorkist policy to support the lower orders against the squirearchy, which was as a whole Lancastrian, and possibly had Richard III. reigned longer he might have made a serious effort to act on the hint thrown out by his chancellor. The Yorkist policy was, however, to some extent adopted by the Tudors, and Acts against this form of "engrossing" were passed in 1489 and 1515. But the most remarkable attempt to repress the evil was the commission which Wolsey appointed in 1517 to inquire into the question. This step has been

[1] This speech is extant in *Cotton MS. Vitellius E.*, x. *ff.* 139 *seqq.*, and is printed extant in *Grants of Edward V.* (Camden Soc.), pp. xxxix. *et seqq.* ; *cf.* Gairdner, *Richard III.*, ed. 1878, p. 194.

attributed with some probability to the influence of Sir Thomas More. Early in 1516 he was reported

Wolsey's commission of 1517.

to be frequently in Wolsey's ante-chamber, and about the same time Erasmus expressed a fear that More would be carried away by a whirlwind of court favour.[1]   No one, moreover, denounced the practice of enclosing more vehemently than the author of the "Utopia," which, after having been read in manuscript by Tunstall and other influential persons at Henry's court, was published in December 1516, a few months before Wolsey's commission.   As a result of this commission, proceedings were at once taken in Chancery against the offenders, and many entered into recognisances to restore decayed tenements and reconvert pasture into arable land.   In furtherance of this policy Wolsey issued on 12th July 1518 a decree for the pulling down and laying abroad of all enclosures made since 1485.   Proclamations to the same effect were again issued in 1526,[2] and from that time it became a stock demand with social reformers.   But Wolsey's measures had only a slight temporary effect, and after his fall Henry's absorption in foreign politics and religious changes allowed the evil to grow unchecked.

The second of these movements—the enclosure of common lands—was somewhat later in date.   It does not refer to waste lands or to the lord's demesne, but to lands on which his tenants had rights of common.   The question of its legality depends upon the view taken of the origin of the manor,

[1] *Erasmi Epistolæ*, No. 21 ; compare *Letters and Papers of Henry VIII.*, iii. 394, &c.   [2] Leadam, *Domesday of Inclosures.*

which is a matter of keen dispute. On one theory
the enclosure movement was one more aggression at the expense of the original owners of the
soil; on the other, it was the revival of a theoretical
and legal right against ancient custom. In any
case it inflicted undeniable hardship on those whose
living depended largely upon the free enjoyment of
rights of common. The enclosure might be made
for one of two purposes, to turn the commons into
either arable or pasture land, but the latter was the
prevalent practice. It has been calculated that the
land enclosed to pasture sheep and cattle bore to land
enclosed for arable purposes the proportion of ten
to one between 1485 and 1490, five to one between
1491 and 1500, two and a half to one between
1501 and 1510, and two to one between 1511 and
1515. The rapidity with which land was enclosed
is explained by the enormous profits which accrued
to the enclosers. A careful computation made from
the returns of Wolsey's commissioners indicates that
the average rent of *enclosed pasture* land as compared
with that of *open arable* land was as twenty-two to
nine; that is to say, that the landlord who turned
open arable land into enclosed pasture land increased
his income by more than a hundred and twenty
per cent. The preponderance of lands enclosed for
pasture over lands enclosed for arable purposes is
similarly explained: the former was, according to
Fitzherbert, fifty per cent. more remunerative than
the latter, and the best modern authority considers
this estimate well within the mark.[1]

[1] Leadam, *op. cit.*

Extent of
the move-
ment
The general effect of this complex movement
was a social dislocation almost unparalleled in
English history.   No attempt has been made—
and it would be a task of infinite labour—to determine the extent of the enclosures of commons, or
the amount of privation it inflicted upon the agricultural labourers.   The havoc caused by the two
other movements, engrossing and the conversion
of arable to pasture, is appalling enough.   In the
" Supplication," which was probably addressed to
Somerset in 1548, and was the immediate occasion
of the appointment of his famous enclosure commission, it is stated that forty " ploughs " had been
" decayed " in Oxfordshire since the beginning of
Henry VII.'s time, and that in other counties the
average was eighty ; that each " plough " (or plough-
land, *i.e.* the ordinary holding of the yeoman) supported a man, his wife, and four others, and that
thus some eighteen or twenty thousand people had
been thrown out of employment.   This was not
the full extent of the evil, for the " ploughs " thus
decayed provided food for at least another twenty
thousand.   These figures are trifling compared with
another estimate given by the same authority, which
states that one plough in each of the fifty thousand
townships and villages in the country was decayed,
and thus three hundred thousand people were thrown
out of work, or at least a tenth of the entire popu-
and its
effects.
lation.[1]   Between   statements   so   widely   divergent

[1] *Four Supplications* (E. E. T. S.), pp. 98-101.   *Cf.* Bishop Scory's
letter to Edward VI., printed in Strype, *Ecclesiastical Memorials*, II.
ii. 482 : " Oh ! what a lamentable thing it is to consider, that there

it is hopeless to form an estimate that is in any way satisfactory, and only a vague conclusion is possible as to the numbers of those who were evicted either because they could not pay the increased rents, or merely to enable the lord to turn his land to more profitable use. These evicted tenants were not only reduced to abject misery themselves, but they constituted a permanent danger to the Government. "Now these persons," said the author of the first "Supplication," "had need to have a living; whither shall they go? . . . from shire to shire, and to be scattered thus abroad . . . and for lack of masters, by compulsion driven some of them to beg and some to steal." The severity of the statutes against vagabondage betrays the alarm of the governing classes, and their frequency testifies to their failure to produce any effect. "They be cast into prison as vagabonds," wrote Sir Thomas More, "because they go about and work not whom no man will set at work, though they never so willingly proffer themselves thereto." It was puerile to threaten with all the rigour of the law those who did not work, when labour was becoming every day more scarce, and when land that formerly employed

are not at this day ten plows, whereas were wont to be forty or fifty. Whereas your Majesties progenitors had an hundred men to serve them in time of peace and in time of wars, with their strength, policy, goods, and bodies, your Majesty have now scant half so many. And yet a great number of them are so pined and famished by the reason of the great scarcity and dearth of all kind of victuals, that the grete shepemasters have brought into this noble realm, that they are become more like the slavery and paisantry of France, than the ancient and godly yeomandry of England."

fifty husbandmen was sufficiently looked after by a shepherd or two.

The same scarcity of labour affected not merely those who failed to obtain work, but those who were employed; for it kept down wages to the same level when the debasement of the coinage, the importation of precious metals, and the dearth of victuals caused an enormous inflation of prices. The rise in prices is the common topic of every contemporary and subsequent writer on the subject, and without burdening these pages with examples that are familiar to every reader, it suffices to say that as a general rule the ordinary necessaries of life, like corn, beef, mutton, white meats, and eggs, trebled in price during the first half of the sixteenth century. The scarcity of food supplies due to land passing out of tillage embarrassed the Government as much as the ordinary consumer. It became as difficult for the king to exact purveyance as it was burdensome for the ordinary farmer to supply it, and one of the remedial measures proposed by Somerset, in the interests both of the Government and of its subjects, was the substitution of a fixed payment for the capricious and uncertain exaction of purveyance. Another result of the decay of the yeomanry placed the Government in even greater difficulties. The employment of mercenaries, who formed a considerable element in the armies of Henry VIII. and Edward VI., has been attributed to all manner of sinister motives on the part of the Government, such as distrust of the English soldiery, and a design to impose religious changes on the people at the point of foreign pikes. It was really due to sheer necessity. The defence of the kingdom had always been a local and not an imperial obligation, and the Government had not the means, if it had the inclination, to maintain a standing army. Though it paid the wages of the levies while on service, they were supplied and equipped by the several localities, and it was a common calculation that in time of need each parish could supply one man.[1] But where the yeomen were evicted in large numbers and their holdings "decayed" this became impossible, not only through lack of men, but because, in the words of a contemporary, "shepherds be but yll artchers,"[2] and neglected those martial exercises for which the yeomen, whose place they took, were noted. The Government was thus compelled to look elsewhere for means of defence, and though their employment caused a further drain on the impoverished exchequer, mercenaries were the only weapon ready to hand. The idea of a national army paid for by the nation was not evolved for more than a century afterwards.

A similar use for theological purposes has been made of one more result of the social revolution. The decay of schools and universities directly followed upon the decay of the yeomanry. There are

[1] This, according to Odet de Selve, was the basis upon which Henry VIII. calculated his forces for the invasion of Scotland which he was contemplating at his death (Selve, p. 64). He puts down the number of parishes at 40,000.

[2] *Four Supplications* (E.E.T.S.), p. 100.

many schools in England to-day whose numbers
and prosperity vary inversely with the degree of
agricultural depression, and the same correlation of
cause and effect obtained in the sixteenth century.
The yeoman who was evicted from his holding could
scarcely be expected to send his children to school,
and the increased rent demanded from those who
retained their holdings is specifically alleged by
contemporaries as the reason why they were compelled to put their children " to labour instead of
setting them to learning." [1] The consequence was
injurious not only to that age; the inability of
yeomen to send their sons to the universities made
those national institutions more and more the pre-
serves of the rich. Even in Henry VIII.'s reign
Sir Richard Rich had proposed that none but the
sons of the well-to-do should become scholars, a
proposal which Cranmer, much to his credit, successfully opposed; but the idea grew up that a
university education was a thing to which only
gentlemen's sons had a right.

Party of
reform.

The evils engendered by enclosures [2] were thus

[1] *Four Supplications* (E. E. T. S.), p. 80.

[2] For mention of some of the grievances caused by the similar
movement in industries and manufactures, see Hales's Defence in
Lansdowne MS., 238. "There wer besides certeyn complayntes
made by weuers of Kent, that they hauyng wifes and chyldren
coulde get no lyuynge, for that the clothiers wer nowe become
also weuers. The weuers beyng journeymen of Worcetter complayned that wher ther was an olde order emonge them that in
euery loome ther shulde be one iourneyman and one apprentice
workynge, nowe because ther was not so great charge in kepynge
of apprentices, for they haue no wages, as ther was of iourneymen,
who of necessitie must haue wages to relyeue them ther wifes and
chyldren, they kepte all apprentices and wold not sett iou₁ ₁eymen

comprehensive and serious enough to claim attention from every one who cared anything for the
welfare of his country, and during Henry VIII.'s
reign there had not been wanting men who had urged
measures for their abatement. They were not confined to one form of theological belief; the greatest
of all was Sir Thomas More, and of similar religious
views were Thomas Starkey and Thomas Lupset, but
for the most part they were, like Henry Brynkelow
and Robert Crowley, Protestants as well as social
reformers. Their ideas were enlightened on other
subjects besides enclosures, and a proposal advocated
by one of the anonymous band of reformers, that
all lands taken from the monasteries should be
devoted to schools, would have made education in
England more splendidly endowed than in any other
country in the world.[1] During Henry VIII.'s reign
these ideas were advocated almost solely by writers, but
under Edward VI. a small but able party, including
divines and politicians, began to form. It was called

on worke. Others complayned that poore labourers in steede of
moneye wer payed ther wages by clothyers with soope, candells,
rotten clothe, stynkynge fish, and such like baggage. The clothiers
of Hadleye openying the falsehed of clothyers, howe they drewe a
clothe from xviij. yerdes to xxvij. or xxviij. yerdes desyred that
redresse might be had therin. Others complayned that a fewe men
had in ther handes a great many mens lyuynges. Others, that one
man occupied dyuers occupations. Others, that artificers and
clothiers wer nowe also ploughmen and grasiers."

[1] Brynkelow, *Complaynt of Roderick Mors* (E. E. T. S.), pp. 47-52;
another of Brynkelow's radical ideas was that both Houses of
Parliament should sit together as one assembly, "for it is not
rytches or autoryte that bringethe wisdome" (*ib.* p. 8). The
political literature of the later part of Henry VIII.'s reign deserves
more attention than is usually bestowed on it.

the "Commonwealth" party, and among its adherents were Latimer, John Hales, and Thomas Lever. Cranmer was also probably in sympathy with them, but the "Commonwealth's men" only became influential because the Protector espoused their cause and adopted their policy. Their cardinal principle was that man was born not to himself, but primarily for the service of God and then for that of the State. "It may not be liefull" [*i.e.* lawful], wrote Hales, "for euery man to vse his own as hym lysteth, but euery man must vse that he hathe to the most benefyte of his Countreie"; and again, "Surely euery honest man ought to refuse no paynes, no trauaile, no studie, he ought to care for no reportes, no sclaunders, no displeasure, no enuye, no malice, so that he myght profett the commen welthe of his countrye, for whom next after God he is ordeyned." "Let us have," he said in his charge when acting as enclosure commissioner, "this godly opinion with us, that nothing can be profitable that is not godly and honest, nor nothing godly and honest whereby our neighbours and Christian brethren, or the commonwealth of our country is hurted and harmed." [1]

---

[1] For the Commonwealth party, see Sir Anthony Aucher's letter to Cecil, 10th September 1549 (*State Papers, Domestic*, Edw. VI., vol. viii. No. 56) : "Sir, as a pore man maye requier you, be plaine with my Lord's grace, that under the pretence of symplyssitie and povertie there maye reste mouche myschyffe. So doe I feare ther dothe in these men called Common Welthes and there aderents."

The quotations in the text are from *Lansdowne MS.*, 238. This MS. contains the fullest information about Somerset's social policy, and all the documents are connected with the enclosure commission on which Hales served. They are (1) Hales's Defence, written 1st September 1549, in answer to various charges brought against

The most important proposals made by this party were the abatement of enclosures and the restoration of tillage. The necessity for some remedy had been forcibly suggested by the sporadic risings of the commons which took place in different parts of the country in the spring of 1548, and perhaps as early as the autumn of 1547.[1] They never gathered head, and have almost completely escaped the notice of historians and chroniclers, whose attention has been diverted to the more serious rebellions

his conduct (*Lansdowne MS.*, 238, ff. 292*b*–304*b*); (2) Somerset's proclamation, 1st June 1548 (ff. 305*a*–308*b*); (3) Hales's exhortation and charge to the presenting juries (ff. 312*b*–314*b*); (4) Somerset's instructions to the commissioners (ff. 315*a*, 316*a*); (5) Somerset's letter to Hales, 21st August 1548, asking whether he had used any words likely to incite the commons (ff. 318*b*, 319*b*); (6) Hales's reply, dated 30th August 1548 (ff. 319*b*–321*b*); (7) Hales's letter to Warwick reproaching him for his opposition (ff. 321*b*–325*b*). About Hales himself there has been much confusion. Strype and every subsequent writer, including Canon Dixon in his " Church History " and in the " Dictionary of National Biography," has made into one person Hales and his nephew, also named John Hales, who was clerk of the hanaper. For a conclusive differentiation of the persons see Leadam in *Domesday of Inclosures*, i. 5, and also in *Trans. Royal Hist. Soc.*, New Ser., xi. 116–118. The late Miss Lamond was the first to suggest that Hales was the author of " The Common wealth of England," originally published in 1581 as by W. S., and absurdly attributed to Shakespeare (see *Dict. Nat. Biogr.*, s.v. Stafford, William, 1554–1612).

[1] In the defence of his conduct Hales says, " Was there not, longe before this commission was sent forthe, an insurrection in Hertfordshire for the comens at Northall and Chesthunt ? Can it be denied that the first rising this yere was in Somersetshire, from Somersetshire it entered into Gloucestershire, Wiltshire, Hampshire, Sussex, Surrey, Worcestershire, Essex, Hertfordshire, and dyuers other places ? " These risings are not noticed in any of the ordinary books, and the fact that the commissioners visited none of these counties is conclusive refutation of the view that the commission caused the risings.

of 1549.   Petitions also began to be presented to
the king against enclosures, and in May 1548
Somerset decided upon energetic measures of reform.   On June the 1st he issued his famous proclamation against enclosures.   " Forasmoche," it read,
" as the kynges Maiestie the lorde protectour's
grace, and the rest of his preue Councell, hathe
byn aduertised and put in remembraunce aswell by
diuers supplicacions, and pytefull complayntes of
his Maiestie's poore subiectes, as also by other wise
discrete men, hauynge care to the good ordre of
the Realme, that of late by thynclosynge of landes
and erable groundes, in diuers and sondry places of
the Realme, manye have byn dreuyn to extreme
pouertie, and compelled to leaue the places wher
they wer borne, and to seeke them leuynges in other
countryes, with great myserye and pouertye inso-
much that wheere as in tyme past, tenne, twentye,
yea and in some place c or cc Christen people
hathe byn inhabiting and kept household, to the
bryngynge forthe and nouryshynge of youthe, and to
the replenysshynge and fulfillynge of his Maiestie's
Realme with faythfull subiectes who myght serve
bothe Almyghtie God, and the kynges Maiestie to
the defence of this realm, nowe ther is nothynge
kept but sheepe or bullocks.   All that land whiche
heretofore was tilled and occupied with so many
men, and dyd brynge fourthe not onlie diuers
famylies in worke and labour, but also capons, hens,
chekyns, small pygges and other suche furnyture of
the markets, is nowe gotten by insaciable gredynes of mynde into one or two mens handes, and

Somerset's
proclama-
tion and
commis-
sion.

scarcelye dwelled vppon with one poore shepherd.
So that the Realme therby is brought to a meracylous
desolation; houses decayed, parysshes dymynyshed,
the force of the Realme weakened and Chrysten
people by the gredie couetousnes of some men eaten
vp and deuoured of brute beastes, and dryuen from
ther houses by sheepe and bullocks. And that
although the same thynge manye sondrie complaynts
and lamentacions hathe ben hertofore made, and
by the most wise and discrete prynces his Maiestie's
father and graundfather the kynges of the most
famous memorie kyng henry the vijth and kyng
henry the viijth, with the consent and assent of the
lordes spyrytuall and temporall in dyuers parlya-
mentes assembled dyuers and sondrye lawes and
actes of parlamentes, and most godlie ordynaunces in
ther severall tymes hathe byn made for the remedie
thereof, yet the most insaciable couetousnes of men
dothe not cease dayly to encroche heruppon, and
more and more to waste the Realme after this sorte,
bryngynge erable groundes into pastures, and lettynge
houses, whole famylies and copiholdes to fall downe,
decaye, and be waste. Wherfore his Highnes is
greatlie moued both with a pytefull and tender zeale
to his most louynge subiectes and speciallye to the
poore whiche is mynded to labour and trauayle for
their lyuynges, and [not] to lyue an idle and
loytrynge lyfe; and of a most necessarye regarde
to the suertie and defens of his Realme, whiche must
be defended agaynst the enemye with force of men,
and the multytude of true subiectes, not with flockes
of sheepe and droues of beastes. And further is

aduertised that by the vngodlie and vncharytable
meanes aforesaid, the saide sheepe and oxen beynge
brought into a few mens handes a great multitude
of them beynge together, and so made great droues
and flockes, aswell by naturall reason, as also it
maye be iustlie thought, by the due ponyshment
of God suche uncharytablenes: great rottes and
murryns bothe of sheepe and bullockes hathe latelye
byn sent of God and seen in this Realme, the
whiche shulde not by all reason so sone fall, if the
same wer disparsed into dyuers mens handes, and
the said cattell also by all lykelyhode of truthe
shulde be more cheape, beynge in many mens handes
as they be nowe in fewe, who may holde them
deare and tarye ther auawntage of the markett.
And therfore by thaduyse of his most entierlie be-
loued uncle, the duke of Somerset, gouernour of his
parson, and protectour of all his Realmes, domyn-
yons, and subiectes, and the rest of his Maiestes
preuye councell hathe wayed most depelye all the
said thynges. And vppon the forsaid consyderacions
and of pryncely and zeale, to see that godlie lawes
made with great travell, and approued by expery-
ence, and by the wyse heddes in the tyme of the
said most prudent prynces shulde not be made in
vayne but put in vse and execution, hathe appoynted
accordynge to the said actes and proclamacions a
viewe and enquyrye to be made, of all suche as
contrarye to the saide actes and godlie ordynaunces,
hathe made enclosures and pastures of that whiche
was erable grounde, or let any house, tenement or
mease decaye and fall downe, or otherwise com-

myted or done any thynge to the contrarye of the
good and holsem articles conteyned in the said
actes and therfore willithe and commaundithe all his
louynge subiectes who knowith any suche defaultes
and offences contrarye to the wealthe and profytt of
this Realme of Englande, and the said godlie lawes
and actes of parlament done and commytted by
any person who so euer he or they be, to insynuate
and gyue informacion of the offence to the kynges
Maiesties Commyssyoners who be appoynted to here
the same, so trulie and faythfullye that neyther for
fauour nor feare they omytt to tell the truthe of any,
nor for dyspleasure name any man who is not giltye
therof. That a conuenyent and spedie reformacione
myght be made herin to the honour of God and
the kynges Maiestie, and the wealthe and benefytt
of the whole Realme." [1]

There was thus nothing novel or revolutionary His work.
in either the aims or the methods of the Protector. They were indeed essentially conservative, and
their object was to stay the agrarian revolution
that was going on in favour of the rich at the
expense of the community at large. The Protector
sought merely to enforce statutes passed in the two
preceding reigns, his policy was the traditional
policy of the Yorkist and Tudor rulers, and the
commission he appointed was closely modelled on
that sent out by Wolsey in 1517.[2] Its object was,

[1] *Lansdowne MS.*, 238, ff. 305 *seqq.*
[2] It has been said that Somerset deserves no credit for the movement against enclosures, which was due solely to Hales's patriot-
ism. Hales himself says : ''I assure you I never was the motioner
nor procurer thereof [the commission], but it onely (as farre as I can

in Hales's words, that "my lorde protectours grace and the Councell myght knowe by parte the whole state of the Realme, and so procede to the redresse of all."[1]   It was merely a commission of inquiry by means of juries into such changes as had taken place since 1485, the number of acres enclosed or converted from arable to pasture, the number of ploughs decayed and "houses of husbandry let down," who had made the enclosures and when, what profit was derived from them, who kept more than two thousand sheep, or occupied more than two houses of husbandry in the same town, village, hamlet, or tithing, and whether the grantees of monastic lands kept on them "an honest continual house and houshold in the same scite or precinct" as they were compelled to do by Act of Parliament.[2]   The presentment of the offenders was delayed in order that each might have the opportunity to clear himself, and for that year (1548) the commissioners[3] were content with collecting the evidence Somerset

lerne) proceded at the sute partlie of poore men as the proclamation declareth, and partlie of some of those that be nowe most ayenst it, whereunto I am preuye, and chieflye for that the kynges Maiestie, my lord protectours grace and many of the Councell sawe what hurte had growen and what was lyke to ensue to this Realme, if the gredynes of grasyers and shepemasters were not in tyme resysted" (*Lansdowne MS.*, 238, fol. 294).

[1] *Ibid.*

[2] See the instructions printed in Strype, *Eccles. Mem.*, II. ii. 360, 361.

[3] The circuits of the commissioners only included some of the home counties, and only in the body of which Hales was a member does there seem to have been any vigorous exercise of their functions. Hales complained that this limitation of scope gave rise to a suspicion that the commission was directed in malice against a few offenders.

required as a basis for remedial measures which were to be introduced into Parliament, and as a weapon for overcoming the opposition which such measures were sure to encounter.

Attempts had been made to check some of the evils consequent upon the hardships which the economic revolution was inflicting on the poorer classes in the previous session of this Parliament. The first bill introduced into the House of Commons in Edward VI.'s reign was one " for bringing up poor men's children," [1] which was no doubt the embodiment of a proposal made by Henry Brynkelow some years before.[2] It was followed six weeks later by a bill [3] to ensure to farmers and lessees the enjoyment of their leases, without fear, presumably, of arbitrary eviction. In the House of Lords, during the same session, a bill was introduced to prevent the decay of houses of husbandry and tillage.[4] But all these measures met with an equal lack of success. The two bills in the Commons reached a second reading, but got no further,[5] and a similar fate befell that introduced into the House of Lords.[6] The one measure that found favour in the eyes of

Remedial measures.

---

[1] *Commons' Journals*, 8th November 1547.

[2] Viz. that a certain number of the poorest children in each town should be brought up at the expense of the community (see Brynkelow, *Complaynt of Roderick Mors*, ed. Early English Text Soc.).

[3] *Commons' Journals*, 17th December.

[4] *Lords' Journals*, 12th November.

[5] *Commons' Journals*, 24th November.

[6] *Lords' Journals*, 14th November. The same failure attended an even more important reform, viz. that of the common law. A bill to this effect was introduced into the Commons, and debated on the 5th of December, but it did not even reach a second reading.

both Houses was the famous Act providing that confirmed vagabonds might be sold into slavery.[1]

Nevertheless Somerset and Hales, whose community of aims and ideas in this matter was complete, were determined to make further and more strenuous efforts in the second session of this Parliament, which began on 8th November 1548. A State Paper in the Record Office, said to be in Hales's handwriting, and entitled " Causes of Dearth," contains several proposals for their abatement, and also for repairing the deficit in the revenue. The first, after pointing out the burden imposed by purveyance on farmers, suggested that it should be made illegal for the purveyor to requisition any provisions, except at a price agreed upon between him and the vendor ; and to make up any loss that the Crown might suffer, a tax of one penny on every sheep kept in common fields, and

---

[1] This Act, 1 Edward VI. c. 3, is the stock quotation used to illustrate the ferocity of the landed classes towards the labourers, but those who quote it limit their extracts to the first sections of the Act, and pass over the latter part "for the relief of poor and impotent persons," which gives a different complexion to the statute. These latter clauses drew the important distinction between able-bodied and impotent paupers. The latter were to be provided for by the localities in which they had been born, and a weekly collection in church on Sundays was ordered for that purpose. As to the slavery, it must be remembered that slaves were fairly common in the sixteenth century (for details of the manumission in Elizabeth's reign of those on the Earl of Derby's estates see Stanley Papers, published by the Chetham Society), and their lot was certainly not harder than that of the vagabonds compelled often to steal, for which the penalty was hanging. This Act was repealed in 1550, but there was a suggestion for its revival under Elizabeth (see Hatfield MSS., i. No. 587).

twopence on every ewe and lamb kept on several [*i.e.* private enclosed] pasture, was proposed, with an export duty of five shillings on broadcloth, and twenty pence on kerseys, the manufacturers of which were accumulating great wealth.[1] The remission of the payment of fee-farms was recommended, in order that the money might be devoted to forming a fund for the purpose of finding work for poor people. Other reforms, that sheriffs should have allowances for their expenses, and that no fines should be exacted " for respite of homage," were designed rather to benefit the land-owning class than those who suffered by enclosures.

Whether these suggestions came from Hales or not—and it is probable that they did not, for he embodied his own remedies in bills which were introduced by himself, and were distinct from those founded on these proposals—they were all carried through both Houses of Parliament. By 2 & 3 Edw. VI. c. 3 all purveyance, except with the consent of the vendor and upon mutual agreement as to price between both parties, was strictly forbidden upon pain of the offender forfeiting treble the price of the article taken, suffering imprisonment for a quarter of a year, and making fine at the king's pleasure. By chapter 5 of the statutes of the same session the payment of fee-farms was remitted for three years, on condition that the funds were devoted to the repair of walls and bridges, " setting the poor on work or other good deeds." The tax on

[1] *Cf.* Dowell, *History of Taxation*, 2nd ed. i. 142.

sheep,[1] which had excited the Lord Admiral's wrath, was embodied in the Act of relief for the king; it was designed to serve two purposes—the re-establishment of the revenue, and the checking of the conversion of arable to pasture land.   The sheriffs got their allowances,[2] and several measures already mentioned were passed to enforce honesty in manufactures and commerce.   Another Act struck at both rich and poor alike.   It was complained that victuallers and others had conspired to sell their victuals at unreasonable prices, "and likewise artificers, handicraftsmen, and labourers have made confederacies and promises, and have sworn mutual oaths not only that they should not meddle one with another's work, and perform and finish that another hath begun, but also to constitute and appoint how much work they shall do in a day, and what hours and times they shall work";[3]

[1] It will be seen presently (p. 272) that this Act never came into force, as its operation was deferred for three years, and before that time arrived Somerset had fallen, and Parliament, under the reactionary influence of the "reformed" Council, abolished these taxes, thus relieving the wealthiest classes of any tax on the wealth which they were acquiring at the expense of the community.

[2] 2 & 3 Edw. VI. c. 4.

[3] *Ibid.*, c. 15.   "To constitute and appoint how much work they shall do in a day, and what hours and time they shall work"; it would be impossible to put more shortly the objects of modern trades unionism; but it is curious to note the different view between that age and this.   Now it is considered in many quarters highly reprehensible to "conspire" to fix the amount of work to be done in a day, though the formation of "rings" and "corners" is regarded as quite justifiable.   Then both were made equally illegal as injurious to the community at large.   Perhaps both may be made so again when, if ever, the State assumes full control of industrial regulation.

and all such proceedings were forbidden under severe penalties.

But the bills which Parliament passed were of Opposition to the Protector's policy. small importance compared with those it rejected. The draft of a bill against monopolising farms which is extant in the Record Office [1] does not seem to have been once read in either House, and the more important bills which Hales introduced met with a fate which he himself has described.[2] "I then deuysed thre bylles to be put into the Parlament, wherunto I made a great many wise men preuye. Thone for reedifienge houses decayed, and for the mayntenaunce of tillage and husbondrye. Thother for regratynge of vittell and other thynges wherin I remembre one pryncipall poynt, that Grasyers nor noo man shulde buye any cattell and sell the same ageyne within a certeyn tyme. For as I had lerned and also nowe knowe of certentie, dyuers grasyers and shepemasters brynge bothe cattell and monye to the markett. If they cannot sell ther owne as deare as them lysteth, they carry them home agayne and buye vp all the rest, whiche two billes wer fyrst put to the lordes. The fyrst boynge redde was not lyked, the causes I will not shew you, but another tyme I doubte not but that, or the lyke byll, will take place. The second they allowed and augmented, and sent downe to the lower house, whiche if ye had there herd debated, and had seen howe it was tossed, and to whose handes at length commytted, and howe it was deferred, if ye shulde haue seen men's affections won-

---

[1] *State Papers, Domestic*, Edw. VI., v. 22.
[2] *Lansdowne MS.*, 238.

derfullye, perchaunce, ye wolde have saied that the
lambe had byn commytted to the wolfe to custodie.
The thyrde bill was set forthe fyrst in the lower house,
and tended to this ende, that euerye man that kept in
seuerall pasture sheape or beastes shulde keape for
euery hundred sheape that he had aboue syx score two
kyen, and for euery of these two kien shulde reare
one calf, and for euery two kyen that he kepithe
besydes, more than tenne, he shulde reare one calf." [1]
Hales does not state what happened to this last bill,
and the Journals of the Houses of Parliament afford
no clue.   But doubtless it met with a fate similar to
that of the other two, as it does not appear on the
statute-book.   A bill for putting down parks, introduced by some other adherent of Somerset's policy,
had a longer career but equally unfortunate end.
It passed its three readings in the House of Lords
between the 21st of January and the 4th of February 1548–9 ; on the 5th it was introduced into the
House of Commons, was read a second time on the
8th of March, but was defeated at the third reading on
the 11th—*vacat per majorem numerum super quœstione,*
as the Journals put it.

The opposition which Somerset's policy, as embodied in these bills, encountered in the House of
Commons is easily explained.   Had Edward VI.'s

---

[1] It is hard to check this account by the Journals ; the first
is perhaps the "Bill for the Commonwealth," which was brought
into the Commons on 25th February 1548–9, but proceeded no
further.   The second might have been supposed to be the bill
against regrators mentioned in the Journals, but that passed its
third reading in the Commons on 12th March, and seems to have
failed in the Lords, instead of *vice versâ,* as Hales says.

House of Commons been elected on a popular basis, it is probable that it would have passed Hales's bills, but in reality it only represented the comparatively wealthy classes. The statute of 1430, limiting the county franchise to forty-shilling freeholders, left outside the franchise at least nine-tenths of the agricultural population, including almost all those who were most affected by enclosures, and practically restricted Parliamentary representation to the class by which enclosures were made. The borough franchise was of every degree of liberality, and in some cases was very democratic, but the representatives of the towns were on the whole no more eager to remedy the social evil than their knightly colleagues from the shires. "It is hard," wrote Brynkelow,[1] "to have it redressed by Parlament, because it pricketh them cheffely which be chosen to be burgessys, for the most part, except thei wold chose their burgessys only for their vertuos liuyng, discrecyon, honest behauor, and ther godly qualytes, be he neuer so pore; such as wold his neyhbor shuld lyue as himselfe. And wold to God thei wold leaue their old accustomed chosing of burgessys! for who do thei chose but such as be rych or beare some offyce in the contrye etc., many tymes such as be boasters and braggars? Such haue thei euer hetherto chosen; be he neuer so very a fole, dronkerd, extorcyoner, aduouterer, neuer so couetos and crafty a parson, yet, if he be rych, beare any offyce, if he be a ioly cracker and bragger in the contry, he must be a burges of the parla-

[1] *Complaynt of Roderick Mors* (Early English Text Soc.), pp. 12, 13.

ment! Alas, how can any such study or geue any godly councell for the commonwelth?" Not only did members of Parliament refuse to pass bills for the redress of these evils, but they were the first to infringe those statutes against enclosures which had been enacted by previous Parliaments.[1]

The opposition which the Protector's policy encountered in Parliament had its counterpart in the dogged resistance with which the Enclosure Commissioners were met in the country. "After that the kynges Majestie had sent forthe the proclamation and commission, what," asked Hales,[2] "dyd they not to hynder it? Somme found the meanes to haue ther seruantes sworne in the Juryes, to thyntent to haue them hazarde ther soules to saue ther gredynes. And as I haue lernyd syns, it is not possible in any of the Shires wher we wer, to make a Jurye without them, suche is the multitude of Reteynours and hangers on. Whiche thynge if it be not remedied the kynge shalbe suer neuer to haue his lawes trulye executed. . . . Somme poore men wer thretened to be put from ther holdes if they presented, somme also as I farther lerned haue no certetie of ther holdes whiche wer wonte to be letten by copie for lyfes and otherwise for yeares, because they at no tyme nor in nothynge shulde offende ther landlordes, but do and saye what soeuer they will commaund them. As it pleasithe my landlord so shall it be. A godlie hearynge in the commen welthe! Somme also wer indicted because

---

[1] Cf. Crowley, *Works* (E. E. T. S.), *passim*.
[2] *Lansdowne MS.*, 238.

they presented the truthe, and somme wer persuaded that thende of the Commyssion shulde be but a monye matter, as it had byn in tyme paste. I could declare unto you a great many slyghtes wherewith somme of them thought to haue blynded us and the presentours, but for very shame I will lett them passe." The frauds to which Hales alludes were ploughing up one furrow in a holding enclosed to pasture, and then returning it as land in tillage, keeping one or two oxen among hundreds of sheep, and then passing the land off as land devoted to the "fatting of beasts," and similar practices. To save all appearance of vindictiveness, Hales obtained from the Protector a general pardon for all offenders presented to the Commissioners, but this act of clemency only encouraged them to renew their illegal courses. "Somme of the Ritchemen as sone as they had the pardon, they retourned to ther olde vomyte, they began immedyatlie to enclose, to take awaye the poore mens Commens, and wer more gredie then euer they wer before. They thought and some saied that the Commission was but a storme for a tyme and soone wold passe ouer, as a great many hoope it will also doo nowe." This opposition was backed by the open or secret support of the majority in the Council. In the proclamation and commission the Council is made to participate in the responsibility for Somerset's attack on enclosures, but it is fairly certain that its assent, if it was obtained at all, was only obtained by those means of which Paget complained when he accused the Protector of "out-reasoning" the councillors, and "wrasting them by reason of your authority to bow to it." Paget himself declared[1] that "these rufflers had the least cause to complain," because "they and their fathers before them have lived quietly above these sixty years, pastures being enclosed." Warwick, whose own park had been ploughed up as an illegal enclosure, took a leading part in the opposition; he denounced Hales as the cause of the rising in Buckinghamshire, and wrote to the Council complaining of the proceedings of the commissioners.[2] Some of the commissioners themselves were no less hostile to the policy they were appointed to carry out. "I remember," said Latimer, "my own self a certain giant, a great man who sat in commission about such matters; and when the townsmen would bring in what had been enclosed, he frowned and chafed, and so near looked and threatened the poor men that they durst not ask their right."[3]

Somerset's persistence.

Such formidable opposition would have daunted any one less determined than the Protector, or less convinced of the righteousness of his cause. On him its only effect was to confirm him in the course on which he had entered. "Maugre the devil," he declared, "private profit, self-love, money, and such-like the devil's instruments, it shall go forward."[4] When Shrewsbury was appointed President of the

---

[1] Paget's letter to Somerset, in Strype, *Eccles. Mem.*, II. ii. 432 *sqq.*, from *State Papers, Domestic*, Edw. VI., vol. viii. No. 4.

[2] *State Papers, Domestic*, Edw. VI., vol. vii. No. 35.

[3] Latimer, *Sermons*, p. 247 (Parker Soc.).

[4] *State Papers, Domestic*, Edw. VI., vol. iv. No. 33.

Council of the North in May 1549, one of his principal instructions was that he should redress wrongful enclosures.[1] Two months later Somerset's only reply to Paget's vehement remonstrances, and the risings of the commons, was to issue circulars to the commissioners, enclosing instructions and enjoining upon them the more vigorous execution of their task. The Protector also set to work to remedy another grievance under which the poor laboured.[2] The same spirit that characterised the opposition to Hales's bills in Parliament and to the commissioners in the country also entered into the law courts. It was found almost impossible for the poor to obtain redress against their wealthy enclosers. Crowley frequently complains of corruption and bribery in the administration of justice, and Brynkelow asserted that it was better to be in hell than in the Courts of Augmentations and Exchequer. " The law is ended as a man is friended " [3] became a proverb, and Hales himself asked, " Who passythe on offendynge and breakynge the lawes when he hathe plentie of moneye to stop the execution of them ? " [4] To afford the poor some chance of justice, and to relieve them from the delays and expenses of the ordinary courts, Somerset adopted the arbitrary expedient of erecting a Court of Requests in his own house to hear their suits, and as a result of com-

[1] *State Papers, Domestic*, Addenda, Edw. VI., vol. iii. No. 47. He was also directed to give " sureties to the poorest against the richest in lawful matters."

[2] *State Papers, Domestic*, Edw. VI., vol. viii. No. 10.

[3] Brynkelow, *Complaynt of Roderick Mors*, pp. 24, 25.

[4] *Lansdowne MS.*, 238.

plaints lodged therein he was frequently under the
necessity of issuing orders even to the most eminent
of his colleagues, to repair wrongs they had committed.[1]

It was this resolute determination to enforce his
policy that stiffened the opposition to Somerset.
The army of enclosers had no objection to laws
against enclosures, provided they remained a dead
letter, and they could put up with commissions for
redress if only they ended in a " money matter," and
passed away like a storm.   But Somerset was in
earnest; there was to be an end of evasion, and
the law was to be strictly enforced.   " The matter
of this byll," wrote Hales[2] of one of those he introduced into Parliament, " dyd not so moche greue
them, as for that ther was a waye founde therbye
to haue it always trulye executed.   For I had thus
deuysed that the parson or curat of euery parisshe
to whome belongithe the tythes, and two honest
men shulde yearelye surueye euerye man's pastures,
and shulde not onlie present who dyd transgresse
this lawe, but who also did obserue it.   This was it
that byt the mare by the thombe.   Men passe not
moche howe manye lawes be made, for they see
very fewe put in execution.   The rytchmen of
Rome were neuer so moche offended with   the

---

[1] *Cf.* his directions to Paulet, Lord St. John, who apparently had
defrauded a widow of her lands, *State Papers, Domestic*, Addenda,
vol. iii. No. 50 (1), and compare Somerset's declaration to his
brother "to receive poor men's complaints that findeth or thinketh
themselves injured or grieved, it is our duty and office so to do"
(*State Papers, Domestic*, vol. v. No. 1).

[2] *Lansdowne MS.*, 238.

makynge of the lawe called *lex agraria* as theye wer
with thother lawe that followed, whereby certeyn
officers called Triumviri wer made to see the same
executed." The landlords of England were of like
passions with the rich men of Rome, and Somerset
found that it required a greater authority than his
to cast out the devil, private profit, self-love, money,
and such-like the devil's instruments. His last
measures were treated with open contempt. " Yea,"
inveighed Crowley[1] against the " gentlemen," " when
ther was a law ratified to the contrary, you ceased
not to finde meanes either to compel your tenants
to consent to your desire in enclosinge, or else ye
found suche maistership that no man durste gaine
saye your doinges for feare of displeasure. And
what obedience shewed you, when the kinges proclamations were sent forthe and commissions directed
for the laying open of your enclosures, and yet you
left not to enclose still? Yea, what obedience
was this which ye shewed at such time as the
kinges most honourable counsell, percieuinge the
grudginge that was emong the people, sent forth the
second proclamation concerning your negligence, or
rather contempte, in not laienge open that which,
contrari to the good estatutes made in Parliament,
you had enclosed? It appeareth by your doinges
that there was in you neither obedience to your
prince and his laws, nor loue to your countrei . . .
yet have you not lacked them that have told you
of it both by wordes and writinges . . . Wittinglye
and willinglye, therefore, ye have boeth disobeied

[1] Crowley, *Works,* pp. 144, 145.

your kinge and his lawes, and also broughte youre
countrei into the miseri it is in."

While the landlords were busily frustrating all
Somerset's remedial measures, the people, who, according to a great French ruler,[1] *ne se soulève jamais
par envie d'attaquer, mais par impatience de souffrir,*
began to weary of seeing filched from them rights
which they and their fathers before them had
enjoyed from time immemorial.   " When poore
men be put in suche desperation of Relief, when
no hope of redresse of ther myserye appereth, when
they thus be made to beleue they shall haue no
ordynarye remedye, what," asked Hales, " shall a
man saye of them ? "   What they said themselves
was, " No remedye, therefore we must nedes fight
it out, or else be brought to the lyke slauery that
the French men are in!"[2] and the smouldering
discontent began to burst into the open flame of
rebellion.   It was kindled first in Somersetshire,
thence it spread eastwards into Gloucestershire and
Wiltshire, southwards into Dorsetshire and Hampshire, and northwards into Berkshire, Oxfordshire,
and Buckinghamshire.   Surrey remained in a state
of " quavering quiet," but Kent felt the general
impulse.   Far in the west, in June, Devon and
Cornwall rose almost to a man.   Staines bridge
was broken down in fear of an advance on London,
and in the city martial law was proclaimed, and
double watch kept at the gates both night and day.
Ere that alarm subsided, the commons of Norfolk
rose, took Norwich, and established a " common-

---

[1] Sully, *Memoirs*, i. 133.   [2] *Cf*, p. 211 note.

wealth " of their own. The Government of England was shaken to its base, its hold on Scotland and on France was relaxed, and at home it was confronted with the prospect of a prolonged and bitter social war. In the midst of the convulsion, the Council bethought itself of saving its face and its pockets by attributing the condition of England not to the original malady but to the remedies that Somerset had prescribed. It prepared to remove not the disease but the physician.

CHAPTER IX

THE PROTECTOR'S FALL

Revolts in
the east
and west. THE popular risings of the summer of 1549 placed
the Protector in an impossible position. He had
done all that in him lay to alleviate social distress
and minimise the risk of revolt, but his schemes
had been baffled and his authority contemned.
The results he feared had come to pass, but instead
of strengthening his position by justifying his policy,
they really cut away the ground from under his
feet. If it had been impossible to carry his social
legislation before, it became doubly so when almost
the whole of the official and upper classes were
exasperated by the revolt of the commons, the
ploughing up of pastures, and destruction of enclosures. A modern minister would have sought
refuge in resignation, but resignation is a modern
expedient, and Somerset would have considered
such a step at such a time a cowardly dereliction
of duty. He continued to hold-a position in which
he was forced, partly by circumstances and partly
by his colleagues, to carry out a policy which he
hated; his authority rapidly waned, and his endeavours to mitigate the severity of repression were met
by more and more open resistance in the Council.

The story of the rebellions in the west and the east has been too often and too well told to need repetition here.[1]   The cause everywhere but in Devon and Cornwall was admittedly social, and even there it is almost certain that the same feeling was at the bottom of the revolt, though it was captured by the priests in the interests of the Roman Catholic religion.   The enclosure of their commons was a more potent irritant with the agricultural labourers than the alteration in the form of their belief, or even the destruction of images in their churches; and the western rebellion has many of the characteristics of a social movement. There was not a peer or a man of wealth implicated in it, and with the exception of the priests the leaders were of the same class as those who headed the rising in Norfolk.   The circumstance that their articles[2] contain reference to only one social grievance is due to the fact that they were drawn up

[1] See for the western rebellion a spirited account in Froude, and a more detailed one in Canon Dixon's *History of the Church of England;* and compare Cotton and Woollcombe's *Gleanings from the History of Exeter.* A more valuable account than either of these, of the Norfolk rising, is given in the Rev. F. W. Russell's *Kett's Rebellion,* 1859, which prints many original documents throwing light on the social condition of the time.

[2] These are printed, with Nicholas Udall's answer to them, in *Troubles connected with the Prayer Book of* 1549 (ed. Pocock, Camden Soc.), pp. 141–193. There was some inconsistency in these articles, as they demanded the restoration of Cardinal Pole at the same time as the Act of Six Articles, by which Pole would have been executed as a traitor. For a list of the ringleaders in the disturbances in Cornwall and Devon in the previous year, see *Cotton MSS.*, Titus, B. ii. f. 25. There is not even a knight among them, though Sir John Arundell was accused of sympathising with the rebellion in 1549.

by the clerical leaders, and possibly the same fact
explains the demand for the re-enactment of Henry
VIII.'s Statute of Six Articles, the repeal of which
can hardly have been an intolerable grievance to the
labourers of Devon and Cornwall. It is also singular,
if the rebels in Devon in 1549 were so passionately
devoted to the old faith, that within a generation
they should have become the stoutest defenders of
the new. It is in truth the social discontent that
explains most of the revolts during the Tudor period;
the Pilgrimage of Grace, Wyatt's rebellion, and that
of 1569, as well as those of 1549. The leaders, of
course, and a portion of their followers rose in defence
of their faith, but the masses who gathered round
their standards were men who had been evicted
from their tenements, or who had been ground down
to the verge of poverty by the loss of their rights
to commons—men who had nothing to hope from
the existing social condition, and nothing to lose in
case of failure.

With this class the Protector was largely in sympathy. Even after the rebellions had begun, he
renewed his instructions to the Enclosure Commissioners to proceed with their remedial measures,
and he openly declared that the covetousness of the
gentlemen had given the people occasion to rise,
and that it was better they should die fighting
than perish for lack of living. He was indeed
compelled to issue a proclamation for the suppression of all attempts to break down enclosures by
force, but one of his Secretaries of State complained
that being only a general exhortation, and not

directed to any one in particular, no one thought himself authorised to take the necessary means to carry it out.[1]   On 20th June Somerset even issued a pardon to the rebels if they would return to obedience,[2] and he treated some of the prisoners with great leniency.[3]   From the same motive he did not take the command against the commons in Norfolk, as he appears to have intended.   He could not do so without alienating the popular support which his domestic policy had brought him, though the other alternative of entrusting the command to Warwick involved him in the more serious danger of opposition from a successful general, with the mass of the gentry at his back.   His sentiments were hateful to the majority of the Council, whose one remedy was repression, and it is said [4] they took the matter in their own hands and issued stringent orders, which were signed by Edward without the Protector's knowledge.

The commotions in England, widespread as they were, necessarily had a most injurious effect upon the conduct of the war in Scotland and France.   In Scotland, Haddington still held out, and on 30th June arrangements were made for an invasion by a considerable force under Warwick's command, which

Their effects.

[1] Sir Thomas Smith in *State Papers, Domestic*, viii. 33.

[2] *State Papers, Domestic*, Edw. VI., vii. 37 ; Russell, *Kett's Rebellion*, p. 95.   This pardon roused even Paget's wrath ; see Strype, *Eccles. Mem.*, II. ii. 432.

[3] Sir Anthony Aucher to Cecil, *State Papers, Domestic*, vol. iii. No. 56 ; and compare the fourth article in the charges brought against Somerset on his fall (*Harleian MSS.*, 353, f. 61).

[4] By Mr. Froude, but I have been unable to confirm the fact.

was to take place about the 10th of August.[1]   Before that day the Norfolk revolt was at its worst, and the army for the Borders was diverted to the eastern counties.   France took advantage of the English embarrassment to declare war, and send an army into the Boulonnais.   Three fortresses fell before it; one was betrayed, another was abandoned as untenable, and the third was carried by assault.[2]

The Council resolves to depose the Protector. These comparatively slight reverses gave the Council a colourable pretext for their attack on the Protector, which was really instigated by their dislike of his social policy.

It is impossible to trace with any degree of clearness or accuracy the growth of the opposition in the Council to Somerset.   The signatures to the " Acts," at best a misleading guide, cease altogether after March 1549, and there is nothing to indicate who did and who did not participate in its deliberations. Nor do the signatures to the State Papers, which are more trustworthy, afford any evidence of a division of parties, and Warwick and Rich, Northampton and Southampton, continue to sign them to the end as frequently as Cranmer or Paget. Nevertheless it is obvious that there was a growing divergence between the Protector and the majority of the Council.   The Council was not without legitimate grievances; by granting Somerset almost unlimited powers, and authorising him to summon what councillors he liked, the councillors had indeed forfeited the best part of their case, but they

---

[1] *State Papers, Domestic*, Addenda, vol. iii. No. 49.
[2] *State Papers, Foreign*, Edw. VI., No. 195 ; *Calais Papers*, No. 173.

were none the less angered by the arbitrary way in which Somerset disregarded their advice, and used Government influence to promote a policy they detested. They knew that his authority was de- Its griev-
ances. rived from themselves, and they bitterly repented having parted with it so freely. If it was true that Somerset used a stamp of the king's signature their complaint of it was just, and the erection by the Protector of a Court of Requests in his own house was equally indefensible from a legal point of view. More damning from a moral point of view, was the rapacity with which Somerset seized on Church lands, and the Council could point with effect to the erection of Somerset House as an illustration of ostentatious arrogance. Such a charge, however, did not lie in the mouth of Warwick or his friends to utter, for, considering his position and opportunities, Somerset's acquisitiveness was trifling compared with that of his accusers. To these general grievances most of the councillors added private wrongs of their own. Considerable as was the patronage in the Protector's hands, he was forced to disappoint nine out of ten suitors who applied to him, and among them were men like Warwick, St. John, and others who were keen competitors for such lands as fell to the Crown. Warwick had another private grievance in the ploughing up of his park, and the same thing had happened to Sir William Herbert. Northampton, the third member of the future triumvirate which ruled England after Somerset's fall, was incensed by the refusal to recognise the legality of his marriage with his second wife while the first was alive, and

Dorset, afterwards Duke of Suffolk, father of Lady Jane Grey, had been the Admiral's chief adherent, and by his fall had been balked of the brilliant prospect which Seymour's scheme for marrying Lady Jane to Edward VI. had opened up for him. These were all professed reformers in religious matters, but it was natural that Catholics should join in a movement against the Protector, in the hope that his fall would involve a reversal of his religious policy. Southampton may also have felt a grudge against Somerset for his ejection from the chancellorship, and he, with Arundel and Southwell, soon ranged himself with the other malcontents.

Out of these discordant elements Warwick, the subtlest intriguer in English history, set to work to organise an effective opposition to the Protector. He had himself been treated well enough by Somerset, and at the beginning of the reign the French ambassador thought that the Protector, Warwick, and Paget kept no secrets from one another.[1] Warwick had been second in command during the campaign against Scotland in 1547, but his cordial co-operation with Somerset had soon given way to a critical attitude towards his Government. His own ambitions and his resentment at the proceedings of the Enclosure Commission combined to stimulate his secret enmity to the Protector, while his victory over the Norfolk rebels made him the hero of the gentlemen, and gave him the opportunity he needed. He returned to his house in Ely Place, London, before the 14th

[1] Selve, *Corr. Politique*, p. 106.

of September,[1] and there, while Somerset was absent
with the king at Hampton Court, the plans for his
overthrow were matured.   Warwick had won the
favour of the Protestants by his simulated vehemence
in their cause; they had come to look on him as
their champion, while they damned Somerset with
faint praise, and regarded his moderation as criminal
lukewarmness.   The same skilful simulation enabled
Warwick to delude the Catholics with the hope of
religious reaction, and the prospect of release from
prison seems to have been held out to Gardiner.
The news of the abandoment of Haddington on the
14th of September [2] gave the conspirators another
excuse for their action.   A few days later Warwick
is said to have waited on Somerset with two hundred
captains who had served in Norfolk, and to have
demanded extra pay for their services.[3]   Somerset
refused, and Warwick thereupon enlisted their support for his coming enterprise.

Meanwhile the Protector was at Hampton Court The
with those of the Council who were his personal struggle.
adherents.   They were Archbishop Cranmer, Paget,
Sir William Petre and Sir Thomas Smith (the two
secretaries), and Cecil.[4]   Somerset had been at

---

[1] Russell, *Kett's Rebellion*, p. 151 *et sqq.*

[2] *Diurnal of Occurrents* (Bannatyne Club), p. 48 ; Lesley, p. 230.

[3] *Chronicle of Henry VIII.*, ed. Hume, 1888, pp. 185, 186, but
this authority is to be received with caution.

[4] Cecil's movements always become mysterious in a crisis. He
was with Somerset late in September, but was not among the
adherents of the Protector who were arrested at Windsor on 12th
October. From a stray note in Cecil's own hand (*Hatfield MSS.*,
v. 69), it appears that he was in the Lord Chancellor's custody on

Westminster until the 12th of September. On the 18th he was at Sion House, and thence he moved to Hampton Court. He had as yet no suspicion of the storm that was brewing, but on the 25th he added, as a postscript to a letter to Russell recommending merciful treatment of the rebels conquered in the west, the sentence, " We do loke for you and Sir Will︤m︥ Herbert, at the furthest about the viii^{th} daie of the next moneth, about which tyme we wold gladlye have you here for matters of importance."[1] Whatever was the significance of this message, Somerset was ill prepared for resistance. His efforts on behalf of the poorer classes of the community had endeared him to the mass of the people, but they were precisely those who had no votes, and no means of influencing the Government or supporting their favourite except by rebellion, and rebellion without organisation or leaders. He had no armed force at his back, and all he could depend upon was moral influence, and such prestige as his position gave him. Thus his fall was easy and rapid.

The Protector and the Councillors with him continued the ordinary transaction of business until the 4th of October. On that day or the next he became aware of the extent of the plot against him. He determined to appeal to the commons, from

27th September. Probably he placed himself there voluntarily, and thus his conduct at Somerset's first fall appears as dubious as his conduct at his second ; see Tytler, i. 237, 244, 245, ii. 24, 31.

[1] *Petyt MS.*, xlvi. No. 538, f. 466, ┊printed by Pocock, *Troubles* (Camden Soc.), p. 77.

whom alone he was sure of support.[1] He issued
orders to all the king's subjects to repair to
Hampton Court armed for the defence of the king,
and he scattered broadcast leaflets denouncing his
enemies. "Good people," were the words he put
into their mouths, "in the name of God and King
Edward, let us ryse with all oure power to defend
hym and the Lorde Protector agenst certen lordes
and gentilmen and chief masters, which wolde
depose the Lorde Protector, and so endanger the
kinges royall person, because we, the poore comens,
being injuried by the extorcionse gentylmen, had
our pardon this yere by the mercye of the king, and
the goodness of the Lorde Protector, for whom let
us fyght, for he lovithe all just and true gentilmen
which do no extorcyon, and also us the poore com-
mynaltie of Englonde."[2] Three couriers were sent,
one after the other, to summon to the Protector's
aid the victorious army of Russell and Herbert
returning from the west. Ten thousand men are
said to have flocked to Somerset's standard, but
they were ill armed and untrained, and Hampton
Court offered no means of defence against a sudden
attack from London. On the night of the 6th of
October Somerset hurried with the young king to
Windsor.

Meanwhile the Council in London professed to
desire a peaceable solution of the dispute. They

---

[1] Mr Froude has been misled by Tytler into dating this summons
the 1st of October instead of the 5th (see Pocock, *Troubles*, p. 76).

[2] *Acts of the Privy Council*, ii. 331; *State Papers, Domestic*,
vol. ix. No. 12.

had, they said, prepared to go and lay their grievances before the king and Protector at Hampton
Court, when Sir William Petre on the 6th arrived
with a demand for an explanation of their assembly,
and a threat to arrest them if they ventured to
Hampton Court.   Accordingly they deferred their
visit and remained all that Sunday in anxious con-
clave at Warwick's house in Ely Place.   Their
numbers included a large majority of the Council.
"That crafty fox, Shebna," as Knox called St.
John,[1] took precedence as President of the Council;
then came Warwick, Arundel, and Southampton.
Petre, instead of conveying to Somerset the Council's
answer, remained to aid in his overthrow, and of
the less influential councillors there were present
the two Wottons, North, Southwell, and Peckham.
Besides the above, whose names appear in the records of the Privy Council, a letter summoning the
people to the Council's assistance, and dated the
same day, is signed by the Earls of Shrewsbury and
Sussex, Sir Thomas Cheyney, and Sir John Gage.
Their first step was to secure the city, and on that
same day the Lord Mayor and aldermen were taken
into the Council's confidence.   There was little
doubt on whose side their influence would be cast;
the profligacy and greediness of the rich merchants
of London, and especially the butchers who bought
up the estates near the city to make them and
their children gentlemen, were the commonest
subjects of the denunciations of the Commonwealth's men; and their natural hostility to Somer-

---

[1] Knox, *Admonition to Professors of the Truth in England*, p. 53.

set's policy made them ready allies of his enemies.[1] They agreed to pay no attention to the Protector's demands for help, and to increase the guards to defend the city in the Council's interest. On Tuesday the 8th a common Council meeting was held, and Rich was selected to declare to it the enormities of the Protector's Government. Rich was believed to have helped Wolsey and Cromwell, both of whom had been his benefactors, to their fall; he certainly did his best to ruin Sir Thomas More[2] and Bishop Fisher, while he tortured Anne Askew and brought Joan Bocher to the stake. He was suspected of having intrigued against Wriothesley in order to step into his shoes, but charity covers a multitude of faults, and posterity forgets his crimes because he founded a public school and took as his motto

---

[1] Throughout, the aldermen and rich merchants of London were hostile to Somerset, while the 'prentices and poorer classes were strenuously in his favour; compare the tales Somerset's enemies told the corporation at the time of his second fall, how he intended to "destroy the city of London and the substantial men of the same" (Wriothesley, *Chron.*, ii. 57). Pamphlets were also scattered broadcast attributing all manner of evil designs to the Protector; cf. *Hist. MSS. Comm.*, 1st Rep., App., p. 42; 2nd Rep., App., pp. 41–45.

[2] Sir Thomas More gave Rich an uncomfortable quarter of an hour at his trial. "You know," he said, " that I have been acquainted with your manner of life and conversation a long space, even from your youth to this time; for we dwelt long together in one parish, where, as yourself can well tell (I am sorry you compel me to speak it), you were always esteemed very light of your tongue, a great dicer and gamester;" and again, "In good faith, Mr. Rich, I am more sorry for your perjury than mine own peril; and know you that neither I nor any one else to my knowledge ever took you to be a man of such credit as either I or any other could vouchsafe to communicate with you in any matter of importance" (Cresacre More, *Life of Sir T. More*, ed. Hunter, p. 263).

Garde ta Foy. He was thus fully qualified to de-
nounce the man who had made him Lord Chancellor, and that afternoon Somerset was proclaimed
a traitor.

Meantime a war of letters had been going on
between the Protector and the Council, but while
only ill-armed peasants came to Somerset's help,
fresh councillors daily joined those at London, and
the gentlemen with their retainers flocked to have
their revenge on the man who had sought to stay
their illegal pursuit of wealth. The balance of
power, however, lay with the army of the west
then encamped at Andover; both sides sent pressing
appeals to Russell and Herbert, and the decision
was in their hands. But they too had grievances
against Somerset; Herbert had seen his park
ploughed up, and Russell had been reprimanded for
exceeding his instructions in his severity towards
the rebels. It was not to be expected that they
would join forces with the man whose victory would
mean further encouragement of the class whose
revolts had just with so much difficulty been re-
pressed. On the 11th they wrote from Wilton to
Somerset expressing a hope that they might be able
to effect a reconciliation between the two parties, and
announcing their intention of moving their forces
up for that purpose, but probably the tone of their
letter left no doubt in the Protector's mind as to
the scale into which their influence would be cast.[1]

[1] Russell's and Herbert's names (as Lord Privy Seal and Master of
the Horse) are entered in the minutes as present at the Council on
9th October, though as a matter of fact they were at Wilton. The

Somerset's cause was now lost unless he headed the peasants in a social war, and this he had perhaps neither the nerve nor the wickedness to do. As early as the 7th he had written to the Council offering "reasonable conditions," and on the 8th Edward VI. wrote deprecating extreme measures against the Protector. Somerset now completely gave up the struggle; on the 9th he allowed Paget and Cranmer to remove his servants, and on the 10th he made no opposition when the Council sent Sir Anthony Wingfield down to Windsor to arrest him. The Council followed on the 12th, and they felt strong enough to countermand the summons they had issued for assistance. On that day Somerset was placed in Beauchamp's Tower in Windsor Castle, and on the 14th he was removed to the Tower of London with his personal adherents, Sir Thomas Smith, Sir Michael Stanhope, Sir John Thynne, Edward Wolfe, and William Gray. Paget had secured himself by assisting in the Protector's arrest, and Cranmer's office saved him from molestation.[1]

entries in the Council-book are therefore quite untrustworthy, and it is not certain that those were present who signed the letters of the Council. On 6th October these were Rich, Northampton, St. John, Warwick, Arundel, Shrewsbury, Sussex, Cheyney, North, and Gage (*State Papers*, ix. 19, 22). On the 7th the names of Southampton, Petre, Sadler, Montagu, Nicholas Wotton, and Southwell are added (*ibid.*, 28). All these signatures, with the addition of those of Sir John Baker and Sir Edward Wotton, are appended to the proclamation dated 8th October, but Russell's and Herbert's signatures are also falsely attached to it. They are not, however, appended to the letter of the Council dated 11th October (*State Papers, Dom.*, Edw. VI., ix. 44).

[1] Somerset yielded on the strength of the assurances brought by Sir Philip Hoby, apparently on 9th October, from the Council at

The triumph of the Council was complete, and they now proceeded to justify their action in the eyes of their countrymen and of foreign princes. Proclamations were issued to explain to the former the " very truth " of Somerset's ill-doings, and letters were despatched to the ambassadors abroad setting forth a similar list of accusations. It was fairly comprehensive; the Protector had sought to sow division between the nobles, gentlemen, and commons, he had been arbitrary in the use of power, had contemned the advice of his councillors, had

London. "They bade me," Hoby said, "declar unto you from them that of their faithes and honour they doe not entende nor will hurte in any case the person of my Lorde the duke nor of none of you all, nor take away any of his landes or goods whom they doe esteeme and tender as well as any of you as they ought and as one whome they are not ignorant no more than you that he is the king's unkle. They doe intende to preserve his honour as much as any of you woulde, nor meaneth not nor purposeth not no maner hurte to him but onely to give order for the Protectorship which hath not bene so well ordered as thei thinke it shoulde have bene, and to see the kinge better answered of his thinges and the Realme better governed for the kinges Maties and the Realme's more safetie. And for you my Lords and masters of the Counsell they will have you to keep your Roomes and places as you did before, and they will counsell with you for the better government of thinges. My Lord (saith he to the Duke) be you not affraide. I will lose this my necke, and so pointed to his necke, if you haue any hurte. Ther is noe such thinge mente, and so they woulde have me tell you, and marke you well what I saye. Then he willed the letters directed to the kinge to be red openly before all the gentlemen of the privie chambere and others, and other letters according to the direction; upon this all the afforenamed there present wepte for ioye and thanked God and preyed for the Lordes. Mr. Comptroller fell downe on his knees and clasped the Duke about the knees and weepinge saide, O my Lord, O my Lord, ye see nowe what my lordes be." This is Sir Thomas Smith's own account of the matter (*Harleian MSS.*, 353, f. 77).

used his office to enrich himself and his satellites, had subverted law and justice, had plunged the country into domestic and foreign war, and had lost strongholds in France which Henry VIII. had won, and others in Scotland which he himself had fortified. The more violent of these charges, the talk about "devilish and evil purposes," the "subversion of law and justice" and traitorous behaviour, may be dismissed as mere stage thunder intended to frighten the people into acquiescence in the revolution. It is inconceivable that there should be any truth in them when it is remembered that those who made them restored Somerset six months later to his place at the Council board. It is obvious that the only charges in which the councillors themselves believed were those of improper and arbitrary use of his power as Protector and of the ill success of his Government. Some of these were partially, if not wholly, true : that Somerset was overbearing towards his colleagues is unquestionable, and we may well believe that he gave offices to his personal adherents. Such deeds were not peculiar to him or to his age. That his Government had been attended by ill success The issues at stake. is obvious, but it is not so obvious that the fault was his. The real cause of failure was the social trouble which finally broke out in rebellion, but this event was precisely what the Protector laboured so persistently to prevent. He knew that no state could be really strong in which the mass of the people were or felt themselves oppressed, and his proclamations, enclosure commissions, and bills in

Parliament were all designed to remove this feeling and to strengthen England against her enemies. The commission which the councillors alleged as the cause of the social disturbances came after they had begun, and to prevent their development. Their real cause was one which the Council found it necessary to ignore, and that was the persistent opposition of the lords and gentlemen which spoilt the Protector's remedies and precipitated social war. Even so, the knowledge that Somerset was on their side probably prevented numbers of the commons from joining in revolt who might otherwise have done so.

Imminent peril at home involved the neglect of distant perils on the Borders or abroad. Levies raised for Scotland or Boulogne were diverted into Norfolk or the west. The wonder is, not that the English suffered reverses, but that those reverses were so slight. In France, Ambleteuse, or Newhaven as the English called it, with its neighbouring fort Blackness, had fallen, as well as Boulogneberg and the "Almayne Camp" in the proximity of Boulogne.[1] But in some of these treachery, for which Somerset could not be held accountable, had done its work.[2] No attempt was made on Calais or in its neighbourhood, and that Boulogne was not so defenceless as the Council endeavoured to make out, is proved by the fact that it resisted the whole force of France all through the winter, until peace was made. That there was war with France

[1] Wriothesley (*Chron.* ii. 31) postdates the fall of Newhaven.
[2] *State Papers, Foreign*, Edw. VI., No. 195.

at all was, moreover, due in no small measure
to the opposition the Council had offered to the
terms which Somerset was prepared to grant the
French king. In Scotland many fortresses still remained in English hands,[1] including Broughty,
Lauder, Home, Dunglass, Roxburgh, Eyemouth, and
other castles, all of which were Somerset's con-
quests. Haddington had indeed been abandoned,
but the chief cause was the plague which raged in
it and carried off a large number of the garrison,
and both its defenders and the military stores were
safely removed, and the fortifications destroyed.[2] Up
to the last Somerset was receiving fresh assurances
of support from the Scots nobles and commoners.
Moreover, the danger at home which had caused
these reverses had been surmounted, and had
Somerset remained in power, the English position
might perhaps have been retrieved. His accusers,
however, did little in practice to justify their
accusations; within a few months of their accession to power almost every fortress in Scotland
which the Protector left them had been recaptured by the Scots,[3] and a disgraceful peace was
made which gave up every point for which the
Tudors had struggled.

[1] See *State Papers, Scotland* and *Domestic*, Addenda, *passim*.

[2] Lesley, p. 230. "Thair wes a vehement plaigue within the
toune of Haddingtoun be the quhilk a gret nomber of thair
souldiours deit . . . be ressone quhairof sone eftir Michelmas nixt
following the erle of Rutland was sende with ane gret army to
Hadingtoune . . ." For an account of the siege see *Archæologia
Scotica*, i. 57–60, and cf. *Diurnal of Occurrents*, p. 48, and *Rutland
MS.*, p. 55, in Hist. MSS. Commission.

[3] *Diurnal of Occurrents*, pp. 49, 50.

These were, indeed, false issues. The real issue was the Protector's domestic policy, his sympathy with the commons, and his determination to enforce the laws that protected them. Fears were expressed in September of further efforts on the part of the "Commonwealth's men";[1] it was said that Somerset had promised redress of grievances in the Parliament that was to meet early in November, and it was believed that he might yet prevail. If the majority on the Council hated Somerset's social policy, they detested with equal vigour his love of liberty, his abolition of treason laws, and the tacit encouragement which they accused him of giving to men who held that all things should be in common. These motives, accentuated by personal jealousy, were at the bottom of their action, and they come out vividly in the policy they carried out as soon as they had seized the reins of Government. Reaction set in under an administration which at home was more arbitrary, more violent, and more repressive than that of Henry VIII., and abroad was more spiritless and aimless than that of Mary. The lenity, which might have reconciled the country even to the rapid religious changes of Edward's later years, was exchanged for a tyranny that hastened and embittered the inevitable reaction.

[1] *State Papers, Domestic,* vol. viii. No. 56.

CHAPTER X

REACTION

It has been remarked by an eminent French his- torian that the first requisite for the avoidance of pitfalls in history is *dater finement*,[1] and the neglect of this precept has led to the treatment of Edward VI.'s reign as one period marked throughout by the same characteristics, methods, and aims. This view originated in the superficial appearance of continuity in religious policy; it has been perpetuated by historians who have written with theological bias, and frequently with an ulterior motive beyond that of faithfully presenting and interpreting the facts. The history of the reign has been dominated by the religious interest to the exclusion of its other aspects, and it has suffered almost as much from those who have regarded the reign merely as a foil to the preceding one, and have been careless as to the exact distribution of the shade, so long as it was dark enough to throw into relief the figure of Henry VIII.

In reality the reign of Edward VI. is divided into two distinct periods, and the fall of the Protector was followed by a reversal of policy far more

[1] Michelet.

radical than is ever now effected by a change of administration. Somerset's ideas were original and peculiar to himself; the spirit of the age, so far from being one of "universal benevolence," was one of violence and callous indifference to personal suffering, and Somerset's successors reverted to the principles and ideas in which they had been trained under Henry VIII. The Protector's experiment in liberty and toleration had broken down, and it was followed by a return to arbitrary and repressive methods in the same way as the Lancastrian attempt at Parliamentary government was followed by the Tudor absolutism. A brief sketch of the characteristics of this reaction is essential to the adequate appreciation of the Protector's rule.

It was felt in every sphere of Government activity. Even in religious reform, though there was an appearance of continuity, the spirit and methods of effecting it underwent a significant change. The first steps of the doctrinal revolution were taken by a man who was a sincere believer in Reformation doctrines, and on that account could afford to be tolerant of those who differed from him. The direction of the revolution then fell into the hands of a man who, if he believed in anything, believed in the dogmas of the Roman Catholic Church, and covered his hypocrisy by the vehemence of his protestations. Somerset, with typical English conservatism, clung tenaciously to many of the forms and ceremonies of the old faith; Warwick, who had no convictions to restrain him, fell in with all the schemes of the zealots who flocked to England from

abroad. He had his reward; he was compared to
Joshua ; Hooper called him " that most faithful and
intrepid soldier of Christ," [1] and declared " England
cannot do without him. He is a most holy and
fearless instrument of the word of God." [2] Others
echoed his praises in equally fulsome terms, while
the unfortunate Somerset was censured for his lukewarmness in the cause of religion, and told that he
owed to it his fall.

Under Warwick's auspices the revolution pro- Altered
ceeded at a break-neck pace, and " in the three of religious
years between the first and second prayer-books of policy.
Edward VI. the country was expected to have prepared itself for a far greater measure of religious
change than the twenty years since Wolsey had yet
effected." [3] For a time, however, there was a period

---

[1] *Original Letters* (Parker Society), i. 82.

[2] *Ibid.*, i. 89. Warwick and Dorset were "considered the two
most shining lights of the Church of England" (John ab Ulmis to
Bullinger, 25th March 1550, *ib.*, ii. 399). The same letter contains
an illustration of the method by which Dorset (afterwards Duke of
Suffolk) ingratiated himself with the Reformers. Ulmis remarks
that Dorset "really seemed to be transported with joy on account
of your intended commendation of him . . . he also liberally increased my stipend, which is now annual, and when I was about to
depart he offered me his hand and presented me by a domestic,
with six pounds for my journey." By a curious mistake, for which,
however, the confused wording of the epistle affords considerable
excuse, Canon Dixon (*Hist. Church of England*, iii. 223) applies
these remarks to Somerset, and takes the occasion to remark that
the commendations of these divines "raised him to childish delight." As a matter of fact the praise recorded by them to Somerset, always faint, ceased on his fall, being monopolised by "that
intrepid soldier of Christ," the Earl of Warwick, and his dupe, the
Duke of Suffolk.

[3] *Social England*, iii. 171. The statement is correct enough, but
the writer with a truly amazing forgetfulness of dates makes it a

of suspense after Somerset's fall, and the letters of
the English divines to their sympathisers abroad
are full of the apprehension of a Catholic reaction.
The Papists were said to be struggling earnestly for
their kingdom; it was by their help that the Protector had been overthrown, and they naturally
expected some share in the Government that succeeded him.   Wriothesley, Earl of Southampton,
and the Earl of Arundel were among the six lords
to whose especial care the king was entrusted, and
Southwell again became an active member of the
Council.   Their hopes were short-lived; they had
served Warwick's purpose, and now they were thrust
aside. He had made up his mind that his interest
would best be served by the Protestant party, and
the Romanists were only an encumbrance. The
precise means by which they were removed are not
known, but that he got rid of them with no open dis-

charge against Somerset, who fell in the year the first prayer-book
was sanctioned by Parliament, and was executed before the second
was completed.   In the seven months that intervened between the
legalising of the first prayer-book—which was Somerset's work, and
is held up as an example of moderation—and his fall he made no
further religious changes, and he had little or no influence on
ecclesiastical or other policy after his fall.   What influence he had
was uniformly exerted to moderate the haste of the Government.
This is, however, a slip trifling compared with those made by the
writer on religion in the same volume (pp. 177, 179), who in less
than three pages succeeds in stating that Tunstall was imprisoned
in 1547 (instead of 1551, and then not for a religious cause, but on
a charge of treason), Bonner in 1548 (instead of 1549), that Joan
Bocher was burnt in 1549 (instead of 1550), that Northumberland
was "Protector," and that within nine months of Edward VI.'s
accession not a "churchman" was left on the Council except
Cranmer.

turbance is singular evidence of Warwick's subtlety
and skill. On 2nd February 1549–50 Southampton
was struck ·off the list of councillors, and he died,
it is said of chagrin, on the 30th of July following.[1]
Arundel was at the same time confined to his house
charged with numerous offences, and fined £12,000 ;
Southwell was in January thrown into the Tower
on the rather mysterious charge of sowing abroad
seditious bills.[2] Those "cruel beasts the Romanists,"
as one evangelical divine called them, who had
already begun to triumph and restore the mass,[3]
found that they had been completely duped, and
that Warwick's finger was a good deal thicker than
Somerset's thigh. If the Protector had lashed them
with whips, they were now to be chastised with
scorpions. If they had resented the doctrinal
changes of Edward VI.'s first prayer-book, they had
far more reason to complain of the second. An
open breach was now made between Catholic doctrine and that of the Church of England ; the "real
presence," which had been implied[4] or at least left
doubtful in the first prayer-book, was explicitly
denied in the second. Anglican doctrine was brought
down nearly to the level of the Reformed Churches
on the Continent, and the difference between the

[1] Ponet, *Treatise of Politike Power*, sh. iii. ; Wriothesley, *Chronicle*,
ii. 41.

[2] According to Ponet, Southwell confessed "enough to be hanged
for." The Protestant divines frequently asserted at the time that
Somerset had been entangled in the wiles of the Papists, and so
had fallen. Compare *Lit. Remains of Edw. VI.*, ii. 247.

[3] *Original Letters* (Parker Society), ii. 464.

[4] The Rev. Nicholas Pocock, in *English Hist. Review*, July 1895.

Church of 1529 and that of 1549 was slight compared with the difference between that of 1549 and that of 1552. In the first Parliament after Somerset's fall, an Act was passed for the abolition and destruction of all service-books, except that prescribed by the Act of Uniformity.[1] Two years later Northampton was rewarded for his support of Warwick by the legalisation of his second " marriage "; and for the first time in English history the principle was recognised that a man might marry a second wife while his first was still living.[2] Similarly the marriage of priests, which before had been but grudgingly recognised as a necessary evil, was now declared to be " true, just, and lawful matrimony, to all intents, constructions, and purposes."

Persecution. These changes, however, were less obnoxious than the methods by which they were enforced. Somerset had always tried every persuasive expedient before he resorted to force; he argued with recalcitrant prelates, wrote to them, and proposed all sorts of compromises before he had them imprisoned. Only two of them suffered that fate; none were deprived, for Somerset withheld his assent from the

---

[1] 3 & 4 Edw. VI. c. 10.

[2] Henry VIII.'s case is of course distinct. He could marry while Catherine of Arragon was still alive, because the view adopted was that his "marriage" with her was void *ab initio* by canon law, and that really there had been no marriage at all. The same theory was adopted in Anne of Cleves's case. Anne Boleyn was of course executed before Henry married Jane Seymour; she died before Anne of Cleves was thought of; and Catherine Howard was executed before Catherine Parr was married. There was, however, no question of the validity of Northampton's first marriage; his wife had only been divorced *a mensa et thoro* on account of adultery.

sentence passed by the Ecclesiastical Courts on
Bonner. Warwick has never been accused of such
leniency. "You know," wrote Terentianus to John
ab Ulmis as a sufficient explanation of the reason
why so many lords had signed against their will
the proclamation of Queen Jane, "you know the
character of the man."[1] From the moment of the
fall of the Catholic party, early in 1550, a systematic persecution of the Princess Mary began. She
was deprived of her license to hear private mass,[2]
her chaplains were imprisoned, and she was ordered
to use the new service-book. To such an extent
did this annoyance, which Somerset vainly endeavoured to mitigate, go that Charles V. laid plans for
Mary's escape from England, and threatened a war
which only the outbreak of hostilities between him
and France prevented. At the same time Bonner
was deprived of his bishopric; Gardiner, Heath,
Bishop of Worcester, and Day, Bishop of Chichester,[3] met with the same fate, while Voysey,
Bishop of Exeter, was forced to resign. Tunstall
was imprisoned in the Tower on a frivolous charge
of treason,[4] and then deprived of his bishopric,
which was dissolved. He was only saved from
attainder by the refusal of the House of Commons
to pass the bill introduced by the Government, and

[1] *Original Letters* (Parker Soc.), i. 365.
[2] *See* Morison's account of her case in *Harleian MSS.*, 353, and
numerous references in the *Acts of the Privy Council*, also *State
Papers, Foreign Series*, passim.
[3] For the proceedings against them, see *Harleian MSS.*, 6195, f. 10.
[4] He was accused of having plotted to raise an insurrection in the
North in connection with Somerset's alleged conspiracy in 1551.

Gardiner is said before his deprivation to have saved his head only by spending half the revenues of his see in bribes.[1]   Others of lower rank were treated with equal severity; Dr. Cole was expelled from the wardenship of New College,[2] and Dr. Morwen from the presidency of Corpus.[3]   Sir Anthony Browne was imprisoned in the Fleet for hearing mass, and a host of other offenders were punished under the new Act of Uniformity.[4] This imposed severe penalties on laymen for mere recusancy or nonconformity, and was the first statute in English history that did since the Act passed under Somerset limited the so, penalties to the more active resistance of priests. It was not merely the adherents of the ancient faith who suffered from religious persecution. The fires at Smithfield, which had remained extinct since Henry VIII.'s death, were once more kindled, and heretics began again to pay forfeit with their lives for their convictions. Joan Bocher, whose sentence, pronounced by Cranmer, Somerset had refused to execute, was burnt on 2nd May 1550,[5] and next year George van Paris was brought to the stake for like opinions.[6]

Foreign policy.   So superficial was the appearance of continuity in religious policy, and so different was the spirit in which it was pursued. In foreign affairs and in

---

[1] Ponet, *Treatise of Politike Power.*   [2] *Hatfield MSS.,* i. 81.

[3] *Acts of the Privy Council,* iii. 287, 305, 307, 311, 316, 317.

[4] 5 & 6 Edw. VI. c. i. This Sir Anthony was son of the one mentioned on pp. 18, 38.

[5] Wriothesley, *Chronicle,* ii. 37.

[6] On 24th April 1551 (*ib.,* ii. 47); cf. *Literary Remains of Edward VI.,* ii. 312.

temporal government at home the reversal of policy
was not concealed by the thinnest disguise.   While
it was high-handed at home, the Government was
cringing abroad; defeat came first, and it was
quickly followed by surrender.   Despite the suppression of the revolts in the west and in Norfolk,
which set free large forces for service in France or
on the Borders, the Government allowed Home Castle
to be captured by the Scots on the 16th December
1549; they gained Broughty Castle on the 6th February 1549–50, "and slewe man, woman, and childe,
except Sir John Luttrell, the captaine, whom they
tooke prisoner,"[1] and the fall of Lauder Castle followed
in March.   Instead of making any effort to retrieve
these losses, the Council gave up the struggle and
made peace with both France and Scotland by the
easy method of yielding everything that was asked.
Boulogne was to be surrendered within six weeks,
four years earlier than had been stipulated in Henry's
treaty with Francis.   The sum to be paid for it
was reduced by half, and the large amount still
owing in the shape of arrears of the French pension
to the English king was remitted altogether.   The
conquest which had cost considerably over a million
and a quarter pounds to achieve and defend,[2] was

---

[1] *Diurnall of Occurrents*, Bannatyne Club, pp. 49, 50 ; *Acts of the
Privy Council*, 1547–1550, p. 407. Wriothesley, *Chronicle*, ii. 31,
misdates the fall of Broughty Castle and also that of Newhaven
(see p. 254).

[2] See the detailed accounts of the expenditure connected with
Boulogne in *Harleian MSS.*, 353, ff. 50 *et seq.* The various strongholds
in France are there enumerated as the High Tower, the Citadel,
the Old Man, Boulogneberg, the Young Man, the Pier, Newhaven,
and Blackness.

surrendered, before the period of English occupation
was half spent, for the paltry sum of four hundred
thousand crowns.   But this was harmless compared
with the criminal abandonment of English interests
involved in the terms of the peace with Scotland.
It was perhaps only to be expected that such Scots
strongholds as remained in English hands should
be surrendered without any countervailing compen-
sation whatever, but no Government with the least
regard for the future of its country could have
weakly submitted to the marriage of the Queen of
Scots with the Dauphin of France.   Yet this is
what the Council did; every point for which Henry
VII., Henry VIII., and Somerset had striven was
abandoned, and it was only the death of Francis II.
without issue by Mary, Queen of Scots, that saved
Great Britain from perhaps the most serious danger
that ever has threatened it.   Even so, the action
of the Council bequeathed to Elizabeth the most
pressing peril that beset the early years of her reign.

After concluding this ignominious peace, the
Council apparently thought that England had little
further need for defences.   Ships of war were laid
up and suffered to rot; no new ones were built, and
the fleet, the creation of which had been one of the
most laudable of Henry VIII.'s achievements, and,
in spite of innumerable obstacles, had been maintained in an efficient 'state by Somerset, was before
the end of Edward VI.'s reign reduced to half
its strength.   Fortifications which had been commenced at Calais and Guisnes, on the Scottish
borders, and on the English coast were stayed, and

some were even demolished.   Garrisons were dis-
banded in some places and reduced to half in
others, and military engineers were dismissed.[1]   The
folly of these proceedings was rendered the more
glaring when the Council proceeded, by their persecution of the Princess Mary, to provoke a war
with England's most powerful enemy, Charles V.
This time it was the French king who saved them
from the results of their conduct; his seizure of
the three bishoprics precipitated a conflict with
the Emperor, and with this and the troubles in
Germany on his hands, Charles was compelled to
defer the satisfaction of his resentment against
England.

While the Government presented to its enemies Domestic
abroad a timorous front, towards its own subjects policy.
its attitude was one of tyranny tempered by corruption.   The Protector's plans for the reform of
internal abuses were abandoned at the same time as
his schemes for the maintenance and extension of
England's external greatness.   Corrupt officials, says
Ponet, took counsel with crafty Alcibiades (*i.e.*
Warwick) how to "make non-accompt,"[2] and Sir
William Sharington, who had been justly attainted as
a coiner of false money, was by one of the first acts
of the new administration released from the Tower,
granted full pardon, and even employed to receive
the French payments for Boulogne.[3]   Sir Anthony

[1] *Acts of the Privy Council*, iii. 43, 44, 47, 100, 104, 209, 225,
364.

[2] *Treatise of Politike Power.*

[3] Mr. Froude (popular ed., iv. 399) notes the fact of Sharington's
pardon and release, but treats it as one of Somerset's delinquen-

Aucher, who was guilty of extensive malversation, and had naturally dreaded the advent of a "Commonwealth's party," not only escaped punishment, but retained his office. Complaints of bribery in the courts of justice became louder than ever, and slight atonement was made when Parliament, by a sort of deathbed repentance, attempted, four months before the end of the reign, to force the revenue officers to render account of their doings.[1]   Another evil, the sale of offices, was admitted, and to some extent even sanctioned by an Act of Parliament passed in the previous session.[2]   It is entitled " Against buying and selling of Offices," but the only penalty imposed on such transactions was that they should be void, and even this was not to apply to any sale or purchase of offices before the following March.   All such offices, moreover, as keeperships of parks, manors, and forests were exempted from the operation of the Act; but more astounding was the final clause, to the effect that the Act was not to apply to offices connected with the King's Bench or Common Pleas.   The calling down of the "testoons" first to ninepence and then to sixpence was a natural result from these ideas of financial morality; the coining of base money, which was prohibited by Somerset three months after he began to rule, was now resumed, but the proportion of base metal was increased

cies. Sharington, however, remained in the Tower till after Somerset's fall, and the Act for his pardon and restitution in blood was passed in the first session of Parliament after that event.

[1] 7 Edw. VI. c. 1.

[2] 5 & 6 Edw. VI. c. 16.

from two to one to three to one, and under Warwick the English currency [1] reached its nadir.

The lands and property of the Church were dealt with on like principles. Early in 1551, when Ponet was appointed to succeed Gardiner in the bishopric of Winchester, he was compelled, as part of the bargain, to surrender all the lands of his see to the Crown, receiving in exchange a salary of two thousand marks. The lands were regranted to the chief members of Warwick's faction in the following summer, with the obvious object of making more sure of their support. A year later, with a similar motive, the bishopric of Durham was dissolved; its revenues were designed to support Warwick's new dukedom, but Mary's accession came in time to prevent the completion of this nefarious scheme. The chantry lands, of which £5000 worth only had been sold under Somerset, the proceeds being devoted to the comparatively legitimate purpose of defending the realm, now began to be granted to private persons,[2] and a mine of wealth was found in the Church plate.[3] It has been assumed that the commission appointed in 1547 to make an inventory of Church plate was merely a preliminary to its wholesale seizure by the Crown, but the conclusion is a little hasty, and at any rate there is another explanation. This is supplied by a letter of the Council, dated 17th December 1547, to the

Spoliation of church property.

Church plate.

[1] See *ante*, pp. 52, 53.

[2] See *Acts of the Privy Council*, vol. iii. *passim.*

[3] For the bibliography of this subject see Mély and Bishop, *Bibliographie Générale des Inventaires imprimés.*

commissioners; there the idea of confiscation was repudiated, and it was stated that the object of the Council was " to see the same preserved entirelie to the churches, without embeselinge or privat salles " [embezzling or private sales].[1] This assertion is borne out to some extent by the remaining references to Church plate in the Acts of the Council under Somerset.   There are only four of them; the first is an order to the dean and chapter of Christ Church, Canterbury, who had already taken down a gold pyx and silver crucifix, and devoted the proceeds to the repair of their " house," to restrain them from further steps in that direction; the second is an order to the Mayor of Feversham to restore to the churchwardens a silver pyx that had been removed from the church.   The last two were orders to the dean and chapter of Christ Church, Canterbury, to deliver up " all such juelles and plate of gould and silver as they have by our late soveraigne lordes permission in their possessyon," and this was an instance, not of the spoliation of parish churches, but of the seizure of monastic property forfeited in 1539.   On Somerset's fall, however, confiscation became general and the numerous references in the Acts of the Council are brought to a close with the order to the commissioners, dated 3rd March 1551, "to take into the kinges handes such churche plate as remaigneth to be emploied unto his Highnes use." [2]

[1] *Acts of the Privy Council*, ii. 536.   There had been a good deal of Church spoliation by private persons before the Reformation began, and Skelton in *Colin Clout* denounces the practice (*Works*, ed. Dyce, i. 326).   [2] *Ibid.*, iii. 228.

The same covetous spirit, reinforced by class- Attitude towards enclosures. hatred and despotic principles, dictated a reversal of the Protector's social policy. It was not to be expected that the men who had successfully opposed that policy under Somerset would give it any countenance when they came into power. John Hales, the chief supporter of the movement, sought safety in Germany when his patron fell, and the Parliament which met four weeks later, instead of carrying out the redress of grievances which Somerset had promised the commons, set to work to make their yoke less easy, and their burden less light. The measures it passed were a reversal, not merely of Somerset's policy, but of that which had been professedly at least the policy of the Tudors and of the Yorkists. Parliament was not content with dropping the Enclosure Commission, and making the proclamations a dead letter, but it proceeded to override all the laws passed against enclosures under Henry VII. and Henry VIII., and to re-enact the Statute of Merton, providing that the lords of manors "might approve themselves of their wastes, woods, and pastures, notwithstanding the gainesaying and contradiction of their tenants," so long as the latter were left "sufficient" commons and free ingress and egress to and from their tenements.[1] It is true that treble damages were awarded to such as should bring a successful writ of novel disseisin against an encloser, but the Act then went on to exempt from this provision all houses built on waste lands to which not more than three acres of enclosed

[1] 3 & 4 Edw. VI. c. 3.

land were attached. Its meaning was apparently that even where an encloser had absolutely no title he could not be proceeded against so long as what he enclosed was waste land, and each enclosure did not exceed three acres. Further relief was granted to the distressed capitalist by the abolition of the taxes on sheep and on woollen cloths,[1] the deficit being made up by renewing the demand for the payment of fee-farms, which Somerset had remitted in order that work might be provided for the poor.[2] A similar object was contemplated by a clause in another statute of the same session.[3] Somerset, it will be remembered, had with an impartial hand made it illegal both for workmen to conspire to raise the price of their labour and for capitalists to conspire to raise that of their merchandise. The former prohibition remained in force, but the policy embodied in the latter was completely reversed, and it was actually made a felony for twelve or more persons to meet together for the purpose of abating rents or the price of corn.

New treason laws.

This statute is indeed the most vivid illustration of the spirit of the party that overthrew Somerset, and in some respects it is unparalleled by any other Act in the Statute-book. It was drawn up with three objects. Besides the protection of capitalists already alluded to, it was

---

[1] Statute 2 & 3 Edw. VI. c. 36 had imposed a tax of 3d. on every ewe sheep kept on private pasture, 2d. on every wether so kept, and 1½d. on every shear-sheep kept on common land; these were all abolished by 3 & 4 Edw. VI. c. 23. The impost of 8d. on woollen cloths was also abolished.

[2] 3 & 4 Edw. VI. c. 18.   [3] *Ibid.*, c. 5.

designed to supply the gentry with the means for crushing the commons, and the Government with the means for stamping out resistance to its authority. It was made felony, without benefit of clergy, if twelve or more persons met for the purpose of breaking down any enclosure, rightful or wrongful, or of enforcing right of common or way over any such enclosure, and refused to retire when ordered to do so. Persons calling such assemblies together with bell, trumpet, outcry, or handbill, were subjected to a like penalty, and if forty or more assembled together for any such purpose, their offence was declared to be treason. If any copyholder refused to help in repressing such assemblies, he was to forfeit his copyhold for life, and the mere inciting to such acts by open word or deed was declared felony without benefit of clergy. A later Act of the same session,[1] after recounting the mischiefs arising from the repeal of certain felonies, viz. the hunting deer or other animals in any park or enclosure whatever, proceeded to re-enact them.

The unique clause of this Act[2] was that by which the Government sought to secure its position by an unparalleled extension of the treason laws. By this Act the members of the Privy Council were granted the same protection as royalty. It was not only declared treason for twelve persons to meet (and remain together an hour after being commanded to disperse) with the purpose of killing a Privy Councillor, but it was to be equally treason if their object was merely to

[1] 3 & 4 Edw. VI., c. 17.   [2] 3 & 4 Edw. VI., c. 5.

imprison him; and, as if that were not enough, the same tremendous penalty was attached to a like assembly for the purpose of "altering the laws." Never in their most arbitrary moments did Henry VIII., Charles I., or James II. deliver such a blow at the liberties and constitution of England. Compared with this, it was a trifling matter that the provisoes, with which Somerset sought to restrain the abuse of what treason laws he left on the Statute-book, found no place in this Act. There was no limit of time within which charges of treason were to be preferred, and no clause requiring the evidence of two witnesses.

The composition of Parliament, and the terror into which the gentry had been thrown by the rebellions of 1549, induced it to acquiesce in these repressive measures. But in spite of all this it was not reactionary or subservient enough for Warwick's purpose. In 1552, after Somerset's death, the House of Commons rejected a fresh Government bill for the creation of new treasons, and substituted a milder one of its own. This was severe enough, and it again erected certain verbal offences into the rank of treason; but it reintroduced the clause about two witnesses,[1] and a limitation of three months within which charges were to be preferred. It was wider than Somerset's limitation of thirty days, but it was at least an improvement

[1] It also made the important addition that the two witnesses should confront the accused at his trial. This proviso has, and I think correctly, been attributed to the indignation Parliament felt at the treatment of Somerset during his trial in the previous December.

on the Government proposal. In the same session
Parliament rejected the Bill of Attainder against
Bishop Tunstall; and its general attitude of independence caused Warwick to dissolve it and
summon another.

The feelings which produced this growing oppo- Treatment
sition to Warwick existed and were known to him of Parliament.
long before. Even during the last days of the
session of November 1549 to February 1550 a proposal had been discussed among certain members
of the Lower House for the restoration of Somerset
to the Protectorate,[1] and the existence of this party
in Parliament strengthened Warwick's resolve to do
without Parliament as long as he could. The result
was that Parliament was not summoned between
1st February 1549–50 and 23rd January 1551–2,
which by a significant coincidence was the day after
Somerset's execution. The means by which Warwick sought to pack Parliament when it did meet
were the creation of boroughs and interference with
elections. The creation of seven new boroughs[2] in
Cornwall, peculiarly subject to Crown influence and
returning fourteen members to Parliament, has
already been mentioned. It has also been pointed
out that under Somerset only one attempt was made
to influence an election, and that was during the
Protector's absence; that one attempt was then explained away, and the person actually recommended
by the Council was not elected for the constituency
to which he had been recommended. The Parliament that met in January 1552 was the same which

[1] Tytler, ii. 15.   [2] See *ante*, pp. 70, 71.

had been elected in 1547, so that the only scope for Crown influence was in filling up the vacancies caused by death. Good use was, however, made of these limited opportunities. On 28th October 1551 the Lord Chancellor was ordered to inquire how many members had died since the last session, " to thintent that grave and wyse men might be elected to supplie theyr places, for thadvoyding of the disordre that hath byn noted in sundrie yong men and others of smale judgement." [1] One of these vacant seats was Reading, which thereupon returned John Seymour. The election of a Seymour at a time when Warwick was seeking to get rid of Somerset was regarded by the Council as an affront, and so on 10th January 1551–2 the electors were peremptorily ordered to return some one else. On 19th January the sheriff of Hertfordshire was directed " to use the matter in suche sorte as Mr. Sadlier may be elected and returned " for that shire. On the 1st of February the sheriff of Surrey was " willed to preferre Sir Thomas Saunders " to its representation in Parliament. Even so, as has been seen, this Parliament proved too refractory and was dissolved ; when the new one came to be elected in the following year, this piecemeal interference was not considered potent enough, and a circular letter was sent round to all the sheriffs ordering the election of such persons as the Council should recommend.

Warwick's treatment of the Council.

Of even more importance than the packing of Parliament was the packing of the Council. Somer-

[1] *Acts of the Privy Council*, iii. 400 ; cf. *ib.*, iii. 457, 459, 470.

set had made practically no change in the Council
during his administration. In the following two
years of Warwick's rule no less than twelve new
members were added to the Council, and all of
them Warwick's devoted adherents.[1] These, with
his adherents among the previous members, gave
Warwick absolute control over the Council, whose
authority was regarded as less than his; proclamations drawn up by the Council in his absence
were sent to him for correction and amendment,
and then published without further consideration by the Council.[2] He was also considered to
be above the ordinary law, and when Sir Clement
Smith (brother-in-law of Somerset) took out a writ
against him, he was promptly summoned before the
Council for his "presumption and lewdness."[3] This
was one instance of the contempt of law evinced
by the Government. A labourer was in 1551
imprisoned and executed merely for presenting a
"Supplication," probably to the Star Chamber,
against certain persons who had destroyed his
corn.[4] •In the same year one Appleyard[5] was
accused of stirring up rebellion in Northampton-

[1] Namely, the Duke of Suffolk, the Earls of Westmoreland
and Huntingdon, Viscount Hereford, Lord Clinton, Goodrich,
Bishop of Ely, Lord Cobham, Sir John Mason, Sir John Gage, Sir
Philip Hoby, Sir Robert Bowes, and Sir Richard Cotton.

[2] *Acts of the Privy Council*, iii. 125.　　　　[3] *Ibid.*, iii. 8.

[4] Tytler, i. 271, 272.

[5] *State Papers, Domestic*, Addenda, vol. iii. No. 79, gives a full
account of this case. It contains the curious statement that
"there is a statute that a man shall not be attainted under two
witnesses"; but this proviso of Somerset's Act of 1547 was not
embodied in the Act of 1549-50 (*see* p. 274).

shire; he was sent before a jury, but there was only one witness against him and he was acquitted; he was then tried before another jury and again acquitted. He was taken for a third trial to Leicester, and the Government took sure means for his condemnation. The Solicitor-General [1] went down and told the jury that "if Appleyard were not hanged, he would be hanged for him," and that if the jury failed to find a verdict for the Crown they would all be summoned before the Star Chamber. Appleyard was hanged, and then a guilty conscience moved his accuser; he confessed that his witness was false, and that, himself under condemnation of death, he had been offered his life if he would accuse Appleyard. It was, however, reserved for the trial of the fallen Protector to show the full extent of the violence and illegality of what has been called the "Reformed Administration." [2]

[1] This Solicitor-General was the chief law-officer consulted for the trial of the Duke of Somerset. Sir Edward Griffin was his name.

[2] Froude.

CHAPTER XI

TRIAL AND EXECUTION OF THE PROTECTOR

THE reversal of his policy and ruin of his work Somerset in opposition. which the Council effected upon the Protector's fall was naturally viewed by him and his adherents with dislike and alarm, and almost from the moment of his liberation Somerset inevitably became the centre of a passive resistance to the new Government. He had been sent to the Tower on 14th October 1549, and two months later thirty-one articles [1] were presented to him for signature, and then laid before Parliament. The strong feeling in Somerset's favour in certain quarters, and the fear that it would prevent the ratification by Parliament of extreme measures against him, made these articles differ considerably from the charges which the Council had originally drawn up. The accusations were indeed so modified as to amount to little more than a vote of censure. The first ten articles, ignoring the patent for his Protectorship which Somerset had obtained from the Council and Edward VI., made various charges based on the terms of the original grant of the office, against the arbitrary way in which Somerset had exercised it, such as

---

[1] *Harleian MSS.*, 353, ff. 78 *et seqq.*

acting without advice (2 and 3), discussing matters
alone with foreign ambassadors (5), threatening to
deprive Privy Councillors of their seats on the
Council (7), erecting a Court of Requests in his
own house (8), granting offices on his own authority
(9), meddling with the sale of the king's lands (10).
The most singular thing about these accusations is
that by his patent the Protector was authorised to
do all the acts therein charged against him.   He
had been empowered to summon whom he liked
to the Council, and, in short, to do anything and
everything a Governor and Protector "ought or
should do."   To make out a case the Council
was apparently compelled to base its charges on
the original grant which this patent had superseded.   The real significance of the objections to
the Protector, however, lies in Articles 12–19, and
22.   It was there stated that Somerset had (12)
declared openly that the nobles and gentlemen were
"the cause of the dearth of things wherby the
people rose and did reform things themselves"; (13)
that he had issued proclamations—"which proclamations went forthe againste the wishes of your
Highnes' wholl counsell—which encouraged the
common people to make divers insurrections"; (14)
"And further caused many and sundry commissions,
with articles thereunto annexed, to be made out
concerning enclosures, giving the commissioners
power to hear and to determine causes"; (15) that
he did not take speedy measures to suppress the
insurrections; (16) that he "comforted and encouraged" divers of the rebels, giving "unto them divers

somes of his owne money"; (17) that he issued
proclamations to the effect that none of the rebels
should be sued or vexed on account of their proceedings in the rebellion; (18) that he said he liked
well their doings, and that the covetousness of the
gentlemen had given the people reason to rise; (19)
that he had said that "the Lordes of Parliamente
were lothe to encline themselves to the reformacion
of enclosures and other thinges. And therefore the
people had good cause to reforme the thinges themselves"; (22) and that he had endeavoured to prevent
the noblemen from repressing the rebels, and had
written letters directing them "to speak fair to the
rebels and to handle them gently"; and (4) had caused
the release of divers persons.[1] Article number 20
charged the Protector with neglecting the defence
of Boulogne, Newhaven, and Blackness, which was
a somewhat delicate accusation, as the Council itself
had in the meanwhile lost several strongholds both
in France and in Scotland. The remainder of the
articles dealt with the Protector's proceedings at
Hampton Court and Windsor after the Council
had begun to seek his overthrow, but, however
violent they may have been, they could scarcely
be urged as justifying the commencement of the

[1] Sir Anthony Aucher made this complaint in September 1549
(Aucher to Cecil, *State Papers, Domestic*, Edw. VI., viii. 56), and also
that "that Common Welthe called Latymer hathe gotten the
pardon of others." It is said that one of Latimer's sermons—
probably the well-known sermon "of the Plough"—first inspired
Somerset with the desire to remedy the social hardships. Latimer
no doubt had some influence in this direction, but the sporadic
disturbances and "supplications" of the commons probably had
more to do with Somerset's action.

Council's action.   These articles amounted to little
more than a vote of no confidence, and when
Somerset had made his submission, the only penalty
inflicted on him was imprisonment without loss of
any lands or goods.[1]   On 6th February 1549–50
he was released from the Tower, and on the 18th
he received a free pardon.   On 10th April he was
readmitted a member of the Privy Council, and
on 14th May was made a Gentlemen of the Privy
Chamber.   On 27th all his property that had not
already been disposed of was restored to him, and
on 3rd June his daughter Anne was married to
Warwick's eldest son, Viscount Lisle.

The reconciliation between the two rivals was,
however, hollow; for Somerset was a fatal obstacle
to the schemes which Warwick had in all probability
already begun to entertain.   Somerset, moreover,
incurred the earl's resentment by the opposition he
offered to the persecuting violence of the new
Government.[2]   In the Council Chamber and elsewhere he strenuously sought to prevent the with-
drawal of the Princess Mary's license to hear private

---

[1] It is generally said that 29 articles only were drawn up, and in
this same MS. Somerset is said to have subscribed 29 only, but
there are 31 given.   It is also said that he was condemned to forfeit
£2000 annual value of lands, but I find no record of this penalty
being inflicted on him.   His lands were, however, given away to
some extent during his imprisonment.

[2] The letter printed by Tytler (ii. 21–24) containing Warwick's
complaints of these proceedings of Somerset is really dated 26th
June 1550, not 1551 as Tytler says, and is naturally connected with
the Council's action against Bishop Gardiner in that month (see *Acts
of the Privy Council*, passim).   The letter is among the State Papers
in the Record Office (Edw. VI., *Domestic*, vol. x. No. 9).

masses, partly, it may be, to win support for himself,
but mainly because he was by nature averse from
persecution, and foresaw the peril it would provoke from Charles V. Similarly in May and June
1550 he did his utmost to secure Gardiner's liberation from the Tower, and the lenient treatment of
the Arundells who had been imprisoned on suspicion
of complicity in the Western Rebellion.[1] This
conduct brought him the support of moderate men
like Paget, the Earl of Arundel, and Lord Grey de
Wilton, and Somerset's party, never quite extinct,
began to threaten Warwick's position. Even on
the morrow of the Protector's fall, Dr. Cardmaker,
preaching at St. Paul's, had said that though
Somerset had had a fall, he was not undone, and
that "men should not have their purpose." Before
Parliament separated in February 1549–50, a movement had been started in the House of Commons
for again making Somerset Protector, and though
the prorogation put a stop to the project, it was
decided to revive it as soon as Parliament should
meet again.[2] The appointment of Somerset as
Lord-Lieutenant of Buckinghamshire and Berkshire
on 10th May 1551 was no doubt some evidence
of his growing influence. But what made him

[1] There were several knights among the Arundell family at this
time ; the two referred to above were Sir John and Sir Thomas.
Strype in one passage makes a hopeless muddle by confusing Sir
Thomas Arundell with the Earl of Arundel, whose family name was
Fitzalan. Strype was even led into falsifying a document he was
copying, in order to explain a confusion he himself created (see
Gentleman's Magazine, 1848, i. 37, 131, 269).

[2] This was one of the reasons why Parliament was not summoned
again until after Somerset's execution.

really formidable was the failure of the Government abroad and its oppressive policy at home, and during 1551 there were many signs of the hatred with which it was popularly regarded.

The danger with which he was threatened by this growing opposition spurred Warwick on to the execution of a deep-laid and far-reaching scheme for the complete vindication of his authority. The precise extent of his designs at this time is, and must probably remain, unknown; the subtlest and most daring of the English disciples of Machiavelli,[1] Warwick was a past master in the art of concealing his motives and aims from his contemporaries, and the scanty indications of them preserved in trustworthy records give little help towards their elucidation. There can, however, be little doubt that the ruin of Somerset was a mere detail in the plan of Warwick's operations: there is no evidence to show that Warwick had any other objection to Somerset than as an obstacle to his ambition, and it was due to the strength of his personal following that Somerset was brought to the block, while the less formidable obstacles to Warwick's aims escaped with imprisonment, fines, and degradation. It is probable that even at this time Warwick con-

[1] Mr. John Morley in his "Romanes Lecture" suggested that it would be interesting to trace the influence of Machiavelli on Reformation statesmen, and quoted Cromwell's well-known commendation of the book. Cecil also asked English ambassadors abroad to procure him copies, and even that harmless gossip, Sir Richard Morison, whiled away his leisure hours at the Emperor's court in perusing it, making frequent reference to it in his correspondence (see *State Papers, Foreign Series*, Edw. VI., *passim; Sloane MSS.*, 1523; and *Harleian MSS.*, 353, ff. 130–139).

templated altering the succession to the Crown;
Edward VI.'s feeble health and constitutional weakness, though carefully concealed from the people,
were patent to his councillors, and it seems impossible that there should have been any other adequate
motive for the creation of Grey as Duke of Suffolk
in October 1551.[1] However that may be, the
scheme included the advancement of Warwick's
adherents and the annihilation of Somerset's party,
the disgrace of Paget and Rich, the imprisonment

[1] His first project in this direction seems, however, to have been
the marriage of his fourth and only unmarried son, Guilford Dudley,
to Margaret Clifford, daughter of Henry, Earl of Cumberland, by
his wife Eleanor, daughter of Mary Tudor and Charles Brandon.
Margaret was thus cousin of Lady Jane Grey, and came next to
the Suffolk family in the line of succession. In 1552 this gossip,
which was founded on fact, was repeated by one Elizabeth Huggons,
formerly servant of the Duchess of Somerset, at Sir William Stafford's house at Rochford. She added the remark "have at the
crown, by your leave," which shows that Warwick's designs were
suspected (see *Harleian MSS.*, 353, ff. 120, 121). What seems conclusive proofs of the aims of Warwick, as early as 1551, is afforded
by a draft letter of the Council among the Hatfield MSS., which
the Historical MSS. Commissioners dated 1551. It refers to Mary's
intention "to resist such ordinances and decrees as the King's
Majesty hath set forth and established for the succession of the
Imperial Crown of this realm" (*Cal. Hatfield MSS.*, i. 93). A brief
examination, however, shows that this is only one of the too
numerous instances in which the commissioners have assigned a
wrong date to the document before them. It should be dated July
1553. Another indication of popular suspicion of Warwick's aims
at this time is given by some entries in the *Acts of the Privy
Council* about the new coinage. On 1st October 1551 a man was
charged before the Council with asserting that Warwick had set
up a mint in Dudley Castle and issued coins, on one side of
which was a ragged staff and the other a bear's face. Next day a
yeoman of the guard was accused of the same offence; other cases
occurred later on. The significance of the matter was that the
ragged staff and bear's face were Warwick's badges.

of Arundel and Tunstall, the deprivation of Gardiner, Heath, and Day, the enhancing of Warwick's authority at the expense of that of the Council, and that of the Council at the expense of the nation at large.

His *coup d'état*, October 1551.

During the whole of September 1551 Somerset was kept from the Council by sickness in his household, and it was probably during this period that Warwick's designs were matured. His first overt move was to get rid of Paget, whose long experience and worldly wisdom gave him considerable influence with the Council and made him by far the most formidable of Somerset's friends. The method by which Warwick accomplished this is a striking illustration of the character which Morison gives of him. He had, said Morison, "such a head that he always conceived two purposes, one of which was sure to be accomplished whichever way things turned out." [1] There had for some time been strained relations with Charles V. on account of Mary's treatment by the Council. The Emperor charged the Council with perfidy in breaking the promise of toleration given by the Council under Somerset to Mary. Paget denied that this promise had ever been given. Charles declared that it had,

[1] *Harleian MSS.*, 353, ff. 130 *et seqq.* It is curious that an exact parallel to this treatment of Paget occurred soon afterwards in the treatment of Sir Thomas Stucley or Stukeley, another partisan of Somerset's. In this case it was the French king whom Northumberland professed to oblige. Stukeley had given information of some hostile design of the French Government. Northumberland believed Stukeley's word, but put him in prison and then told the French king it had been done to show the English Government's respect for his word, because he had denied the alleged plot.

and to smooth over the difficulty, though he had
no intention of carrying out the promise, Warwick
informed Charles on 16th October that a fortnight
before he had confined Paget to his house, and
forbidden him to communicate with any one, for
doubting the Emperor's word.[1]   As, however, the
Lord Treasurer (William Paulet, Baron St. John,
then Earl of Wiltshire, and afterwards Marquis of
Winchester), who had equally with Paget doubted
the Emperor's word, was left at liberty, it is fairly
obvious that that was not the true cause of Paget's
confinement.

The next step was to enhance the dignity and
authority of Warwick and his adherents.   On 4th
October it was determined in the Council (though
the private arrangements must have been made
some time before) that on the following Sunday
Warwick should be created Duke of Northumberland; Dorset, Duke of Suffolk; Wiltshire, Marquis
of Winchester; and Sir William Herbert, Earl of
Pembroke.[2]   To these honours were added knight-
hoods for Cecil, who had sold himself to Warwick;[3]

Promotion
of his
partisans.

---

[1] See *State Papers, Foreign Series*, Edw. VI., No. 461.

[2] *Acts of the Privy Council*, iii. 379, 380. The smaller fry of
Warwick's adherents had to be content with large grants out of
the lands of the bishopric of Winchester; see the Council's warrant-
book in *Royal MSS.* 18, C. xxiv. f. 135, where the bishop is ordered to
deliver over the deeds to Sir John Gates, Andrew Dudley, Henry
Neville, Sir Philip Hoby, and others. This was on 27th September 1551.

[3] There is really no other conclusion to be drawn from the fact
that Cecil was knighted at the very time of the fall of his first
friend and patron. The surprised congratulations showered on
Cecil on his escape from the fate that overtook Somerset confirm

Henry Sidney, who in the previous March had married Warwick's daughter; Henry Dudley, one of Warwick's brothers; and Henry Neville. The ceremony of these creations was got through without disturbance at Hampton Court on Sunday the 11th of October, and Northumberland now considered himself strong enough to strike at Somerset. For some days there had been a curious number of arrests in various shires, and of summonses of Northumberland's adherents to the Council.[1]   On 1st October Somerset, who was either at Sheen or Sion, was requested to come to court; the request

Arrest of Somerset. was repeated on the 3rd, and on the 4th he came. Three days later Sir Thomas Palmer, a brilliant but unprincipled soldier of the swashbuckler type, revealed to Northumberland—so at least the Duke told Edward VI., whose "Journal" is the only authority for the date and the fact—a conspiracy which he said Somerset and his friends had entered into about St. George's day (23rd April) to "raise the people." Other plots were detailed in Palmer's subsequent confessions, but for some days the matter was kept a secret. On the 11th, however, the same day that the elevation of Warwick and

the supposition. Pickering wrote from Paris congratulating him on his good fortune in being "found undefiled with the folly of this unfortunate Duke of Somerset," and Morison wrote that he was glad Cecil was "as far from shentings as void of fault; for it were a way to make an end of amity if when men fail their friends should forthwith be troubled therefor." He then added the cryptic remark that he perceived that the mark Cecil had "now a good while shot at was the service of their master" (*State Papers, Foreign Series*, Edw. VI., No. 488).

[1] *Acts of the Privy Council*, September and October 1551, *passim*.

his adherents took place, the Council directed an inquiry into the debts Somerset owed the Crown. This roused Somerset's suspicions that something more serious was in store for him than the loss of influence consequent upon the recent promotion of Warwick. On the 14th he made inquiries of Cecil, who returned a cold and formal answer; nevertheless he continued in attendance on the Council, and on the 16th, after dinner, he was arrested and sent to the Tower. Lord Grey, the Earl of Arundel, Sir Miles Partridge, Sir Michael Stanhope, Sir Thomas Arundell, Sir John Thynne, Sir Thomas Holcroft, the Duchess of Somerset, and other partisans were arrested on that or the following days, and either sent to the Tower or confined elsewhere.

So far Northumberland's plot had proved successful, but Somerset's hold on the popular imagination rendered his arrest a hazardous operation, and extraordinary precautions had to be taken to prevent commotions. The fathers of the city were ordered " to be greatly circumspect to see good and substantial watches and warding " kept, and to quicken their sense of duty they were informed that Somerset had schemed " to destroy the city of London and the substantial men of the same."

The new standing army—an institution so un-English that a French word, *gens d'armes*, had to be found to describe it—which had been organised a few months before, was summoned,[1] and in order to bribe the people into acquiescence the proclama-

Other measures.

---

[1] *Warrant-Book*, in *Royal MSS.*, C. xxiv. f. 158. "Letters to have the king's gendarmery and bands of horsemen which be herein ap-

tion for a new and purified coinage was hastened forth'.[1] In the prevailing state of opinion it was deemed inadvisable that Parliament, which was to have met on the 4th of November, should assemble, and on the 18th of October a commission was appointed for its prorogation.[2] Early in November a further important change took place in Northumberland's authority; hitherto all warrants, bills, and State Papers had been countersigned by six members of the Council, and in September Lord Chancellor Rich had refused to allow some documents to pass the Great Seal, because fewer than six signatures, besides the king's, were appended to them.[3] For this scruple he was taken to task by Northumberland, and on the 10th and 14th of November the Council decided that henceforth no signatures were to appear on such documents except that of the king, who had just reached the mature age of fourteen years.   This rendered Northumberland almost independent of the Council;[4] even the compliant Rich was terrified by this abuse of power, and feigned illness to avoid exercising the functions of his office under such conditions.

Meanwhile Northumberland was busily engaged in

pointed in a redynes. . . . The like to my Lord Marquis of Northampton . . . with all the pensioners and men at arms attending on the court."

[1] *Acts of the Privy Council*, iii. 400, "to hast forthe the Proclamacion for the coyne for the satisfaction of the people."

[2] Council *Warrant-Book*, in *Royal MSS*. 18, C. xxiv. f. 142*b*.

[3] *Ibid.*, f. 137 ; *Acts of the Privy Council*, iii. 411, 416.

[4] This regulation about countersigning had been in force during the Government of Somerset, who had been accused of such "arbitrary" proceedings.

the attempt to collect sufficient evidence to hang his
rival. According to the information that was given
to the young king, Crane, the principal witness
against Somerset, had by the 26th of October confessed "almost as much" as Sir Thomas Palmer ;[1]
but his confessions really amounted to very little,
and the victorious faction now had recourse to a
practice from which contemporary writers boasted
that England was free. On 5th November the
Council authorised the commissioners appointed to
examine the prisoners in the Tower to put them
" to suche tortours as they shall think expedient ; "[2]
and throughout November they were examined one
by one, sometimes by commissioners in the Tower,
and sometimes before the Council.[3] Only the deposition of Crane survives,[4] and that with the Earl of
Arundel's confession, or rather Northumberland's
version of it, constitutes the sole material now
extant on which to base an estimate of the truth of
the charges against Somerset. He himself confessed
nothing, and one day during the last week of
November[5] Northumberland wrote to Sir Philip
Hoby and the Lieutenant of the Tower complaining

[1] Edward VI.'s *Journal*, in *Literary Remains* (Roxburghe Club).

[2] *Acts of the Privy Council*, iii. 407. Tytler, whose examination
of Somerset's case and trial is by far the most complete and satisfactory, has overlooked this important fact, that the evidence
against the duke was obtained by the use of torture.

[3] Cf. *Acts of the Privy Council*, iii. 417.

[4] *State Papers, Domestic*, Edw. VI., vol. xiii. No. 65, printed in
Tytler, ii. 38–41.

[5] *Harleian MSS.*, 523, f. 26. An adequate treatment of the whole
question of the trial of Somerset would occupy far more space than
can here be given it. I have accordingly limited myself to the

of Somerset's silence, and ordering them to strip
from him the garter and collar of the order, even
at the cost of personal violence.   At the same time
they were to inform him that he was to be tried on
the following Tuesday (1st December), "so in the
meantime may he be the more readie to bewaile
his offences, as he hath great cause to do."   To
which Somerset replied that "he trusted the king
neither with right and justice could do [it], nor of
his goodnes and equitie would do [it]."

Somerset's
trial.

The official formalities for the trial were now
completed.   The special commission for taking the
indictments had been issued on 16th November,[1]
and on the same day were directed to the sheriffs,
the justices' precepts for the return of grand juries
in the city of London, the shire of Middlesex, and
county of Kent.   Those who have had the mis-
fortune to serve on a grand jury are aware that its
functions are not very important, and that even now

more important points, and, as far as possible, to documents which,
so far as I am aware, have not previously been used.   The letter
here quoted is one of these.

[1] The following details are all taken from the *Baga de Secretis*.
A portion of this important collection, dealing with the attainder of
Anne Boleyn, &c., was printed in an appendix to vol. i. of
Wriothesley's *Chronicle* (Camden Society).   All the documents to
the end of Elizabeth's reign are calendared in the Fourth Report of
the Deputy-Keeper of the Records, Appendix ii.   These documents
throw considerable light on the question of Somerset's trial.
Tytler, whose industry in bringing fresh documents to light was
extraordinary, remarks that only one of the indictments is extant ;
the whole series is, however, extant in the *Baga de Secretis*, in the
Record Office, which extends from the reign of Edward IV. to that
of George III., and contains the indictments and other records for
trials on charges of treason and other State offences.

true bills are, almost without exception, found as a
matter of course; and in those days the Crown
experienced even less difficulty in procuring indictments.   The Middlesex grand jury returned two
indictments; in one Somerset was charged with
having on 20th April 1551 compassed and imagined
with other persons at Somerset Place in the Strand
to deprive the king of his royal dignity, and to seize
his person.   In order to effect this end he, Sir
Michael Stanhope, Sir Miles Partridge, Sir Thomas
Holcroft, Francis Newdigate, and others assembled
for the purpose of taking and imprisoning John,
Duke of Northumberland, then Earl of Warwick,
one of the king's Council, and of seizing the Great
Seal and Tower of London.   "And furthermore
incited the citizens of London to rebellion and
insurrection against the king with drums and trumpets, crying out in English, 'Liberty! Liberty!'"
The other indictment was to the effect that on
20th May, at Somerset Place, the duke procured
Partridge and others to rise against the king, and
take and imprison Northumberland, Northampton,
and Pembroke (then Sir William Herbert).   The
indictment returned by the city jury was similar in
character, but found that the high treason had been
committed in St. Andrew's parish, Holborn.   The
jury of Kent found that on 21st April, at Greenwich, Somerset had conspired to rise and rebel
against the king, and take and imprison Northumberland, Northampton, and Herbert.

These indictments are more significant in their Charges
omissions than in the charges they make.   A great against him.

deal of ingenuity and industry has been expended
by historians on the question whether Somerset was
guilty of a scheme for assassinating Northumberland, Northampton, and Pembroke; some have answered in the affirmative and some in the negative,
but no one has pointed out the all-important circumstance that no hint of such a plot is contained
in the indictments on which Somerset was tried.
Such an omission seems fairly conclusive proof
that there was not the slightest evidence to support
the accusation. If there had been, the charge
would certainly have been made, for the indictments
did actually include accusations for which the evidence was so inconclusive that even a tribunal
packed by Northumberland was compelled, on these
counts, to acquit the prisoner. Nor does this
omission from the indictments stand alone; there
is a precisely similar and significant omission from
the questions addressed to Somerset during his
examination.[1]   Moreover, Paget, at whose house the
intended assassination was to have taken place, and
the Earl of Arundel, another accomplice, were never
brought to trial, though they were pronounced
enemies of Northumberland. Paget apparently was
never even questioned on the subject, and Arundel
affirmed on oath that no harm had been intended
to the persons of the supposed victims. The evidence for the assassination plot, which has by some
historians been regarded as conclusive, was thus in
reality so slight that the counsel for the prosecution did not even venture to charge the accused

[1] Printed in Tytler, ii. 48–51.

with it in public, or question them on it in private.[1]

The only charges that need be discussed are those contained in the indictments. These, it has been seen, amounted practically to two: the assembling together with others on one or two occasions for the purpose of "taking and imprisoning" the Duke of Northumberland, Northampton, and Pembroke; and inciting the citizens of London to rebellion and insurrection with drums and trumpets, crying out in English, "Liberty! Liberty!" By Act 3 & 4 Edward VI., c. 5, it had been declared high treason for twelve or more persons to assemble for

---

[1] The only authority for the charge is Edward VI.'s *Journal*, and it amounts to this, that some one, probably Northumberland, told the king that Palmer had made this accusation, and that Crane also had confessed it. The entries are in the Journal under date 7th October and 26th October. The first reports that Palmer said "a device was made to call the Earl of Warwick to a banquet [the king first wrote 'toure' (Tower), and then crossed that out and wrote 'banket'] with the Marquis of Northampton and divers others, and to cut off their heads." The second entry declares that Crane confessed that "the place where the nobles should have been banqueted and their heads cut off, was the Lord Paget's house." Whether Palmer made such an accusation or not, it is impossible to say, but it is practically certain that Crane made no such confession. It does not occur in his "information against the Duke of Somerset" in *State Papers, Domestic*, vol. xiii. No. 65, and it is doubtful whether he had made any confession at all by this time, for a week later it was found necessary to apply torture to the prisoners in the Tower, of whom Crane was one. These are only two among many instances in which the young king makes charges against Somerset that are entirely uncorroborated, or rather disproved by other evidence, and they show that those about the king instilled into his mind all sorts of suspicions of his uncle, with a view to securing Edward's acquiescence in the Protector's execution. More will be said about the value of his Journal when Somerset's trial is described.

the purpose of killing *or imprisoning* a Privy Councillor, if such persons refused to retire when ordered to do so by the sheriff.[1] Now, no evidence was adduced to show that Somerset and his accomplices had ever been ordered to disperse, and on this ground Coke delared that the verdict found against Somerset was not justified. The verdict, however, did not find him guilty of treason, but of felony, and it was probably through the above circumstance that the treason charge broke down. The same Act, however, made it felony for any one to call unlawful assemblies together by bell, trumpet, handbill, or outcry, and also to incite to such assemblies by open word or deed. One of the counts in the indictments was that Somerset had so incited the citizens of London, and it must have been on this count that a verdict was found against him.[2]

If to determine exactly on what count Somerset was condemned is difficult, it is impossible to decide with any certainty whether the charge on which he appears to have been condemned was true or not. Considering the total lack of corroborative evidence of Somerset's having incited the citizens of London to rebellion by drums, trumpets, and outcry, the accusation is scarcely credible. There

[1] *Statutes of the Realm*, Record edition, iii. 104–108.

[2] This is quite a different conclusion from those reached by all other writers on the subject, but I am the less deterred from suggesting it because no one has as yet made a comparison of the statute by which Somerset was condemned, the indictments against him, and the accounts of his trial. The usual course has been to say he was condemned for the other offences mentioned in Edward VI.'s *Journal*, though they do not occur in the indictments.

are some half-dozen chronicles or diaries extant which were kept by people living in London at the time,[1] and in none of them is there any hint of such a proceeding; the State Papers are equally silent, and it is sheer impossibility that, had such public incitement taken place, it should have been five months before the Government heard the least whisper of it. There remains the last possible charge, that the incitement was only by " open word." Of an offence like that there could be no evidence except that of the person who spoke the words and those to whom they were addressed; and then, of course, comes the conflict of evidence. The accuser swears to the affirmative and the accused to the negative, and it becomes a question of the veracity of men like Palmer and Crane on the one hand, and Somerset and his partisans on the other. There is little room for hesitation, and one final and significant circumstance goes far to remove what little doubt might otherwise remain. Somerset's three partisans— Vane, Stanhope, and Partridge—one and all with their last breath solemnly denied the charge, while there is good evidence [2] that both Northumberland

---

[1] *e.g.* Wriothesley's *Chronicle*, Greyfriars' *Chronicle*, *Narratives of the Reformation* (Camden Soc.), Edward VI.'s *Journal*, Grafton's *Chronicle*, to say nothing of the numerous letters printed in Ellis's *Original Letters* and the Parker Society's *Original Letters*, but the strongest argument is in the entire silence of the State Papers.

[2] The statement is made by Renard in a letter to Charles V. that Northumberland confessed this to Somerset's sons just before his execution. There was no possible motive for Renard to invent the story, and as it was a private and not a public confession, it is not strange that the chroniclers do not mention the fact.

and Palmer just before their execution confessed
that these same charges were false.   Such was the
evidence and such the accusations on which Somerset was condemned.   Sympathy has been denied to
Thomas Cromwell because he fell a victim to the
bloody laws which he himself procured.   By a
converse method of reasoning sympathy may be
claimed for Somerset, because his condemnation
would have been doubly impossible had the laws
as he left them remained in force.   The whole of
the case against him was based on the iniquitous
Act passed immediately after his first fall—an Act
in some respects unparalleled in English history.
By it alone was it made treason to conspire the
death or imprisonment of a Privy Councillor, by it
alone was it made felony to summon assemblies
which it alone declared illegal, or to incite to them
by " open word."   Nor was this all; the Act by
which Somerset abolished the majority of treasons
provided, with respect to the few that were left,
that accusations must be made within thirty days
of the commission of the offence.   The Act passed
on his fall contained no such provision, and five
months elapsed from the time of the offences with
which Somerset was charged and Palmer's accusation.   This Act, however, was only temporary; it
was to expire at the end of the following Parliament,
and for this, besides many other reasons, the proceedings against Somerset were completed before
Parliament was allowed to meet.

Methods of
his trial.

Had Somerset been a criminal of the deepest dye,
no casuistry could palliate the methods by which he

was tried.   It has been the practice of some historians to compare his trial with that of his brother
the Admiral, to the disadvantage of the latter
method.   It would be hard to mistake the form for
the reality more completely.   The charges against
the Admiral were discussed by the whole Council,
who waited on him and endeavoured to procure
answers to them : the witnesses against him were
men whose word, if any in that age, could be relied
upon, and his case was then discussed fully and
openly by both Houses of Parliament.   Contrast
the treatment of Somerset : there is no mention of
the Council as a whole ever having been consulted
on the charges.   The misdeeds of which Somerset
was accused were directed against Warwick's partisans : it was they who ordered his arrest, it was
they who drew up the charges and examined the
witnesses.   After having acted as accusers and
counsel for the prosecution, it was they who
assumed the function of judges; and finally it was
they who, having condemned their enemy, decided
whether he should be executed or not.

On the 28th of November Winchester was appointed Lord High Steward for the trial.   On the
30th the Lieutenant of the Tower was ordered to
bring up his prisoner for trial before his peers on
1st December at Westminster Hall.   The citizens
of London were commanded to remain indoors that
day, and a large force had been summoned to over-
awe the capital.   At five o'clock, in the darkness
of a December morning, Somerset was brought by
water from the Tower in order to avoid the risk of

a commotion or attempt at rescue. The court before
which he appeared was carefully selected; twenty-
six only out of forty-seven temporal peers had been
summoned, and the first three names were those
of Suffolk, Northumberland, and Northampton, and
lower down was Pembroke—the prisoner's bitterest
foes. Lord Chancellor Rich, who, as the highest
judge in the land, should have been prominent at
the trial, was suspected of leanings in Somerset's
favour, and he was kept away; Paget, Arundel, and
Lord Grey de Wilton were in the Tower. Among
others not summoned were the Earls of Oxford
and Shrewsbury, and Lords Clinton and Willoughby.
The accused was not confronted with the witnesses,
except Lord Strange, and he swore only to the trivial
charges that Somerset had employed him to secure
Edward VI.'s favourable consideration of a proposal
of marriage between the young king and one of
Somerset's daughters, and to give the Duke secret
information of the proceedings of the Council—both
of which Somerset denied on oath. "Then[1] was

[1] The manuscript from which I have transcribed this account of
Somerset's trial is extant in *Harleian MSS.* 2194, in a volume entitled
The Lord High Stewards of England. This volume contains most of
the treason-trials presided over by Lord High Stewards from the
time of Henry VII. to 1635. At first I thought it was a compilation
of about the latter date, and therefore not entitled to much
credence; but on examining the volume more closely, I found that
it was written in three different hands. On consulting the experts
in the British Museum MSS. Department I was told that the
handwriting of the earliest portion was probably about 1580 or
1590; this was confirmed when the volume was examined, and it
was found that this handwriting ceased with the trial of Philip
Howard, Earl of Arundel, in 1589. It was therefore almost certainly written by some one who was alive at the time of Somerset's

the examination of his accusers read, namely that
of Sir Thomas Palmer, a man neither lovinge nor
beloved of him.   Palmer's speech was seconded by

trial.   The officials were unable to give any particulars whatever as
to the history of the manuscript, except that it came to the Museum
with the other Harleian MSS.   It is obviously written by a sym-
pathiser with Somerset, and is not an official account of the trial ;
it is, however, quite impossible to say where the writer obtained
his information.   The account seems to me extremely probable ; it
fits in better with the indictments than any other account, and is
confirmed in many other details by independent evidence.   From
it Hayward has taken almost verbally his description of the Protector's trial.

The expression describing Palmer "a man neither loving nor
beloved of" [Somerset] is singular, because it is so like the phrase
"hating the duke and hated of him," which was inserted, in a
sixteenth-century hand, in Edward VI.'s Journal, where the young
king gives an account of Palmer's first information against Somerset.
I have carefully compared the two hands ; they are similar but not
the same.   The insertion in Edward's Journal was afterwards
crossed out.   It would be interesting to discover who made the
insertion ; for the MSS. of the Journal remained in the Royal
Library until about 1610, when it passed into Sir Robert Cotton's
hands (it is now in the British Museum, *Cotton MSS.*, Nero, C. x.).

There is another brief account of the trial in a letter from John
ab Ulmis to Bullinger (*Original Letters*, Parker Soc., 439 *et seq.*)
written nearly two months later, but it is not of much authority,
and only represents what Northumberland wished the foreign Protestants to believe.

The young king's account of the trial, on which alone modern
historians have been content to rely, is as follows : "1st Decem.
The Duke of Somerset came to his trial at Westminster Hall.   The
Lord Treasurer (Paulet, Marquis of Winchester) sat as High
Steward of England, under the cloth of estate, on a bench between
two posts, three degrees high.   All the Lords to the number of
twenty-six, viz. [he then gives a list of them].   These sat a degree
under, and heard the matter debated.   First, after the indictments
read, five in number, the learned counsel laid to my Lord of
Somerset, Palmer's confession.   To which he answered, that he
never minded to raise the north ; and declared all ill he could
devise of Palmer ; but he was afeard for bruits, and that moved him

one Crane, a man who, having consumed his owne estate, had armed himselfe to any mischeife; thirdly,

to send to Sir William Herbert; replied it was again, that the worse Palmer was, the more he served his purpose.

"For the banquet, first he sware it was untrue, and required more witnesses; whence Crane's confession was read, he would have had him come face to face. For London, he meant nothing for hurt of any lord, but for his own defence. For the gens d'armery, it were but a mad matter for him to enterprise with his one hundred against nine hundred. For having men in his chamber at Greenwich, confessed by Partridge, it seemed he meant no harm; because, when he could have done harm, he did it not. My Lord Strange's confession, he swore it was untrue; and the Lord Strange took his oath it was true. Newdigate's, Hammond's, and Alex. Seymour's confessions he denied, because they were his men.

"The lawyers rehearsed, how to raise men at his house for an ill intent, as to kill the Duke of Northumberland, was treason by an Act anno 3° of my reign, against unlawful assemblies; for to devise the death of the lords was felony [it was in reality treason]; to mind resisting his attachment was felony; to raise London was treason; and to assault the lords was felony. He answered, he did not intend to raise London, and sware that the witnesses were not there; this assembling of men was but for his own defence. He did not determine to kill the Duke of Northumberland, the Marquis, etc., but spake of it, and determined after the contrary; and yet seemed to confess he went about their death.

"The Lords went together. The Duke of Northumberland would not agree that any searching of his death should be treason; so the Lords acquitted him of high treason and condemned him of treason felonious; and so he was adjudged to be hanged. He gave thanks to the Lords for their open trial, and cried mercy of the Duke of Northumberland, the Marquis of Northampton, and the Earl of Pembroke, for his ill-meaning against them, and made suit for his life, wife, children, servants, and debts, and so departed without the axe of the Tower. The people, knowing not the matter, shouted half-a-dozen times so loud that from the palace hall-door it was heard at Charing-cross plain, and rumours went that he was quit of all."

This account has been treated as though it were that of a skilled law-reporter, who was present in person at the trial. Now, Edward was not present at the trial, and he was only fourteen years old. All he knew of the trial must have been told him by somebody, and

affirmed by one Whally,[1] a busie-headed man, desirous to be sett on worke. Against these persons
were obiected many thinges by the Duke; especially
against Sir Thomas Palmer he spake much evill,

as Northumberland's *coup d'élat* of October had removed every
one from court except his devoted adherents, that somebody must
have been Northumberland himself, or a tool whom he could trust.
The version in Edward's Journal is therefore practically Northumberland's version of the trial. It must not be forgotten that
Northumberland's aim was to remove Somerset, and in order to do
so it was necessary thoroughly to prejudice the young king's mind
against his uncle. The young king's account is exactly what might
be expected under such circumstances. There is no mention of
Somerset's effective retort (see p. 304) to the remark that the
worse Palmer was, the more fitted he was to be Somerset's instrument ; the dissensions among the peers is passed over in silence,
and all the credit for clemency is given to Northumberland, Suffolk
not being mentioned (see p. 304) ; and the remark that "Somerset
seemed to confess" is utterly unsupported by any evidence whatever. The fact, all-important as it would have been, is not mentioned in Winchester's account of the trial written on the following
day (printed in Tytler, ii. p. 63–5). Similarly the whole story of
Somerset's thanking the Lords for open trial and throwing himself on their mercy is probably fiction. At the time of his execution the report was spread about that it was just because he refused
to throw himself on their mercy that he was put to death.

As if to clinch the argument against the genuineness of Somerset's
plot, all the chief witnesses who had been implicated were soon
after released. Palmer, who was supposed to be such a villain,
became Northumberland's right-hand man ; Crane and Hammond
were released without penalty. Berteville, who is alleged to have
been the instrument selected by Somerset for the assassination of
Northumberland, had been set at liberty on 1st November, and on
28th February 1551-2 was, by order of the Council, provided with
a house "where he may be well intreated, and his charges shall be
allowed" (*Acts of the Privy Council*, iii. 491).

[1] For Richard Whalley see *Dict. Nat. Biogr.*, lx. 399. He had
previously been imprisoned for intriguing in Somerset's favour,
and was again sent to the Tower on 18th October 1551. As a
reward for turning king's evidence he was never tried for his own
share in the alleged conspiracy.

and yet in the opinion of many farr short of the trueth.   Wheretoe noe answere was made but that the worse they were the fitter they were to be his instruments.   'Fitt instruments, indeed,' said the Duke, 'but rather for others than for me.'   The Lords went togeather, and first the duke of Norfolke[1] nobly said that he heald it not reasonable that beinge but a meane action shoulde be drawne to intention of Treason.   The duke of Northumberland in countenance bearinge shewe of sadnesse (but in trueth stifly obstinate) denyed that he woulde ever consent that any practise against him should bee either imputed or reputed treason,[2] yett this was not taken to proceede from modesty, as hee expected, but that he could not with his honour or reason so enforce it.

"The Marquess of Northampton was crossinge and contentious with many, but replyed not to any answeare, a manifest token of no strong spirit. Some of the rest brake forth that they held it unfitt that the duke of Northumberland, the marquess of Northampton, and the Earle of Pembroke, should bee of the tryall because the prisoner was

---

[1] So the MS.   The Duke of Suffolk is obviously meant.

[2] This was afterwards interpreted as magnanimity on Northumberland's part, and so Winchester represented it in a letter he wrote to Clinton the day after the trial (printed in Tytler, ii. 63–65).   The cant of this was nauseating ; death was the penalty for the felony as well as for the treason ; the advantage felony gave the prisoner was that it did not affect his lands, but a special Act of Parliament was passed immediately after Somerset's execution, taking away his lands (see the Act of Parliament passed in September 1660 in favour of his descendant William Seymour, Marquis of Hertford, thereby restored to the Dukedom of Somerset).

cheifely charged with practices intended against them : but hereto answere was made that a Peere of the Realme might not be challenged. After much variation of opinions, the prisoner at the barr was acquitt of treason; but by voyces most favouringe the Duke of Northumberland he was found guilty of felony and had judgement to dye."

Somerset was led away with the axe of the Tower turned back. Outside Westminster Hall the people in thousands awaited the result of the trial. Seeing the axe turned away from the prisoner, they thought the duke was acquitted, and throwing their caps in the air, they raised a shout of joy which pealed up Whitehall and was echoed across Long Acre fields. The crowds that lined his route back to the Tower cried " God save him ! " all the way,[1] and far away at Bath church bells were rung and bonfires lighted in honour of the " good Duke's " supposed acquittal.[2] Felony, however, served Northumberland's purpose as well as treason, and Somerset went back to the Tower under sentence of death. His previous imprisonment had been whiled away in writing a preface for a devotional

[1] Wriothesley, ii. 63. " The people . . . made such a shryke and castinge up of caps that it was heard into the Long Acre beyond Charinge Crosse, and also made the Lordes astonyed, and word likewise sent to London, which the people reioysed at ; and about v of the clock the sayd Duke landed at the Crane in the Vintre, and so had thorough Canwyke Streete to the Tower, the people cryinge God saue him all the way as he went. . . ."

[2] *Acts of the Privy Council*, iii. 462. For this offence the Duke's sympathisers were summoned before the Council.

work[1] and in translating a letter from Calvin. He now again turned to the consolations of religion, and some of his reflections on the day before his death have been preserved.[2] Meanwhile Parliament had been summoned to meet on 23rd January 1551–2, and Northumberland felt it necessary to get rid of Somerset before that date. There was no expectation that he would be executed, and to prepare men's minds for such a step he spread reports that pardon had been offered the fallen Protector, but that he had refused to make his submission. There was no time to be lost, but, packed as the Council was by Northumberland's nominees, and poisoned as the king's mind was against his uncle by the misrepresentations of his enemies, Northumberland still anticipated difficulty in bringing king and Council to assent to the Protector's execution. The tale of his evil deeds was not yet complete. On 18th January 1551–2 Edward drew up in his own hand "certain points of weighty matters to be immediately concluded on by my Council." Among them was the following note: "The matter for the Duke

---

[1] *i.e.* Wermueller's *Spiritual and Precious Pearle*, which went through many editions ; see Hazlitt's *Bibliographical Handbook* and *Collections.*

[2] In *Stow MS.*, 1066, which a few years ago was acquired by the British Museum. It is a little calendar on the fly-leaf of which Somerset wrote, " Fere of the Lorde is the begynning of wisdome." " Put thy trust in the Lord with all thine hart." " Be not wise in thyne owne conseyt but fere the Lord." " From the Towar the day before my dethe 1551 [–2]. E. Somerset." This little book afterwards belonged to Somerset's daughter-in-law, Catherine Grey, Countess of Hertford, who also used it in the Tower. Inside the cover she wrote her name, "Catherine Seamoure, Catherine Hartford."

of Somerset's confederates to be considered as aparteineth to our surety and quietnes of our realme, that by their punishment example may be shewed to others." In other words, the Council was ordered to take measures for bringing to trial Somerset's confederates, who were in prison but had not yet been tried. The Council met to discuss the matter on the following day, but before Edward's memorandum was submitted to its consideration, it had, by means of interlineations and erasures, been made to read as follows: " The matter for the Duke of Somerset *and* his confederates to be considered . . . that by their punishment *and execution according to the lawes,* example etc." [1] The order for the trial of Somerset's confederates had become an order for the execution of the duke. He was not directly referred to in the king's original note; in the amended version laid before the Council, his was the only execution contemplated, for arrangements could scarcely be made for his confederates' execution before they had been tried. There can be no doubt under whose pressure the king made the alteration—if he made it. On this point experts differ; one thinks the interlineations to be in Edward's own hand, another considers them forged, and in either case the moral obliquity is about equal. Armed with this instruction, Northumberland apparently secured the

---

[1] This document is extant in *Cotton MSS.,* Vespasian, F. xiii. f. 171; the officials in the MSS. Department of the British Museum were kind enough to give me their opinion on the authorship of these alterations.

consent of the Council to Somerset's immediate execution, though no record of its deliberations or decision occurs in the Council's official register. The same precautions that attended his trial were observed in the arrangements for his execution. It was fixed for the 22nd of January at eight o'clock in the morning, "when no one expected such an event."[1]   Nevertheless Tower Hill was crowded when the duke mounted the scaffold. His speech, often printed, is too characteristic to be omitted.[2]

His execution.

" 'Masters and good fellows,' he began, ' I am come hither for to die; but a true and faithful man as any was unto the Kings Majesty, and to his realme.   But I am condemned by a law whereunto I am subject, and as we all ; and therefore to shew obedience I am content to die ; wherewith I am well content, being a thing most heartily welcome unto me ; for the which I do thank God, taking it for a singular benefit, and as great a benefit as ever might come to me any otherwise. For as I am a man, I have deserved at God's hand many deaths ; and it hath pleased his goodness, whereas he might have taken me suddenly that I should neither have known him nor myself, thus now to visit me and call me with this present death as you do see, when I have had time to remember

---

[1] *Original Letters* (Parker Soc.), ii. 731, 732.

[2] This account was printed by Sir Henry Ellis from a Cotton MS. in his *Original Letters*, 2nd Ser., ii. 215, 216; slightly different accounts are given in Stow and in Burgoyne's Letter to Calvin, *Original Letters* (Parker Soc.), ii. 731–737.   It is confirmed by Wriothesley, *Chron.*, ii. 65.

and knowledge him, and to know also myself; for which thing I do thank him most heartily.   And, my friends, more I have to say unto you concerning religion.   I have been always, being in authority, a furtherer of it to the glory of God, to the uttermost of my power, whereof I am nothing sorry, but rather have cawes and doo rejoyce most gladlye that I have so done for the greatest benefyt of God that ever I had, or any man myght have in thys world; besechyng you all to take yt soo and to follow yt on styll, for yf not ther wyll follow and come a worse and great plage.'

" Sodenly came a wonderous ffeare apon the peoplle after thos wordes of hym spoken, by a great sowend whych appered unto many abowe in the element as yt had byne the sowend of gunpowder set on fyre in a close howes burstynge out, and by a nother sowend apon the growend as yt had byn the syght of a greate nomber of greate horses ronnynge on the people to overe ronne them; so greate was the sowend of thys, that the peoplle fell dowen one apon the other, many with bylles, and other rone som thys waye some that waye, cryeng alowed, ' Jesus save us, Jesus save us.' Many of the peoplle cryeng ' Thys waye thaye come, that waye theye come, awaye, awaye.'   And I loked when one or other shuld stryke me on the hedd, so was I stonned.   The peoplle beyng thus amassed, espyes Syr Anthony Brown apone a lytell nage rydyng toward the scaffold, and therewythe burste out cryenge in a voyce, ' Pardon, pardon, pardon,' heorlyng up their cappes and clokes wythe thes wordes saying, ' God save the kynge, God save the kynge.' [1] The good Duke all thys whyell stayed, and wythe his cappe in hys hand wayted the peoplle to come together, saynge these wordes to ther wordes of pardon, ' Ther ys no such thynge good peoplle, there ys no such thynge, yt ys the ordynans of God thus for to dye where wythe we moste be content; and I praye yow now lette us praye together ffor the Kynges Maieste, to whouse Grace I have bynne allwayes a ffaythefull, trewe, and moste lovyng subjecte, desyros allwayes of hys moste prosperos succes in all hys affayres; and ever glad of the ffurtherance and helpyng ffortheward of the Commen Welthe of thys Realme.' At whyche wordes the peoplle awensewered, ' Ye, ye, ye '; and som sayd wyth a lowed voyce, ' That is fowend now to trew.' ' To whouse Grace I beseche God to send and grant to rayngne moste prosperoslye to the pleasor of God.' " Then murmuring " Lord Jesus, save me," he laid his head upon the block, and as the executioner's stroke fell the people started forward to dip their handkerchiefs in the blood of one they looked on as a martyr in their cause. So died Somerset, without a word of reproach against his enemies, without a regret for the life he was losing, and with a confidence born of a clear conscience, that whatsoever he had done he had done for the glory of God and the welfare of his country. Exactly nineteen months later Northumberland

---

[1] See also Elizabeth Huggons's testimony in *Harleian MSS.*, 353, f. 121. She said that Somerset might easily have escaped in the confusion had he wished to do so.

stood on the same scaffold. In abject degradation
he declared that he had lived the life of a hypo-
crite, that his faith had really been that of the
bishops he deprived and the priests he persecuted,
and piteously he begged for life, " yea, even the
life of a dog." [1] In politics a simple faith may be a
poor substitute for the arts of Macchiavelli, and
Somerset may have been no match for the craft
and subtlety of his rival, but when the hour came
he could at least die with decency and spirit.

The death of Somerset was the crowning-point
of Northumberland's infamy; it burnt deep into the
minds of the people, and from that time they only
awaited an opportunity for throwing off his yoke.
His own daughter-in-law declared that he was
" hated and evil spoken of by the commons," and
that " his life was odious to all men "; and when
on Edward's death Northumberland sought to
secure for her the crown and the crown matrimonial for his son, these pent-up feelings broke out.
The tide of popular enthusiasm which bore Mary to
the throne was not primarily a reaction against the
Reformation, and had the question of deciding between Mary and Northumberland been confined to
Protestants, the issue would have been the same.
In Norfolk, the scene of Northumberland's triumph
over the commons, these commons, Protestant
though they were, rose as one man and flocked
to Mary's standard. In London the people who
had dipped their handkerchiefs in Somerset's blood

[1] Northumberland's speech on the scaffold is preserved in British
Museum *Royal MSS.*, 12 A. xxvi.

wept for joy as Mary rode through the streets to claim her rightful inheritance, and never in the memory of man had there been such demonstrations of delight.[1] They welcomed in Mary not merely the representative of hereditary right, nor the champion of the Roman faith, for when Gilbert Bourne a month later began to preach up the old doctrines these same citizens of London broke out in riot,[2] but they welcomed in her their deliverer from the violence and iniquity of Northumberland's rule. Nor was this hope of better government altogether vain.   The first words of the first Act of Mary's first Parliament declared that the " state of every king, ruler, and governor of any realm, dominion, or commonalty standeth and consisteth more assured by the love and favour of the subjects towards their sovereign ruler and governor than in the dread and fear of laws made with rigorous pains and extreme punishment." With pointed allusion to Somerset, it recalled the fact that " Many as well honourable and noble persons as others of good reputation within this her Grace's realm of England have of late (for words only, without other opinion, fact, or deed) suffered shameful death not accustomed to nobles." Thus echoing the sentiments and even words of the statute by which Somerset had swept away the treasons created since 1352, the first Act of Mary's reign proceeded to

---

[1] Contemporary letters in *Harleian MSS.*, 353, ff. 139 *et seqq.* ; Wriothesley, *Chronicle*, ii. 88, 89 ; *Chronicle of Queen Jane* (Camden Society) ; Stow ; Holinshed.

[2] Wriothesley, ii. 97, 98.

repeal those which Northumberland had again placed on the Statute-book.[1] It is true that this early promise soon withered away. Wyatt's rebellion was followed by a new treason law,[2] and the traditions of arbitrary government were handed down through the reigns of Elizabeth and the Stuarts. It was nearly a century and a half before England again secured the measure of freedom and toleration she had enjoyed under the government of Protector Somerset.

[1] Statute 1 Mary c. 1.
[2] Statute 1 & 2 Philip and Mary c. 10.

CHAPTER XII

THE PROTECTOR'S WORK AND CHARACTER

THE heated atmosphere of theological controversy which clings around the history of the sixteenth century has distorted and obscured, in the eyes of posterity, the lineaments and features of the men who made it. The Protector has been included somewhat indiscriminately in the diatribes which Catholic writers have levelled at the whole class of Reformers, but a corresponding exaltation at the hands of Protestants has been effectually checked by the fact that the bitterest of Somerset's foes were men who professed more fanatically than he the Reformed religion. To the poor of his time he was affectionately known as " the good duke," and their view has been adopted by some eminent historical writers, while others have found in Cæsar Borgia [1] the nearest parallel to the Protector. These divergent views merely accentuate the good or evil elements out of which was formed Somerset's, like every other, character. He was indeed a man of many faults, some of them serious, and one at least amounting to a vice; but at the same time he possessed virtues which stand out in sharp contrast with the prevailing characteristics of his age.

[1] Sharon Turner.

314

The blot that has left the deepest stain upon his memory is the rapacity with which he profited by the spoliation of the Church. His original inheritance, some £2400 a year, had by 1547 been nearly doubled, and before his death another £3000 had been added, of which a considerable portion at least consisted of Church lands.[1] While the treasury was exhausted, the extravagance of Somerset House was an offence in the eyes of all men, and when, in order to provide materials for it, the Protector demolished the aisle of St. Paul's, containing the "Dance of Death," he incurred the charge, not merely of sacrilege, but also of vandalism. In this respect Somerset was tainted like his contemporaries. "We," wrote Sir William Petre, "which talk much of Christ and His Holy Word, have I fear me used a much contrary way; for we leave fishing for men and fish again in the tempestuous seas of this world for gain and wicked mammon."[2] The confession was unique, but the vice was universal. Catholic and Protestant were equally guilty. Petre himself was a Romanist at heart, but his angling brought him thirty-six thousand acres in Devon alone, and the iron will of Mary, in the fervour of religious reaction, failed to wring from her Catholic nobility lands that had been robbed from the Church. Somerset had at least the excuse that

---

[1] These figures must be multiplied by ten at least to bring them into relation with the value of our present currency. See *Wiltshire Archæological Magazine*, xv. 189 ; for details of Somerset's property see also *Cartæ Edwardi Ducis Somerset* and *Grants of the Forfeited Lands of Edward, Duke of Somerset*, both privately printed by Sir Thomas Phillipps, London, 1866, fol.   [2] Tytler, i. 427.

monastic endowments were to him unclean things,
but it would have been better for his memory had
he refrained from touching them.   Against his
participation in ecclesiastical spoliation, however,
must be set the Protector's championship of the
Commons against enclosures.   This has been attributed to mere love of popularity on his part, but
when this charge is made, it may well be asked how
many seekers after the favour of the multitude
have done what Somerset did, and used their influence to procure special Acts of Parliament in
favour of their tenants and to the detriment of
themselves.   In 1548 the Protector carried through
Parliament a bill[1] giving his mesne tenants, who
were tenants at will, equal privileges with copy-
holders on other men's lands, and a security which
they could not have enjoyed by common law or
any statute then in force.[2]   The Protector's appropriation of Church lands may not have been
justifiable, but at least the tenants on those lands
were vastly the gainers by the change, and no
more conclusive proof is possible of the genuineness
of his sympathy with the poor.

Compared with his rapacity Somerset's other
failings were trivial.   It is said he was ambitious,
and copy-book morality would have it that ambition
is a grievous fault.   That entirely depends upon
the motive that lies behind it, and the only test of
its character comes when private ambition conflicts
with public welfare.   By that test Northumberland

---

[1] 2 & 3 Edward VI. c. 12.
[2] Leadam, *Court of Requests* (Selden Soc.), p. lviii.

fails, but Somerset does not; he regarded power not
as an end in itself, but as a means to achieve ends
which he was profoundly convinced were just and
necessary—the union of England and Scotland, the
mitigation of the hardships of the poorer classes
and of the severity of the laws, and the purifying of
religion. Had he been less eager to attain these
objects, and more mindful of his own immediate
interests, he might have retained his power until
the end of Edward's reign. Ambitious he certainly
was; the mere seizure of power on Henry VIII.'s
death is enough to prove it; yet his was an ambition
animated by no mean or selfish motives, but by the
desire to achieve aims that were essentially noble,
however ill-judged the means that he took to attain
them. Their success was indeed largely impeded
by the methods the Protector adopted. When the
younger Pitt was asked what quality he considered
most essential to a statesman, he replied, " Patience,"
and patience was what Somerset most lacked.
Ardent and enthusiastic by nature, he fixed his
gaze on a distant goal and overlooked the obstacles
that beset his feet. Gladstone remarked of Peel
that he was clear-sighted rather than far-sighted.
Somerset was far-sighted but not clear-sighted.
Gifted with no little political imagination, he perceived better than any of his contemporaries some
of the lines on which the development of Great
Britain was bound to proceed, but he was little
fitted to carry out in detail the policy he knew to
be right. He was a man of ideas rather than a
statesman; one of the few idealists who have at-

tempted to govern England, he had all the idealist's impatience of the petty arts of management which enter so largely into the successful government of men. He thought his own will and authority strong enough to overcome the "devil, private profit, self-love, and such like the devil's instruments," and when he found he had underrated the power of the forces opposed to him, he became headstrong and irritable. He upbraided his inferiors with such vehemence that sometimes they burst into tears,[1] and his obstinate self-will offended many who might otherwise have supported him.

These outbursts were the temporary aberrations of a nature singularly lovable. Nothing is more extraordinary than the personal affection which men most opposed to him felt for Somerset. His widowed duchess was one of the prisoners in the Tower whom Mary kissed and called "her prisoners," and released on her first arrival in London;[2] and she is said to have wished to restore the Protector's sons to their lands and dignities. Gardiner had similar feelings, and a few weeks after his fall Wriothesley was seen conversing in a friendly and confidential manner with Somerset. From all quarters came tributes to his "mildness," and not infrequently it was made a matter of reproach. It sprang from a sensitiveness which was at the root of Somerset's nature, and distinguishes him most strongly from all the statesmen of his time. In the

---

[1] See Paget's letters of complaint printed in Strype, *Ecclesiastical Memorials*, vol. ii. Part II.

[2] *Harleian MSS.*, 353, f. 140.

whole of his correspondence and reported sayings there is scarcely to be found a coarse or brutal word, and his personal morality seems to have been singularly pure.[1] The same almost feminine sensitiveness came out in Somerset's aversion from violence in every shape or form, and was probably not without influence in producing that love of liberty which is now held to be Somerset's chief virtue, but was then regarded as reprehensible weakness. It was against "liberty" that Paget warned him while still Earl of Hertford, and "liberty" was the cry with which he was accused at the end of his career of having sought to raise the citizens of London.

---

[1] In the "Lives of the Berkeleys," by John Smith or Smyth (1567-1640), the pedigree is given of the descendants of one John Seymour, who is described as "base" son of the Duke of Somerset (see *Lives of the Berkeleys*, ed. Sir John Maclean, ii. 238, 239). Though Smith and Maclean were careful genealogists, this epithet "base," is, I believe, a mistake. The John Seymour referred to was one of Somerset's two sons, by his first wife, Catherine Fillol. The statement in the peerages, made on the authority of an MS. note in Vincent's "Baronage," in the College of Arms, to the effect that this first wife was divorced on account of misconduct, though I have adopted it in the "Dictionary of National Biography," is probably an error. Somerset's first wife was dead at any rate before 1540, and almost certainly before he married his second wife. The entail which settled his estates and titles on the issue of his second marriage was confirmed by Parliament in 1540. It was no doubt due to the influence of his second wife, Anne Stanhope, a lady of "haughty stomach" and royal descent. The line of this younger branch died out in the eighteenth century, when the elder branch succeeded to the dukedom, in which branch it still remains. An ineffectual attempt was made in 1553 by Sir Edward Seymour, the surviving son of the duke's first marriage (John died in the Tower on 19th December 1552), to persuade Parliament to break the entail in his favour. It is a curious fact that Somerset had three sons named Edward.

It was to his feelings that the wrongs of the commons appealed, and his vehement expressions of sympathy seem exaggerated and sentimental unless the grievousness of those wrongs is realised. A similar strain of feeling, quickened by religious conviction, led him to regard duelling as an immoral practice—a view which took three centuries to prevail in England. He declared it "a heathenish custom, whereas Christians by a just hearing avoid the chance of losing both the body and soul of one party; therefore we forbid fights that tend rather to vain glory than to true trial." This sensitiveness was the result of highly-strung nerves, and though highly-strung nerves produce delicacy of feeling, they were a serious impediment to a ruler in that age of violence, and Somerset's failure was due as much to his hatred of compromise and the baser arts of the politician as to a certain inflexibility of character. This lack of suppleness is evident in his somewhat wooden handwriting and in his portraits.[1]

The iconoclasm of the Reformers has led to the

---

[1] The engraving by Houbraken from Holbein's portrait gives Somerset an austere and almost melancholy expression. The forehead is high and broad, the nose straight and large, the beard and thin moustache are long. The features are regular and handsome, and the general impression is of a refined personality. His portraits are absolutely different from those of any other Tudor statesman, except his brother the Admiral. The Holbein portrait belongs to the Duke of Northumberland. Two anonymous portraits are at Sudeley Castle, and two others, also anonymous, are known (see *Cat. First Loan Exhibition at South Kensington*, Nos. 168, 174). Houbraken's engraving is given in Birch's " Lives," and another in Holland's " Herwologia."

impression that as a whole they were an ignorant class. The reproach does not apply to Somerset; the parallels he quotes in his "Epistle" to the Scots in 1548 show that he was well read in the history of his own and other countries, and like most Tudor statesmen he was a good linguist. It is a curious fact that the French ambassador to England did not understand a word of English, and that the members of the Privy Council were quite able to converse with him in French. Somerset was also—and this too was a matter of course in that age—a competent Latinist, and he probably had a fair knowledge of German. As a theologian he was not contemptible, and he had some acquaintance at least with the works of the Fathers. Nevertheless he was undeniably an iconoclast; he was entirely devoid of those æsthetic and artistic feelings with which even a Puritan like Milton was so deeply imbued, and his nearest approach to an artistic accomplishment was his gift of eloquence and mastery of good English prose.

In doctrinal matters the Protector's views are said to have tended towards that unlovely form of theology which pitilessly consigns the greater part of mankind to foredoomed and everlasting perdition, but his was a Calvinism with few Calvinistic features. In any case, what a man believes matters little compared with the spirit in which he believes it. If Somerset was a "rank Calvinist," it is insignificant compared with the fact that he burnt no Servetus. In the long roll of martyrs to the Roman faith, in the piteous catalogue of tortured sectaries, there is not one who owes injury in life or limb to the Protector. Henry VIII. burnt Gospellers for heresy, and hanged Catholics for treason : Somerset blotted out heresy laws and treason laws alike from the Statute-book. While he ruled, the Smithfield fires remained unlit, and the thumbscrew and the rack stood idle in the Tower. When he fell, religious persecution once more resumed its wonted sway. Anabaptists and priests under Northumberland, Reformers under Mary, and priests and Puritans under Elizabeth and the Stuarts were tortured or proscribed for opinions and beliefs. The torch of political and religious liberty which the Protector had kindled was for many generations quenched in smoke.

Failure, indeed, is written scornfully across the history of Somerset's career. Men who grant the nobility of his intentions, contemn him as a weak enthusiast whose aims and ambitions led but to the block. Many another shining light has gone out that way, but failure is not the verdict on their life and work. Unless might is to be identified with right, and the physical to be confused with the moral order of the world, aims, rather than achievements, must be the final test applied to man. With all his faults of method and defects of character, Somerset had instincts of genuine statesmanship, which raised him above the personal ambitions and unprincipled time-serving of his colleagues. His means were inadequate, his time was short, and the men with whom he worked had no eye for

the loftiness of his aims, and no sympathy with
the motives that impelled him.   Yet his achievements were of no mean order.   He was born
before his time, a seer of visions and a dreamer
of dreams; but his visions were visions of the
future, and his dreams were dreams that came
true.   Immediate failure was but the prelude to
ultimate success.   His repeal of the heresy laws,
his removal of the restrictions on the printing-press,
his refusal to persecute for religious opinion, anticipated some of the reforms which are justly ranked
among the greatest of the privileges enjoyed by
Britons.   The policy of sympathy towards the poor
which the Protector by means of a transient
authority sought to enforce, is now compelled by
the surer method of a liberal franchise.   England
and Scotland have become the Great Britain of
which Somerset dreamt, a realm having " the sea
for a wall, mutual love for a garrison, and no need
in peace to be ashamed, or in war to be afraid
of any worldly power."   The religious revolution, so
far as he carried it, has been permanently established.   The treason laws which he abolished are
now a byword, and that love of liberty which
proved a stumbling-block to his contemporaries is
become the corner-stone of the British constitution.
So long as civil and religious freedom remain ideals
of English-speaking peoples, the Protector Somerset
will be entitled to grateful remembrance as one
who brought his country at least one step nearer
toleration, and added at least one stone to the
temple of liberty.

APPENDIX

APPENDIX

A DESCRIPTIVE CATALOGUE OF MATERIALS FOR, AND WORKS ON, THE HISTORY OF SOMERSET'S PROTECTORATE

A. Manuscript Sources

The most important source for the history of the period is the State Papers in the Record Office. They are now arranged in three classes—papers relating to domestic affairs, to Scotland, and to foreign affairs. Of the Domestic State Papers, there are nine volumes in the original series relating to the years 1547–1549. But a number of State Papers relating to domestic affairs were discovered comparatively recently, and they are described as "Addenda" to the Domestic State Papers. Three volumes of the "Addenda" are concerned with the first three years of Edward VI.'s reign, and they relate almost exclusively to matters connected with the Scottish Borders. Four volumes of State Papers relating to Scotland cover the period of Somerset's rule. The State Papers relating to foreign affairs are not so numerous.

State Papers are, however, but a small portion of the materials for the history of the period preserved in the Record Office. The voluminous records of the Court of Star Chamber have already been mentioned in the text.

Scarcely less voluminous and equally unexplored are the records of the Court of Augmentations. There are also records, but much more scanty, of the Court of Requests, and some of these have been used by Mr. I. S. Leadam in his "Select Cases" (Selden Society, 1897). Other documents to which reference must frequently be made are the Close and Patent Rolls and the *Inquisitiones Post-Mortem*. The *Baga de Secretis* has already (p. 292) been mentioned, and other materials of a miscellaneous character are dealt with in the various reports of the Deputy-Keeper of the Records, in Mr. J. Scargill-Bird's "Guide to Documents Preserved in the Record Office," 1896, and in the "Lists and Indexes" now being issued by the Record Office.

Owing, however, to the lax views as to property in State Papers which prevailed down to the eighteenth century, the vast bulk of them passed out of the possession of the State into private hands, some to be destroyed, others to be preserved with equal if not greater care than would have been their lot had they remained under State control. The theory was that State Papers were the property of the particular holder of office to whom they were addressed or by whom they were written. Of these, fortunately a great number found their way to the British Museum, and in some respects the manuscripts in the British Museum are even more indispensable to the student than those in the Record Office. The two finest collections are the Cottonian and Harleian, made respectively by Sir Robert Bruce Cotton and Sir Robert Harley, afterwards Earl of Oxford. It is quite impossible to give here a list of the manuscripts in these collections bearing on the history of the Protectorate, and unfortunately they are arranged and catalogued in a most confused way. Some help is rendered by the chronological catalogue of separate MSS. which is kept in the Manuscript Department of the British Museum, but the dates there assigned to documents are almost as frequently wrong as they are right. A few of the more important volumes are Caligula, E. iii. and iv. ; Galba, B. xii. ; Titus, B. ii. ; Vespasian, D. xviii. In the Harleian collection the most important volume is Harleian MS. 353. This consists of transcripts made by Ralph Starkey (*d.* 1628) from originals, many of which are now lost. Starkey's collections on Parliamentary history and practice are also extant among the Harleian MSS. On Starkey's death his collections were bought by Sir Symonds d'Ewes, whose grandson sold them to Harley. Other volumes of great value among the Harleian MSS. are Nos. 283 and 288, containing the Calais Correspondence, 249, 289, 417, 419, 523, 2194, 6986.

The third great collection in the British Museum is the Lansdowne MSS., which the British Museum purchased for £4925 on the death of the first Marquis of Lansdowne, better known as Lord Shelburne ; but though of enormous value for the history of Elizabeth's reign as containing Burghley's original papers, it is of much less importance than the two preceding collections for the history of Edward VI.'s reign. It contains, however, all the documents relating to John Hales — the chief source of information on Somerset's agrarian policy. Other important collections are the Royal MSS. and Stow MSS., the latter of which was only acquired six years ago. The most valuable of the Royal MSS. is No. 18 C. xxiv., consisting of the Warrant-Book of the Privy Council ; and the Stow MSS. contain a contemporary copy of Henry VIII.'s will, and the calendar Somerset used in the Tower.

All these collections are, however, dwarfed in size by the miscellaneous " Additional Manuscripts," which now comprise nearly forty thousand volumes. The most important of these are Nos. 32091, 32647–8, and 32654, 32657, which refer to the affairs of the Borders. They were originally deposited among the archives of the Council of the North, then in Hamilton Palace, whence they acquired the name "Hamilton Papers"; in 1883 they passed into the hands of the German Government, but six years later they were repurchased by the trustees of the British Museum. They contain some hundreds of Somerset's letters, mostly written during Henry VIII.'s reign. The excellent catalogues of these manuscripts and indexes render superfluous any further enumeration of them. Another collection among the Additional Manuscripts equally important contains Bergenroth's transcripts of papers at Simancas. The volumes covering Edward VI.'s reign are Additional Manuscripts 28595–7.

Outside the Record Office and the British Museum the most valuable collection is perhaps that made by William Petyt (1636–1707), known as the Petyt MSS., and now in the library of the Inner Temple. It contains many original letters to and from the Protector. It is also necessary occasionally to consult the original MS. Register of the Privy Council, which is in the Privy Council Office, White-hall. The numerous private collections of manuscripts which have been calendared by the Historical Manuscripts Commission are mentioned among the printed sources, because the original manuscripts are not accessible to the ordinary student.

B. CONTEMPORARY MATERIALS THAT HAVE BEEN PRINTED OR CALENDARED

All the collections of State Papers in the Record Office have been calendared under the direction of the Master of the Rolls. The calendar of the original series of Domestic State Papers (by the late Mr. Robert Lemon) was the first to be undertaken, and was unfortunately begun on a very inadequate plan. It is a catalogue rather than a calendar, giving merely a list of the papers, with no attempt to indicate their contents. The calendar of "Addenda" by the late Mrs. Everett Green is done in a much more satisfactory manner, and leaves little to be desired. No calendar, however, can be a completely satisfactory substitute for the original documents; the signatures to a State Paper, for instance, and the hand in which it is written, are often more significant to the student than its contents. The calendars of State Papers relating to Scotland (ed. Thorp, 1858, and ed. Bain, 1898) and to foreign affairs (the latter containing a calendar of the Calais Papers) are also adequately done; and to these must be added the Calendar of Venetian State Papers preserved at Venice, and calendared by the late Mr. Rawdon Brown. The Calendar of Spanish State Papers does not cover Edward VI.'s reign, the series commenced by the late Dom Paul de Gayangos having only reached 1544, and that edited by Major M. A. S. Hume beginning with Elizabeth's reign. It is much to be regretted that the same plan was not followed for Edward VI.'s reign as was adopted for that of Henry VIII. by Drs. Brewer and Gairdner. The "Calendar of Letters and Papers relating to the Reign of Henry VIII." will, when it is finished, be the most complete collection of documents for the reign of any monarch that has ever ruled over any country; it calendars all letters and papers known to be extant relating to the reign, instead of being limited, like the other calendars of State Papers, to those documents preserved in the Record Office.

Next in importance are the various reports and appendices to the reports of the Historical Manuscripts Commission. Here, again, there is great variety in the quality of the work done by the commissioners; some of the collections calendared are very adequately represented; others, not

to put too fine a point on it, have been disgracefully
scamped. Of the collections thus brought to some extent
within the reach of the historical student, by far the most
important is that of the Marquis of Salisbury at Hatfield
House, which has been referred to throughout the text as
the Hatfield MSS. The first of the eight volumes already
published covers the reign of Edward VI., and with regard
to this collection the commissioners did their work con-
scientiously. But not having an intimate acquaintance
with the history of Edward VI.'s reign, they have misdated
many of the documents—nearly one in five. The next
important collection is that of the Marquis of Bath at
Longleat House, which is not at all adequately represented
in the report of the commissioners. This collection contains a number of documents relating to the Protector's
private life, their presence at Longleat being due to the fact
that Sir John Thynne, ancestor of the Marquis of Bath
and builder of Longleat, was the Protector's steward. Several
of the most interesting of these documents have been printed
by Canon Jackson in the Wiltshire *Archæological Magazine*, vols. xv., xvi. The only other collections that need
special mention are those of the Duke of Rutland and Mr.
W. More-Molyneux, though nearly all the commissioners'
reports contain some mention of the Protector and events
during his Protectorate.

Beyond these there are various miscellaneous collections
of State Papers, such as Haynes's Burghley Papers, the
Hamilton Papers, 2 vols., 1890–1892 (printed from the
MSS. in the British Museum, already described); Kempe's
Loseley MSS., 1836 (a printed selection from the MSS. of
Mr. W. More-Molyneux, at Loseley House, Guildford);
Lodge's " Illustrations of British History," 3 vols , 1791 (con-
sisting of MSS. from the Howard, Talbot, and Cecil collec-
tions in the College of Arms); Teulet's *Relations politiques*

de la France et de l'Espagne avec l'Écosse, and *Papiers d'État*
(Bannatyne Club); Ribier's *Lettres et Memoires d'Estat*,
1666; Weiss's *Papiers d'État du Cardinal de Granvelle*,
1842, and the very important *Correspondance politique de
Odet de Selve*, published in 1888, under the direction of
the French Ministry for Foreign Affairs. A number of
State Papers from the Petyt MSS., Record Office, and
other collections are printed by the late Rev. Nicholas
Pocock in his "Troubles connected with the Prayer Book
of 1549" (Camden Society).

Other official sources are the "Acts of the Privy Council,"
ed. J. R. Dasent, which also contains a portion of the
Council's letter-book printed from Starkey's transcript, the
original being lost; the Journals of the House of Lords
and House of Commons, printed by the Record Commission; the Statutes of the Realm, of which the only
trustworthy edition is that published by the Record Commission; Rymer's *Fœdera* and its foreign counterpart,
Dumont's *Corps Universel Diplomatique*, 1725; and for
ecclesiastical matters Wilkins's *Concilia*.

The next class of materials consists of contemporary letters,
chronicles, and other writings. There are two most valuable collections of original letters, Sir Henry Ellis's, in three
series, each consisting of three or four volumes, and the
Parker Society's Original Letters, ed. Robinson. The latter
deals exclusively with religious affairs, and consists of letters
written by Reformers in England to their sympathisers
abroad. Of contemporary chronicles there is a considerable
number. Those of Grafton, Stow, and Holinshed, on which
most subsequent histories have been based, were not strictly
contemporary chronicles, though written by men who were
of mature age when the events they describe happened.
This criticism does not, however, apply to many chronicles
and diaries published during the present century by various

clubs and societies. The most important of these is the
"Literary Remains of Edward VI." (Roxburghe Club),
containing the young king's diary (extant in Cotton MS.,
Nero, C. x.); it was edited by John Gough Nichols, who
illustrated it by publishing a great number of other contemporary MSS. The next in importance is Wriothesley's
Chronicle (Camden Society, 2 vols., 1877). It was written
by Charles Wriothesley (1508–1562), a cousin of Lord
Chancellor Wriothesley, and an official in the Heralds'
Office. Other strictly contemporary works are Machyn's
Diary, Greyfriars' Chronicle, and "Narratives of the Refor-
mation" (all published by the Camden Society). Another
contemporary chronicle, more curious than credible, is that
of Antonio de Guaras, a Spanish merchant resident in
London; it is among the Additional MSS. in the British
Museum, and was unearthed by Major Hume, who pub-
lished it in 1888. Although styled a "Chronicle of Henry
VIII.," it deals largely with Edward VI.'s reign.

The history of the period is also illustrated by a number
of contemporary writings which have been published recently by the Early English Text Society and the Parker
Society. The former relate chiefly to the social condition
of the people, and the principal of them have been mentioned in the text (p. 206). The latter deal chiefly with
religious affairs, and the most important are the works of
Cranmer, Latimer, Hutchinson, and Becon. Equally important are John Knox's "Works" (Bannatyne Club) and
Bishop Ponet's much-neglected "Treatise of Politicke
Power," 1556.

C. Non-Contemporary Writers

This list exhausts most of the more important general
works relating to the period which are strictly contemporary.
A few others, dealing with special questions like enclosures

and the relations with Scotland, have been mentioned in the text under those chapters. Sir Thomas Smith's *De Republica Anglorum*, written in 1561, but not published till 1583, is, however, a contemporary description of the highest value of the English constitution in Tudor times. The most important works on the history of the Protectorate published within the succeeding generation are the Chronicles of Grafton, Stow, and Holinshed, and the martyrologies of Foxe on the Protestant side and Nicholas Sanders and others on the Roman side. These were followed early in the seventeenth century by Speed's "Historie" and Sir John Hayward's "Life and Raigne of Edward the Sext." Neither is, however, of much authority, coming after the period when personal knowledge remained and before the period when serious investigation into records took its place. Seventeenth-century historians were concerned almost exclusively with the religious aspect of the period. The earliest of these writers was Thomas Fuller (1608–1661), a moderate if not low Churchman, whose "Church History" appeared in 1655. His history marked a great advance on previous works, and in 1845 it received the compliment of being edited for the Clarendon Press by Dr. J. S. Brewer. It was, however, attacked from a High Church point of view by Laud's friend and biographer, Peter Heylyn (1600–1662), in his *Ecclesia Restaurata*, 1661. Both Fuller and Heylyn were eclipsed by Gilbert Burnet (1643–1715), and John Strype (1643–1737). Burnet's "History of the Reformation," published in three folio volumes (1679–1715), has passed through many editions, the standard one being that of the late Rev. Nicholas Pocock, Oxford, 1875, 7 vols., which contains corrections of the numerous errors pointed out by Wharton (Anthony Harmer). It is still in many respects the best history of the Reformation. Many additional documents are supplied in Mr. Pocock's edition, but as a collection of records Burnet was almost immediately superseded by the monumental works of Strype. The most important of these for Edward VI.'s reign are the " Ecclesiastical Memorials," " Memorials of Cranmer," " Life of Sir Thomas Smith," and " Life of Archbishop Parker." These were published during the last years of the seventeenth and early years of the eighteenth century, but the edition almost invariably used is the collected Oxford edition, in twenty-six volumes (1820). Strype makes no pretence at elaborate historical composition, but his industry in searching out and transcribing original documents has rarely if ever been surpassed; his collections are still the basis of most works written on the period. Sometimes, however, Strype's zeal led him into grave errors; his blunder about Edward VI.'s foundation of schools is mainly responsible for the erroneous ideas prevalent on that subject, and his method of transliteration of his originals into the English of his time led him into some misconceptions, and his readers into more; on one occasion at least he was guilty of altering his originals to make them fit in with a confusion he made himself between the Earl of Arundel and Sir Thomas Arundell (see *Gentleman's Magazine*, 1848, i. 47, 131, 269), and in the Oxford edition these errors are increased rather than diminished. Nevertheless Strype's works remain an invaluable repertory of materials for the history of the period.

For a hundred years after Strype no new light of any value was thrown on Edward VI.'s reign, for the histories of Carte, Rapin, and Hume, though admirable in their way, made no original study of that particular period, and the authors were content to rely on the labours of Strype and Burnet. Nor can the histories of Sharon Turner ("Modern History of England," 2 parts, 1826–9), Dr. Lingard (8 vols., 1819–1830), and Mackintosh (1830) establish for their authors much claim to have brought any new materials to light; for the most part they contented themselves with drawing exactly opposite inferences to those which their predecessors drew from the same materials; and subsequent research has shown that these historians are not very trustworthy guides, at least for the reign of Edward VI. A few years later, however, two eminent historical scholars, Patrick Fraser Tytler and John Gough Nichols, published a great deal of new material. Tytler's "History of England under Edward VI. and Mary," published in 1839, is comprised almost entirely of State Papers printed from the collections in the Record Office. Nichols, though he wrote no connected history, did equal service by his editions of the "Literary Remains of Edward VI." (Roxburghe Club), of the "Chronicle of Queen Jane," "Narratives of the Reformation," and "Greyfriars' Chronicle" for the Camden Society, and by numerous contributions to *Archæologia*, the *Gentleman's Magazine*, and other periodicals.

These two writers were concerned mainly with the secular history of the reign, but the theological controversies of the middle of the century soon affected the views taken of the Reformation. In 1849 Dr. S. R. Maitland published, in his "Essays on Subjects connected with the Reformation," an acute examination of some of the stories embodied in Foxe's "Acts and Monuments" (to which attention had been called by Townsend's edition in 8 vols., 1843–1849), which had up till then been accepted almost as gospel. Dr. Maitland convicted Foxe of carelessness in some instances, considerable exaggeration in others, and no little credulity; but he failed to shake the general credibility of the work, or to convict Foxe of offences which are not easily explained by the religious passion of the times. A new edition of Maitland's "Essays" was published in 1898, with an introduction by the Rev. A. W. Hutton. A somewhat similar line

was taken up by the Rev. Nicholas Pocock, whose services to
the history of the Reformation were much more considerable
than those of Dr. Maitland. His collection of "Records of
the Reformation," which would have been invaluable had
it been completed, only reached the year 1535 and two
volumes, the Clarendon Press refusing to publish more on
account of their inadequate sale; and the remainder of Mr.
Pocock's collections remained in manuscript, except the
volume on the "Troubles," published by the Camden
Society, and occasional papers published in the *English
Historical Review* and *Church Quarterly Review*.

It was between 1856 and 1870 that Mr. Froude published
in twelve volumes his brilliant and fascinating "History of
England." The view which he took of Henry VIII. and
his methods of dealing with the evidence have been the
subject of a good deal of criticism, some very bitter, but
on the whole not unjust. His treatment of Edward VI.'s
reign is more satisfactory, but it is to some extent warped
by the assumption that Henry VIII. left England in a
sound position, and that it was the bungling of his successors
that caused all the trouble. There is also the unconscious
desire to contrast the rule of Edward VI.'s ministers with
that of Henry in order to glorify the latter. Yet, on the
whole, the removal of Henry VIII. from the scene restores
Mr. Froude's balance of judgment, and few of his estimates
of the statesmen of Edward's reign seem to me grossly
unfair. Of the literary qualities of his work and his industry in searching through manuscript collections, it is
superfluous to speak. It is true that he never understood
the sanctity of inverted commas, and often puts in inverted
commas what is merely an abridgment of the document he
is quoting; but though I have compared a considerable
number of his quotations with the originals, I cannot say
that these abridgments are unfair representations of them.

It was, however, Mr. Froude's tone on ecclesiastical matters that gave most offence, and in 1878 Canon R. W. Dixon began a counterblast in his " History of the Church of England," which is the most complete and detailed account, not merely of the religious history, but of the general history of Edward VI.'s reign, and is an indispensable authority on the period. It makes, however, no allowance for the difficulties with which statesmen had to deal, and seems to find in heresy an explanation of most of the evils of the time.

GENERAL INDEX

INDEX TO REFERENCES AND BIBLIOGRAPHY.

THE END